SEASON OF ADVENTURE

Traveling Tales and Outdoor Journeys of Women Over 50

edited by Jean Gould

Adventura
BOOKS
AN IMPRINT OF SEAL PRESS

Seal Press
3131 Western Avenue, Suite 410
Seattle, Washington 98121
Email: sealprss@scn.org

Text design by Stacy M. Lewis
Cover design by Clare Conrad
Cover photograph by Bert Sagara/Tony Stone Images

Acknowledgments: "Wild Voice of the North" from *Wild Voice of the North* by Sally Carrighar. Copyright © 1959 Sally Carrighar. Used by permission of Doubleday, a division of Bantam Doubleday Dell Publishing Group, Inc. "My Journey to Lhasa" from *My Journey to Lhasa* by Alexandra David-Neel. Copyright © 1927 by Harper & Row, Publishers, Inc. Renewed 1955 by Alexandra David-Neel. "Drinking the Rain," Chapter 4 from *Drinking the Rain* by Alix Kates Shulman. Copyright © 1995 by Alix Kates Shulman. Reprinted by permission of Farrar, Straus & Giroux, Inc. "Have Saddle, Will Travel" from *Women, Animals, and Vegetables: Essays and Stories by Maxine Kumin.* Copyright © 1994 by Maxine Kumin. Reprinted by permission of W. W. Norton & Company, Inc. "Polar Bear Pass" is reprinted with the permission of Simon & Schuster from *Polar Dreams* by Helen Thayer. Copyright © 1993 by Helen Thayer.

Printed in the United States of America
First printing, October 1996
1 3 5 7 9 10 8 6 4 2

Library of Congress Cataloging-in-Publication Data
Season of adventure : traveling tales and outdoor journeys of women over 50 / edited by Jean Gould.
1. Middle aged women—Recreation—Case studies. 2. Aged women—Recreation—Case studies. 3. Middle aged women—Travel—Case studies. 4. Aged women—Travel—Case studies. 5. Middle aged women—Self-actualization (Psychology)—Case studies. 6. Aged women—Self-Actualization (Psychology)—Case studies. I. Gould, Jean
GV191.64.S43   1996   796.5'082—dc20   96-24635
ISBN 1-878067-81-8

Distributed to the trade by Publishers Group West
In Canada: Publishers Group West Canada, Toronto, Canada
In Europe and the U.K.: Airlift Book Company, London, England

for
Irving Gould

and for our daughters
Deborah Colgan
and
Cheryl, Kim, Jane and Malaya Gould

ACKNOWLEDGMENTS

When women collaborate, exceptional results are possible. Holly Morris and her colleagues at Seal Press prove this every day in terms of the respectful process by which books such as *Season of Adventure* are developed. I am grateful for the encouragement and wisdom so generously available to me as I worked on this anthology.

Additionally, it has been my privilege to be associated with women whose active engagement with the outdoors has influenced my vision of this project, particularly: Connie Archibald, Enid Bone, Edith Bulle, Sophie Freud, Florence Gaylin, Rose Gotsis, Alice Hershfelt, Gladys McKinnon and Muriel Parks.

I am also grateful to those whose presence in my life—short, long or intermittent—has led me to this book about women who dare to be: Diane Aronson, Miriam Bronstein, Daphne Carvela, Sally Collini, Ginny DeLuca, Ginny Work Evans, Sue Pekarsky Gary, Nancy Gertner, Karen Kahn, Ellen Miller, Edith Welch

and especially Norbett Mintz.

CONTENTS

"And now I am very old, gently traversing my sixty-fifth year. By some freak of destiny I am stronger and more active than I was in youth. I can walk farther. I can stay awake longer. My body has remained as supple as a glove. My sight is somewhat blurred, so that I have to wear spectacles, but they have increased my interest in natural history, as they enable me to see in the grass and sand tiny objects I might have overlooked. I go bathing in icy water and find it pleasant. I never catch cold, and I have forgotten what rheumatism is. I am absolutely calm."

George Sand
The Intimate Journal
September 1868

INTRODUCTION

To celebrate my fiftieth birthday, I climbed in the Everest foothills, making my way up and down the slopes in and around the sparkling Dudh Kosi River on the trail toward base camp. The blue-purple skies and high altitudes held me as I had known they would. I slept outdoors in zero degree temperatures to the melodies of gentle yak bells, developed a yen for rice and lentils, and found a home among steep mountains. Lacing my boots each morning, my breath drifting through the thin air like a signal of smoke, I was warmed by the harsh extremes and delicate balances of the natural world and my place in it.

We gather renewal where we can. Few things in human lives are certain. The structure of our days can be altered without our control. Nevertheless, the sun will rise and set. A bird may sing by the feeder. Some old ruins remain to tell us stories of our earlier selves. When we place seeds in the soil with love and attention, the chances that they will flourish are good. We have much to learn from animals, both wild and domestic. Despite the settled lives some of us live, we are nomadic creatures: we wander and explore and test our limits. A rope climb can be as terrifying as an avalanche or as calming as the rhythm of ocean tides. With age, we may begin to embrace nature in new ways: exhilaration and inspiration, triumph and defeat, are no less moderated, but they are often accompanied by a seasoned balance; what my high school history teacher used to call the "balance of powers."

I grew up wanting to be a horse in the wild, or at the very least a blade of grass in my own back yard. In those days, there was a course in my school entitled "Social Graces." I was lucky to find Carol Brink *(Caddie Woodlawn)* and Willa Cather *(My Antonia)*, who wrote fiction about the adventures of girls in the outdoors, and Osa Johnson *(I Married Adventure)*, a writer and explorer of Africa. Theirs were the books that gave me permission to prefer outdoors to indoors, blue jeans to formal gowns, the wisdom of tall trees to corsages of gardenias. But as I take another look at the girl I was then, neighing and cantering around our Philadelphia back yard, I wish that child had known about Alexandra David-Neel's experiences in Tibet *(My Journey to Lhasa)* and Elinore Pruitt Stewart's life in Wyoming *(Adventures of the Woman Homesteader)*, both of which are excerpted in this collection. For me, the "balance of powers" has always been about carving out space for serious exploration among my responsibilities and balancing conventional demands with a wild spirit.

Women born prior to 1945 were supposed to be reined in by the "Goldilocks factor," the "Red Riding Hood lesson." And so on. What was contributor Sally Carrighar doing up there in the Arctic, anyway, studying lemmings, while Mamie Eisenhower was such a good wife to our hero-general? On the radio, Harriet Hilliard, perfect mother to David and Ricky Nelson, taught us everything we needed to know. And if a girl actually wanted to do anything else—leave home, for instance— she might take herself to Atlantic City and become Miss America, as Bess Myerson did. Good girls didn't sweat. And certainly, women over a certain age—shall we say fifty?—had no authority to wander the world, to wear bathing suits, to ride camels.

The lines of transition in my life have never been clearly defined in terms of chronological age. At four, I was in the first grade, I didn't menstruate until fifteen, and although I had my first child at twenty-four—which was more or less the norm in those times—I was forty-five when my first novel was published; now, at fifty-seven, I consider graduate school. Only lately, as some of my younger friends occasionally refer to me as a role model, or when wilderness guides offer to carry my pack, does the word *old* occupy me. But I am puzzled about the differences between *old* and *older.* At ninety-three, my grandmother spoke about those old people, as she tended her garden and baked her own bread each day. But lately I have also heard that I may be "irresponsible." I have no retirement plan or life insurance and I care more about saving the earth than the accumulation of money; even my college roommate was shocked when she visited not long ago. "You have furniture!" she declared. I do not smoke corn silk or sleep, as a rule, in barns. Nevertheless, I suspect there is some quality about me people might label "uncivilized" or not quite "grown up." Something about my independent nature can rankle others.

Ah, labels: old, civilized, or—and here it is—"feminine." Definitions of these concepts are complex, personal and highly charged. The point is that none of us is one-dimensional: we can be and are adventurous and cautious, brave and frightened, rebellious and conforming, old and young, and even feminine and masculine at the same time. The truth is that most women over fifty are active, healthy and self-supporting.

Recently I met and interviewed Alix Kates Shulman about the publication of her memoir *Drinking the Rain*. She said she thought the critics were taking this new book more seriously than her previous work. Are we less threatening, I wondered, because we are perceived as asexual, now that we are finished with the bearing of children? Is it only now that we can reclaim our bodies for other endeavors? We left these questions open between us. Perhaps as older women we are only continuing our patterns, with applications to new opportunities. After all, we have juggled the pieces of our lives for a long time; women's lives require such juggling.

Or is it true that women, older women, define themselves primarily by human relationship, as psychologists hypothesize? I wonder. That may be one way of defining the self. Today, I think we are also what we *do* and have grown less willing to be shaped by others for their use. We have new relationships with our bodies and have learned or are learning to value them for how they work, as well as how they may appear to others. The truth is that as we map new territory outdoors and indoors, most of us accommodate, sometimes can even honor, the aging process. In the end, however, although relationship with self and other may set a context for these essays, I think the primary connection put forth by writers in this anthology is with nature. Where, each woman asks, is her place among natural phenomena?

This collection informs its readers about nature as a way of life, as a means to travel, and as physical sport. For some, their experience has been a one-time adventure. For others, it is one of a series of connected experiences over a lifetime. Interaction with nature can also be meditative. For all, such exploration facilitates renewal and discovery, as if, in fact, we need such experiences to remember who we are and can be.

So. We ride horses, swim, climb mountains, garden, sail, canoe, walk in the wind, report from the Sahara, play tennis at home, go with others to the Amazon or to Guyana, climb Indian ruins, have fun with grandchildren or learn to climb ropes. We are confident and curious and lively. We are bold and brave. We accept risk as part of living, seeking it out. Outdoor adventure surely is its own reward. Yet, in the middle or late-middle or close-to-the-end of our lives, our perspective lets us know what has value. We are not fearless. And that's the human thing: we are at home with our lives and know that vulnerability does not signal weakness of character.

My grandparents homesteaded in Illinois during the last century. When, after my father's death, the farm buildings were removed from his birthplace for tax purposes, I was devastated. I had secretly harbored the fantasy of living on the plains and tilling the soil that was so rich and dark. We had visited the place when I was small, and the courtyard water pump, the dirt floors in the farmhouse, the gigantic barn and the fragrance of animals welcomed me home. Today, I am instructed not to garden without gloves, that there are germs and fungus in the soil, and that my skin will dry up, dry out, or fall off. Perhaps I am foolish. There is always some small possibility that the "authorities" could be right. But sometimes, the tradeoffs require too much.

Two years ago, I returned to the Himalaya to explore Bhutan and northern India. However difficult the lives of people in that part of the world, I am drawn there by simple daily acts of acceptance of the place of human beings in the scheme of things. When the natural world dominates, and animals and trees so clearly outnumber people, our place in the natural order becomes evident. Today, as older women construct their lives, we have more options, and many of us lead more privileged lives than our forebearers. But not all. I am mindful of that fact, as I am in touch with older women, outdoors and homeless, here and abroad, whose experience deals more with survival than adventure or sport.

As I write this, snow falls steadily. The wood stove throws heat to most of the house's corners. Our Siberian husky-in-residence buries tennis balls in the drifts, retrieves them, and buries them again. I make final plans for another journey to the Himalaya, this time to connect with women's groups for sustainable development, and later, to watch black-necked cranes on their spring migration path through the

Bumthang Valley. The errant zipper in my sleeping bag has been repaired. I continue to be led by that quality of mountain light that is pink and gentle and receptive. When I go outside to play now with the dog, the freezing air lifts my lungs and my body into their most efficient modes. Shoveling a path to the road, my bones and muscles cooperate almost musically.

In my enthusiasm for this collection, I imagine that all of the contributors gather in a place outside this book. Maybe we hike the Appalachian Mountain Trail, take a canoe trip in Ontario, or even ride horses through a dappled wood. Because we are writers, we will measure our words with each other and be at home with our silences. We will listen to a paddle in the water, a hoof beat or footstep on the trail, the call of thrushes or sparrows or bumblebees. We may float candles on a lake at twilight and make wishes while fresh water laps the shore, as we did at my childhood summer camp. Not all of us will want to be outdoors at nightfall, listening for owl sounds or letting our fingers play with stones by the fire. But each of us will sleep well after we tell our stories again and again and again.

The director at that camp of floating candles was a local schoolteacher, well-known in Philadelphia environs for her no-nonsense approach to both students and campers. One summer, she left us in the hands of her sister, another teacher, while she went around the world on a sabbatical. Unmarried, unattached, she was out to find her life partner, rumor had it. She may then have been a bit younger than I am now. But when she returned the following summer with a star sapphire on one finger and tales of Indonesian jungles, I knew the trip had been about something else, although I had no words for it then.

As I contemplate the making of this book and some imagined get-together of its contributors, there are others whose less concrete contributions are ever more poignant in memory. That oh-so-proper camp director created a place where girls could safely learn the rules of games and how to play them well, while being herself a figure, for me at least, of possibilities. Not too long ago, I played a competitive badminton game with an elderly Tibetan nun outside the nunnery in Dharamsala, India. Once I had a Viennese landlady in her sixties who swam from April through November in her New England pond, sometimes in a wet suit. It is important to take note of such mentoring.

This is the first anthology of its kind: a collection in which older women speak about their experiences in the outdoors. Blended as they are with the accumulating power and pathos of long lives, these accounts chronicle more than specific journeys. For older women, in particular, it is valuable to connect the past to the present, assessing our beginnings in terms of the persons we've become and the legacies we leave to those who come after us. In gathering these pieces, I have been especially struck by the importance the writers attach to generational connections. For those who value activity in the out-of-doors, passing on that appreciation to others in terms of preservation and joy is one of the forces that drives us.

The stories of others inspire and validate our own lives. They transport us to new places, particularly to those places where women have dared to be themselves.

In an Indian mountain village, I inquired about finding other women writers. "Oh, there may be a few," I was told, "but they write only of their own lives." "Only." *Only.* These accounts enrich and offer us a vigor that, matched with our own, creates a more natural wholeness and integration. They are great gifts, provide nourishment, self-awareness, models for being in the world that can change both those who read and those who write. They inform the indomitable spirit of doing.

Jean Gould
Natick, Massachusetts
March 1996

SEASON OF ADVENTURE

My Journey to Lhasa

Alexandra David-Neel

All necessary arrangements had been made. We stood, Yongden and I, in the thick jungle, alone and free. The novelty of our situation bewildered us a little. For months, during the long journey from the sands of Gobi to Yunnan, we had been discussing the way in which we could "disappear," as we used to say, and assume other personalities. Now, the hour had come and we were to start that very night for the Dokar Pass, which now forms the border of independent Thibet.

"Let us drink a cup of tea," I said to the young lama, "and then you will start on a scouting tour. At any rate, we should reach the foot of the Kha Karpo track without meeting anybody, and be out of sight from the village before daybreak."

Hastily I revived the fire. Yongden brought water from the stream, and we prepared the Thibetan tea, with butter and salt, in the simple manner of poor travellers who cannot enjoy the luxury of a churn to mix it.

I may as well explain immediately the composition of our cantine. We had only one aluminum pot, which was our kettle, teapot, and saucepan all in one. There was also one lama wooden bowl for Yongden, an aluminum bowl for myself, two spoons, and a Chinese travelling case containing one long knife and chopsticks, which could be hung from the belt. That was all. We did not intend to indulge in refined cooking.

---

* Please note that the original spelling and syntax of this piece has been retained.

Our meals were to be those of the common Thibetan travellers; that is to say, tsampa, mixed with buttered tea, or eaten nearly dry, kneaded with butter. When circumstances would allow, we would make a soup. Forks were useless with such a diet, and even our two cheap spoons could not be produced freely, as they were of a foreign pattern such as only affluent Thibetans possess. *Arjopas* (pilgrims travelling on foot and often begging their food), as we pretended to be, have none. In fact, these spoons became, later on, the occasion of a short drama in which I nearly killed a man. I shall tell the story in due course.

The tea drunk, Yongden started. Hours passed; night had fallen. I remained seated near the fire which I did not dare to let blaze, fearing that it might be seen from afar and betray our presence. The remains of the tea, kept as a last cordial to cheer our departure, were simmering on the embers; the rising moon tinged with bluish and russet hues the melancholy depths of the valley. All was silence and solitude.

What had I dared to dream? . . . Into what mad adventure was I about to throw myself? I remembered previous journeys in Thibet, hardships endured, dangers that I had confronted . . . It was that again, or even worse, which lay before me . . . And what would be the end? Would I triumph, reach Lhasa, laughing at those who close the roads of Thibet? Would I be stopped on my way, or would I fail, this time forever, meeting death at the bottom of a precipice, hit by the bullet of a robber, or dying miserably of fever beneath a tree, or in a cave, like some wild beast? Who knew?

But I did not allow gloomy thoughts to overpower my mind. Whatever might be the future, I would not shrink from it. "Stop here! Go no farther!" Such were the commands of a few Western politicians, to explorers, savants, missionaries, scholars, to all, in fact, except their agents, who travelled freely, wherever they were sent, in this so-called "Forbidden Land." What right had they to erect barriers around a country which was not even lawfully theirs? Many travellers had been stopped on their way to Lhasa, and had accepted failure. I would not. I had taken the challenge by my oath on the "iron bridge" and was now ready to show what a woman can do!

As I was thus musing, Yongden emerged suddenly from the bushes. Strangely lit by the moon, he looked a little like a legendary mountain spirit.

Briefly he reported the result of his scouting: To avoid the village we should have to cross a rickety footbridge higher up the valley, and follow the stream downward on the opposite bank. Perhaps it was possible to make a direct descent by wading in the river itself past any village house that might be perched upon the bank. This would certainly be a short cut, but, as people were in the fields nearby, he had not been able to test the depth of the water.

Whichever road we might choose, we could not avoid passing in front of a few houses between the small bridge on the stream flowing out of the valley where we pitched our camp, and the large one on the tributary of the Mekong, which we had seen on our arrival.

When we crossed that second bridge, we could look for the bypath which was to lead us to the pilgrimage road. Yongden had seen it clearly, winding up the steep slope, but he had failed to discover the exact point from which it branched from the bank of the river.

With these vague ideas, I hurriedly set out. It was already late and we could not guess how many miles we should have to tramp that night until we could reach a spot which afforded some degree of safety.

Was my load heavy on my shoulders? Were its rough straps cutting my flesh? Indeed they were! I felt it later, but at that moment I was not aware of it. I was aware of nothing. I knocked myself against sharp rocks, I tore my hands and my face in the thorny bushes. I was dead to all sensation, stiffened, hypnotized by the will to succeed.

For several hours we trudged in the valley. We had first climbed up to the main road, and then, skirting isolated farms, tried the passage in the stream. It proved impossible at nighttime. The water was rather high, the current swift and breaking against boulders. We should have fallen in two minutes. And so we again directed our steps in search of the footbridge. Several times we lost our road. The trails that my young friend had marked in the day were difficult to find by the dim light of the moon, veiled in mist. At last we found ourselves on an easy but very winding track on the opposite bank. It led tortuously beside the stream, and we were exasperated by the precious moments lost in following it. When at last we caught sight of the village, we put our loads down, drank a draught of the clear water that flowed past us, swallowed a granule of strychnine to rouse fresh energy in our tired bodies, and took the dreaded passage on the run.

A bridge, the houses, the second and larger bridge . . . safely passed. We stood at the foot of the wild and solitary hill on which a narrow, twisting trail led to other tracks and paths and roads leading into the very heart of Thibet, the Forbidden Capital of the Lamas.

A dog had given a low, suppressed bark when we were near the river— a single dog, in that village where a dozen or more of these rather fierce animals wandered to and fro all night! It reminded me of the Indian tales relating the nightly flight of those sons of good family, who, in quest of the "Supreme Deliverance," abandon their home to take to the religious life of the sannyasin. In order, we read, to make their flight easier, "the gods lulled the men to sleep and silenced the dogs." So had it been with me, and smilingly I returned thanks to the invisible friends who protected my departure.

In our haste to be off we overlooked a small landslide just in front of us, which was in reality the beginning of the bypath leading upward that had fallen in. We searched for the road along the river bank until we neared a steep gorge which afforded no means of ascent and we were thus forced to return to the bridge. Another half-hour was wasted here; we were in full sight of the village and trembled for fear of being no- ticed! Moreover, the right track, which we found a little after midnight, happened to be extremely steep and sandy. Heavily loaded as we were, we could only make slow progress, in spite of our strenuous efforts, being compelled to stop frequently, out of breath. It was terrible, and my feelings could well be compared to those of a nightmare in which the dreamer imagines himself to be pursued by murderers and tries his utmost to run away, but cannot move his feet!

Toward the end of the night we reached a gloomy spot sheltered by large trees. Our steps awakened a number of big birds perched on the branches, which flew away noisily. A streamlet flowed nearby and Yongden, who had not enjoyed a minute's rest since the morning of the previous day, craved a refreshing bowl of tea.

Thirst parched my mouth and I shared the desire of my companion, but nevertheless I was most reluctant to stop. This dark place, the only one where water was obtainable, did not appear to me very safe. It might possibly be haunted by leopards and panthers, of which there are many on these hills. Above all, I wished to put as great a distance as possible between us and Londre. Had I been alone, I would have suffered no matter what agony, and would have crept on my knees if I could no longer stand, rather than delay a single minute. But the exhausted lama's fatigue overcame prudence. Nothing could be done; he fell rather than sat upon the wet ground, and I went in search of fuel.

The hot drink was most comforting. Unfortunately, his new sense of well-being lulled my companion to sleep. I could have cried. Each minute wasted on that path diminished our chances of success. However, in such cases nothing is to be done; sleep is a necessity that cannot be resisted. Nevertheless, Yongden was not allowed a long rest and we continued on our way.

The solitude reassured us. The sun had long since risen and we were still climbing when we heard a voice above us. Then, without exchanging a single word, panic-stricken, Yongden and I threw ourselves out of the path and rushed like scared game, through the thick jungle, our only idea being to escape from sight.

I found myself, without being able to remember how I had come there, on an old stony landslide surrounded by thorny bushes. Of my companion there was no trace.

However, he had not gone far and we soon found each other. But we did not dare to walk again in broad daylight. Woodcutters, cattle drovers, or others might be going down to Londre and talk about us there. Pilgrims might perhaps follow that path, overtake us, notice something peculiar in our appearance, and repeat it in gossip on the other side of the border. We expected the worst, anxious to give bad luck as little chance as possible. We therefore spent the first day of our journey squatting under the trees. From our resting-place we could hear, higher up, invisible folk driving equally invisible cattle. A wood-cutter appeared on an opposite slope. I watched him for some time; he sang prettily as he piled his logs and doubtless was not in the least aware of the agony he was causing a foreign woman. The autumn foliage probably screened us completely from the gaze of distant observers, and the villagers did not suspect our presence. Nevertheless, in my fear of having been seen, I was filled with the most pessimistic ideas. I almost believed that failure was awaiting me and that I had come here in vain from far away Turkestan, across the whole of China.

Soon after sunset we began our nocturnal tramp. When darkness came we saw several fires higher up on the hill. We could not be sure that the winding path which we followed would not lead us to them, and we were very much worried. Coal men or, perhaps, pilgrims were camped there and the prospect of arriving at night amongst Thibetans by the Londre track did not please us in the least; for such a meeting would have been the occasion for many embarrassing questions from inquisitive people.

We remained for a long time seated on the grass in a clearing, waiting for the moon to rise. We could not see the trail, yet all the time we *could* see these alarming, glowing fires! They gave a peculiarly disquieting and demoniacal aspect to the black, indistinct landscape of pines and huge rocks jutting around them in the dark starlit sky. How thankful we were when we saw them far behind us and were certain that we could not meet the people near them.

Soon afterwards we arrived at a small *chorten* marking the junction of our track and the pilgrims' road. The latter was a rather large mule path, and walking became easy and pleasant. To have reached this spot without meeting anybody was indeed fortunate. If my luck held out, I might, with equal fortune, cross the Dokar Pass and reach the district of Menkong. I could then congratulate myself on having made the most important step toward final success, for in that country many roads cross, bringing together travellers from various directions. Our tracks would be easily lost, and with a little cleverness we could lose ourselves in the anonymous mass of poor Thibetan pilgrims whom the officials do not condescend to honour with so much as a single glance.

Thirst was torturing us still more than upon the previous night when we reached a large roaring mountain torrent which cut across the road. A small bridge spanned it rather high above the water which rushed, white with foam, amidst a chaos of boulders. Yongden thought only of his thirst, and wished to go down the road immediately to drink. This was dangerous, since, in the darkness, he could not see the obstacles which might cause him to stumble and roll into the torrent, which would have immediately carried him away. I remonstrated with the obstinate fellow, but he argued that as water was so scarce, seeing that we had found none since the previous night, it was indeed possible it would be hours before we struck water again. I could not contradict him, but thirst was preferable to being drowned. I therefore ordered him to cross the footbridge. On the other side, the bank was less steep and an easy way down could be seen. Although time was precious, and I did not like to light a fire so close to the road, I was thinking of halting, when, to our dismay, we heard a voice calling us. It was that of a man who offered us red embers to kindle a fire, and even a cup of ready-made tea to begin with!

We remained motionless, speechless. We had talked in English a few minutes before. Had that man heard us?

"Who are you?" asked another voice. "Why are you walking at night?"

We still could see nobody, but the sound came from a huge tree. I thought it might be hollow and that travelers had taken it as hostelry for the night.

"We are pilgrims," answered Yongden. "*Dokpas* from Amdo. We cannot bear the heat of this country. When we walk in the sunshine, we get fever. So we tramp around the Holy Hill at night."

That was quite a plausible reason. The man who had asked the question asked nothing more, but Yongden continued:

"And you, who are you?"

"We, too, are pilgrims."

"Well, good-bye," I said, to cut the talk short. "We will still walk a little, and camp the next time we find water."

So ended the first chance meeting on our way to Lhasa. We congratulated each other that it did not happen while we were still on the track climbing from Londre, but at the same time we learned that even night marches were not absolutely secure, and that we had to be prepared at any hour and at any place to explain, in a way that awoke no suspicion whatever, the reason of our doings.

We continued our way for several hours without finding further traces of water. I felt exhausted and walked mechanically, half asleep. Once I thought that we were approaching a hut built on the road and turned over in my mind what I would say and do if I met Thibetans. But the "hut" turned out to be a passage between two great rocks. At last utter exhaustion compelled us to rest. The site was not in the least fit for camping; the exceedingly narrow trail skirted a stony, natural wall, and, on the other side, ended perpendicularly. We lay down on a rocky mattress whose roughness we unpleasantly felt through our clothes and endeavoured to remember even in our sleep that we were perched on the edge of a precipice whose depth was unfathomable in the night.

In such wise we spent the second happy night of our wonderful adventure. Day had not yet broken when Yongden and I loaded our burdens on our backs and continued the tramp through the forest. More than twenty-four hours had now elapsed since we had eaten and drunk. We had not yet become accustomed to prolonged fasts, and this first one was hard to bear.

We proceeded as fast as we could in order to reach some stream before hiding ourselves for the day. It was a race with the sun, which was now rising rapidly. It appeared somewhere above a summit hidden in the thick foliage, and its heat soon began to light and warm the underwood. The time had come for us to take shelter in the forest. The men whom we had met during the night might overtake us, and that would mean a long talk, a lot of explanations, and, what was still worse, our showing ourselves in broad daylight.

We crept between the thickets that extended beyond some *do-chod* until we were completely invisible from the path. Looking down, I discerned some blue smoke floating far below between the trees. A distant noise of running water could also be heard. Travellers or wood-cutters were enjoying their morning meal, an idea which so increased our hunger that Yongden decided to risk himself on the road with our kettle in search of water.

While alone, I hid our baggage under some branches, and lay down flat on the dry leaves and threw others over me. Any wanderer through the wood could have passed very near without detecting my presence. Indeed, this happened to Yongden when he came back with his kettle full of water. I had fallen asleep and he roamed a long time in the jungle looking for the place where he had left me. He did not dare to call aloud, and had I not been awakened by the noise he made in wading through the dry leaves and got up, he would have wandered still longer.

We had discussed, during the previous night, the question of our disguise. Till then we had worn our Chinese robes, which would not have compromised us even if I were recognized as a white woman, for, as a rule, all foreigners in these remote parts of Thibetan China dress in this way. But we now hoped that no one who could detect us would come along our road. Our fellow-travellers would probably be pilgrims from various regions of Thibet and our best plan was to merge at once in their number, like inconspicuous, common *arjopas*.

The *arjopas* are those mendicant pilgrims who, all through the year, ramble in thousands across Thibet, going from one to another of its sacred places. The *arjopa*, not necessarily, but for the most part, belongs to the religious order—either as a monk or as a nun. He or she may be a true pauper or even a professional beggar, but the mass of them have homes and means of subsistence in their own countries, although they cannot afford to ride on horseback during their pious journeys.

Some *arjopas* start without any money and rely entirely upon charity during their pilgrimages; others are not entirely penniless, but keep carefully the few coins they possess for the unlucky days when alms-givers are few or none. A third category is rich enough to purchase the simple food of the ordinary Thibetan diet. However, for the most part, the pilgrim passes easily from one to another of these different classes. A lama capable of reading the Scriptures, who can perform the different lamaist ceremonies, and can, above all, act as exorcist and fortune-teller, may at any time find himself so well provided with food, clothing, and even money, that he may dispense with begging for several months. On the other hand, the owner of a heavy purse may fall ill, be delayed on his way by other circumstances, or be robbed—a thing which happens frequently—and have to take his place, in the same day, amongst the poorest of his colleagues.

I had chosen to travel as an *arjopa* because it is the best disguise to pass without attracting notice. Yongden, who is an authentic and well-read lama, looked his part perfectly, and I, his aged mother, who had undertaken a long pilgrimage for devotional reasons, constituted a rather touching and sympathetic figure. These considerations had their full weight when I decided upon our disguises, but—and why should I not confess it?—the absolute freedom of the *arjopa*, who, like Diogenes, carries all his possessions with him, and who is free from the care of servants, horses, luggage, sleeping each night where he pleases, attracted me greatly. I had had a taste of it during a previous short trip in Kham, and wished to enjoy it more fully and longer. And now that I have thoroughly experienced the joys and the hardship of the *arjopa*'s life in Thibet, I deem it to be the most blessed existence one can dream of, and I consider as the happiest in my life those days when, with a load upon my back, I wandered as one of the countless tribe of Thibetan beggar pilgrims.

WILD VOICE OF THE NORTH

Sally Carrighar

Fate was starting to do some weaving for the blue-eyed Siberian Husky. Not immediately, but within a year, his life would have a new pattern composed of three strangely assorted threads: lemmings, a gaunt gold-rush house, and myself. These, none of which now concerned him, would be determining whether he might survive. But before the threads could be put together they had to be spun, and that process would take a little time.

If the Husky had been a sled dog instead of a "family dog," lemmings would have been very familiar to him. Those small arctic rodents are the most relished food of the Northern wolves and therefore of Huskies, who share the inheritance of the wolves. When a lemming scent crosses the trail of a team of dogs, even a very dependable leader may swing off to follow it, although some leaders will fake an interest in other, imaginary scents to divert the team's attention. The flesh of lemmings is so palatable, in fact, that lemmings are eaten roasted by people in some parts of Northern Europe. An Alaska bush pilot who had crash-landed up on the arctic slope saved his life by subsisting on lemmings during the three weeks before he was found.

A lemming hunt was my own reason for stopping at Nome that summer. For a year I had been in the North in order to gather material for a book about arctic animals. Many are rare and little-known species, and heading the list as the most important were lemmings.

The significance of the little animals is both scientific and literary. Few biologists ever have seen them, although lemmings are a key species and determine the populations of many others. Their effect is due to the way they increase explosively and then, in companies numbering millions, migrate down to the sea and drown. So few are left that one could believe they had become extinct; but again, in only three or four years, they have reached their fantastic density.

During the time when so many of them are available, a whole group of predators live on little else—and being so well fed, themselves breed at an abnormal rate. Other creatures like squirrels and hares, that ordinarily would be prey, are left alone, and they too increase. Wolves ignore caribou, which they hunt at other times, when their hunger is satiated with lemmings. The results extend a long way from the arctic. Snowy owls, a far Northern species, thrive and multiply at the peak of the lemmings' cycle. When they can find no more lemmings, the owls' hunger takes them south even into the Carolinas—and small birds and mammals there become the victims of owls they otherwise never would see.

For their importance biologically, then, lemmings had aroused my curiosity, especially since no scientist has given an undisputed explanation of why they go on their suicidal migrations (suicidal in effect, if not in intention). Some biologists are convinced that the lemming hordes leave their birthplace because they have exhausted the mosses and grass in those area. Examinations of lands over which they have passed, however, have proved that much nourishment still may be there.

For centuries it has been part of the folklore of Europe to believe that the migrating lemmings were seeking a former home on the lost Atlantis or, to speak scientifically, on lands which existed during the Miocene period and now are covered by parts of the North Sea and Baltic Sea. I don't know of any biologists who take that theory seriously—although they do sometimes speculate as to whether the northward migrations of birds every spring could be due to the birds' racial memories of arctic homes in the distant past.

But the legends aren't all found in Europe. In every far Northern country, on every continent, the primitive people call lemmings "mice from the sky." The Eskimo word is *kay-loong-meu-tuk*. Several serious-minded Eskimos told me of seeing the lemmings come down, "falling in bigger and bigger circles that turned same way as sun" or, as we would say, clockwise. Eskimos who had not seen the lemmings descend all could describe lemming tracks that "start where the lemmings landed, without any footprints going out to that place." The late Reggie Joule, an Eskimo bush pilot and son of intelligent native teachers, said that the familiar spurs of lemming tracks often are found on the roofs of the Eskimo cabins at Point Hope, where he grew up, "and there weren't any tracks outside the cabins." He concluded, "I think lemmings fly."

The more common Eskimo explanation is that lemmings float down to the earth from some distant star. (The very smallest spacemen—and Eskimos have prehistoric beliefs about flying saucers or, as they say, flying baskets, but the lemmings weren't passengers. It is believed that they drift down freely.)

I did not take the stories about the tracks very seriously—until a day when I had a chance to see some of them for myself. It was early in April when Frank Ryan, the Eskimo postmaster at Unalakleet, told me that lemmings had landed that day, from the sky of course, on the end of the airstrip. I hurried out. The blacktop was covered with less than an inch of new, light, soft snow—too shallow for any lemming to tunnel under it without thrusting up a ridge on the surface. And there, indeed, were the mysterious little trails, just as the Eskimos had described them. In fifteen places a track began rather faintly for a couple of inches, as if an animal had come down and gently coasted onto the snow. The tracks then continued more deeply, the individual footprints showing clearly, and also the slight brush marks between the footprints where the hairs on the lemmings' feet dragged. They were not mouse tracks, for then there would have been a tail mark between the footprints; but lemmings have only half-inch tails, which they carry turned up as they run. In each case the tracks led off the blacktop to a clump of grass, where the lemming evidently had burrowed down among the roots.

And how could those tracks just begin suddenly, out there on the smooth white surface? I have no idea. Lemmings cannot jump even a fraction as far. They have no membranes between their forelegs and hind legs, as bats have, and therefore they cannot fly. They do have long, soft, thick fur, and briefly I wondered if the wind could have picked up the fluffy little creatures and set them down on the airstrip. That possibility would have been reasonable, perhaps, if the wind had been strong enough on that day to have drifted the snow. It wasn't; the snow was as light as eiderdown and it lay as level as it had fallen. That owls did not pick up the lemmings as they were venturing out on the surface is obvious because the tracks led *to* the clumps of grass, not away from them. An owl (owls and ravens were the only large birds present in the North in that month) might have dropped one squirming lemming—but hardly fifteen in a space about twenty yards square. Naturally I do not believe that the lemmings arrived from a distant star. But the tracks and some other mysteries that developed later remain just that: mysteries, and I don't belittle the Eskimos for devising what must have seemed a logical explanation for them.

I had been trying to find some live lemmings ever since I first came to Alaska. I wanted to take a colony of them to San Francisco, where they were going to be housed and studied by others besides myself at the California Academy of Sciences. Unfortunately I had arrived in the North during the crash period of the lemming cycle, and they had proved very elusive. All the natives at Unalakleet, where at times lemmings are very common, knew I was hunting for them, and six had been seen by various people who tried to capture them, unsuccessfully. In fact, my need for lemmings had been publicized throughout Alaska, and many others were looking for them. The fact that no lemmings were found showed how scarce they were at the sag in their cycle, but when I saw the tracks out at the airfield, late that afternoon, I thought that my problem was solved. Wherever they came from, at least and at last they were here. In the morning I'd dig up the grass roots where they had gone, and I felt certain that I would find them.

By morning I had a fast-developing case of pneumonia and, as soon as a mercy plane could be sent, was bound for Nome and the hospital. It was another instance of the frustration that had characterized the lemming hunt all through the year. When I returned to Unalakleet a month later, the lemmings had vanished, leaving only a few little dried-out pellets which could be identified and which proved that they had, indeed, been there temporarily.

There was new hope, however. On the day that I left the hospital I had met, at Nome, an Air Force major who told me the welcome news that there were "thousands" of lemmings on St. Lawrence Island. They were "running all over the place," he said. A geologist, he had been out on the island surveying an airfield, and, since he was a scientist, I felt sure I could trust his word. In July, then, I was back at Nome, with the objective of getting myself to St. Lawrence Island.

The island lies out in the Bering Sea within view of the coast of Siberia. Its principal Eskimo settlement, Gambell, is 210 air miles from Nome. No commercial planes or ships made the trip in that summer, but the Air Force and Navy went out very often and sometimes they took civilians, who had no other way of getting there. The major assured me that the Air Force would give me a lift. By July he himself had gone back to the States.

The Air Force, when interviewed at Nome, refused my request for a ride. The Navy also refused. I explained the project to numerous officers, who listened with patience but little sympathy, and persisted in calling the lemmings mice. Radio messages flew back and forth between Nome and more distant headquarters, but the answers were all the same: catching some mice was not considered a need urgent enough to breach the security program.

By the end of July I had given up hope of reaching that island where lemmings were running all over. I would return to San Francisco, my base, and make another trip to the arctic the following summer. It was a disappointing and expensive compromise, and the work of the winter would be handicapped by having no firsthand knowledge of the significant lemmings. But there seemed to be no other choice.

Very briefly, during this trying experience with the military, I had thought of the Coast Guard. During the ice-free months a Coast Guard cutter cruises around in the northern Alaska waters. There, where no lifesaving stations or lighthouses are maintained, other ships do at times need the cutter's help. Besides standing by for emergencies, it is one of the peacetime duties of the Coast Guard "to send a cutter to remote parts of the Alaskan coast to carry medical aid and the benefits of law and civilization to the whites and natives." Wouldn't a survey of arctic wildlife be one of the benefits of civilization? I thought so and had inquired whether the cutter might indeed go, but except for rescue work no woman had been allowed on a Coast Guard ship for eight years. The ban was due to the fact that one woman, permitted to ride on the cutter for a short distance, had refused to get off. For several months she thus avoided a legal summons from a husband who wished to divorce her.

I therefore abandoned all hope of the Coast Guard too, without knowing that officers of the cutter then in the arctic, the *Clover*, had heard the radio messages about the woman who wanted "mice," and had felt that the other services were a little ungallant, and had wanted to come to my aid. The director of the Guggenheim Foundation, which was financing my project, also had presented the problem to the commandant; but unaware that wheels, or rather propellers, had started to turn, I left Nome, bound for Kotzebue, where I planned to take a plane out of Alaska.

On the way to Kotzebue I stopped over at the Eskimo hamlet of Shishmaref for the year's final lemming hunt. When the bush plane came down on the beach, several natives gathered to greet the pilot, and they had reassuring answers to my questions about the lemmings. Not thousands but maybe hundreds of them had been seen on the sand dunes since spring—some within the last week. The plane left and I hired an Eskimo with a shovel.

Few human settlements anywhere have as slight a toehold in nature's impersonal element as Shishmaref. Its residents speak of living on an island, but it's only a sandbar, really, with a few acres of beach grass. Yet the scene is attractive in a spacious and airy way—this stretch of sand all surrounded by water as clean, clear, and blue as if it were the earth's first, original sea.

The Eskimo, Foster Olanna, and I walked to the eastern tip of the island, then back from the shore to low mounds of salt-green sedges and cotton grass. Everywhere they were crisscrossed with little trails, used so lately that the new shoots of grass on the floor of the trails showed only as pale yellow tips. The runways led to the burrow entrances, which were up on the sides of the mounds, Foster said, in order to be above the spring meltwater that would lie in the dune trenches. He started to dig out the tunnels, while I stood poised with a butterfly net to capture the lemmings as they might run out.

The burrows were intricate, curving passages up to a dozen feet long, all interconnected and with chambers opening off to the right and left. In each network one "room" was used exclusively for the animals' droppings. Some of the others were filled with the empty casings of grass stems, cut in three-quarter-inch lengths, amazingly uniform. These seemed to serve as padding for nests after the nourishment in the stem had been eaten. Outside the burrows Foster pointed out many stubs of stems, cut off just above the rootstocks. When he would be walking over the snow on his snowshoes in winter, he said, he often had seen a stalk of grass suddenly shrink and disappear as some lemming beneath had pulled it down through the snow and run away with it to the burrow.

We excavated a dozen or more of the tunnel communities—little ghost towns from which every resident had departed. To go where? Since this was a small, narrow island, the only direction the lemmings could have taken was towards the sea. They could only have crossed the wide, smooth beach, festooned at the tide marks with flowerlike shells—a migration of two hundred yards, but a death march.

Why?

The burrows looked comfortable, and the runways the lemmings had made in the sunny grass led through food that was still abundant. In what way were their lives so intolerable that they gave them up? What seemingly "unnatural" instinct overcame the instinct of self-preservation, so that young and old took themselves out of this pleasant place to enter the cold salt waves?

Now, more than ever, I felt I must find some live lemmings—capture enough to have a colony of them, keep them where I could see them continuously as I was working, and hope that they would reveal some hint of the curious impulse that destroyed them. Certainly I would come back the following summer. The population of lemmings should have begun to increase by then.

And would the walls of a cage, if not their own wish to survive, force them to live? For how long? A project like this has avenues opening out and out.

While I was waiting at Shishmaref for the return of the bush pilot, I heard the most whimsical of the numerous lemming legends. It concerned the white species. Of two closely related lemming strains, one remains brown in all seasons, whereas the other, whose members climb up out of the snow to eat the bark of berry bushes, turns white in the winter—no doubt an example of nature's camouflage. Carson, the Eskimo storekeeper, told this little story about the white lemmings, as we were sitting outdoors in the crisp arctic sunshine.

He had been talking about the Little People, who "used to come down from the clouds all the time, but we don't see them so much any more." I asked if they came to help human beings, and he said, "No, they just come to visit, but sometimes they do something friendly. One winter day some of them came ashore from the sea ice and told the people that they'd seen a lot of the white polar bears out there. The hunters got their harpoons and the Little People led them to the place on the ice where they'd seen the bears. But they weren't bears, they were only white lemmings, which looked big to the Little People because they are small. The men hit the lemmings this way and that with their spears: 'That's how we kill your polar bears,' they said.

"The Little People came back to the shore, and we saw them making harpoons for themselves. Then they went out on the ice to try to kill their own bears. Pretty soon they found some, and they tried to knock them out the same way they'd seen the men do—only these were real polar bears and they turned on the Little People and chased them. They would have caught them, too, but the Little People took themselves back to the clouds in a hurry."

With my bags on the plane at Kotzebue and forty minutes to wait before it would leave—there, too, still looking for lemmings, I went for a walk. A boat pulled up on the beach and a sailor jumped out.

"Can you tell us where to find Sally Carrighar?" he asked. "We have come to take her to St. Lawrence Island."

When the plane soared up from Kotzebue, I was in the boat, on my way to the *Clover,* which was anchored twelve miles out to sea.

There were signs of a gale approaching. I had been out in other storms on these Northern waters and was glad that I need not dread this one—for in what ship, if not a Coast Guard cutter, could one ever experience, intimately and yet securely, the ocean's wild fury? As it happened, the cutter's radar equipment went out of commission. Our route led along the arctic coast and down through Bering Strait into the Bering Sea, but the strait is a treacherous channel, strewn with rocky islands and approached past a shoal that has wrecked many ships. Without radar Captain Shannon did not wish to risk the passage, not in the racing fog and tremendous waves that soon were whipped up. Therefore we headed north, straight for the North Pole, in waters where there was little chance of collision with any other ship, though we might be encountering ice floes. The waves were as big as the cutter itself, and I said to one of the officers, "Even you will admit that this is rough water?" And he laughed: "Yes, I'd say this is almost a full sea."

A full sea: wonderful phrase! I took it to mean that the waves were about as high as waves ever become.

Due to the storm it took us four days to travel the four hundred miles from Kotzebue to the island. By the end of that time all the men on board had become interested in lemmings, and from one, Chet Frogle, the chief engineer, I learned something that may clear up one of the lemming mysteries.

While I was in Kotzebue an Eskimo woman had told me that once, when she had caught a lemming "coming down from the sky," she killed it and cut open its stomach, which was filled with very fine grass, bright green, she said. "And it was winter, when nothing is green down here, so that lemming came from a star."

Engineer Frogle, hearing this tale in the wardroom at dinner one night, said, "The green stuff in their stomachs is probably dried grass turned green by the action of the stomach juices. I was brought up on a farm, and I know that after a cow eats hay it turns back into green grass in her stomach."

A radio message had been sent ahead from the ship to the St. Lawrence weather station, asking that some Eskimos be employed to catch lemmings before our arrival. The next day a report came back that two or three dozen lemmings were caged in some boxes on the beach.

We anchored late in the morning in the channel between St. Lawrence Island and the Siberian coast. It is always a turbulent strip of water and that day the waves were about fifteen feet high. Nevertheless, an Eskimo skin boat came alongside while we were having lunch. The men in the *umiak*, more enterprising than some of their neighbors, had brought out their ivory carvings to sell in advance to the crew. The *umiak* was hoisted up onto the deck, and when the officers and I went out, Captain Shannon said to the natives, "We have brought Sally Carrighar to your island to see some lemmings. And we hear by radio that you've caught some of them and they're on the beach."

"On the beach, all right," said one of the Eskimos. "Only—not lemmings."

Stunned by a terrible premonition, I said, "No *kay-loong-meu-tuk?* I was told there are thousands—'running all over,' a scientist said."

"Maybe few *ka-loong-meu-tuk* back in mountains some place. I never see any here. I see them on mainland one time, different from what we catch for you. Little animals, run every place on St. Lawrence Island, just mice."

I looked around at the faces of all these men who had spent four days bringing me here on this ship, and I remembered the woman who had duped the Coast Guard eight years before, and all I could gasp was, "Right now I would risk my life to find lemmings."

It's the kind of thing that one shouldn't say, because fate takes us up on those proclamations.

The captain was courteous and kind. He apparently was convinced that I had been given the wrong information and that I almost was overcome with embarrassment. We went ashore to make sure that the captive animals were not lemmings, and they were indeed mice, tundra voles, of which I already had kept more than a dozen caged at Unalakleet, for months. I paid the mouse-hunters and we returned in the launch to the ship.

The *Clover* is not only a cutter but an ice-breaker, with a bowl-shaped hull so that her prow can be driven up on the sea ice to break it. Because of the ship's incurring sides, the Jacob's ladder for mounting up to the open deck dangled lose in the air for ten to fifteen feet, and swayed in and out with the roll of the ship in this channel. It had not been hard to go down it—one could just drop off the end into the launch below, but getting onto a Jacob's ladder isn't easy for anyone when the water is very rough. I had already heard about one of the seamen who had lost his life a month earlier as he tried to board the Coast Guard weather ship in the Aleutian Trough. The captain warned me therefore to jump onto the ladder fast, when a wave would lift the launch to its fullest height—and I tried. My hands caught the ropes at the sides of the ladder, but my rubber-soled shoepaks slipped off the wet bottom rung. There I hung, with the extra handicap of a large press camera suspended around my neck between me and the ladder. With the ladder swinging so widely my feet could not find the rung again quickly, and I didn't dare try to drop into the launch because, strung up as I was, I couldn't look down. I could look up, though, and I saw the faces of several crew members peering over the edge of the deck. All were taut and some even quite pale, and their concern struck me as very nice and also a little humorous, and helped me to keep my head until I could get and keep my feet back on the ladder.

The ship was to take me to Nome. As we steamed away from St. Lawrence I was not only troubled about the fruitless outcome of this generous effort—although the officers had assured me that they were in the North on a standby basis and might as well be going out to the island as anywhere; but also, what about the reaction of the Nome officers in the other services? They, who had insisted on calling lemmings mice and had refused their help in securing them: how now would they comment on the courteous gesture made by the officers of the *Clover?* Those were my unhappy musings—but only till midnight. At that time we sailed into the center of a scene so rare that, as far as I know, no other naturalist ever has had a chance to observe it.

I was up on the bridge as we moved along in the arctic's unearthly twilight, surrounded by silence so vast that even the sound of the engines seemed hushed . . . when there ahead we discovered a carnival of the giant humpback whales playing. More than a dozen were rolling about in the waves, chasing each other, diving up into the air to descend in slow, graceful arcs, with often a frolicsome toss of their flukes just before the water closed over them. Theirs was the most complete release of high spirits I ever had seen, by some of the largest animals in existence, on one of the most remote seas.

The ensign on duty signaled for slower speed, and the cutter slipped into the very center of the whales' playground. Yet the whales, all around us now, continued to tumble. Possibly they were too possessed with joy to conceive of danger arising from this other, even more massive bulk.

It was hard to think of the whales as animals. They were so huge they seemed almost cosmic, as if this were nature itself at play—free and spontaneous and entirely benign. I wished the ensign and I had not been the only ones watching. I wished everyone who thinks of nature in tooth-and-claw terms could have been there on the ship, for none could have failed to see the innocence of that play, innocent as play only is when it arises from the heart's impulse.

The whales were still splashing and diving, their immense bodies so light, when we left them, when the ship, trailing its thin, long line of smoke, disappeared eastward beyond their horizon.

This undreamed-of opportunity to be in the very midst of the animals in their unguarded gambols—not hunted, not migrating, just amusing themselves as if humans didn't exist—was the climax of the entire year I had then spent in the arctic. Lemmings could and would be found elsewhere, but only the trip to St. Lawrence provided the prize.

I would write about it, of course. The play of the whales would become some of the most important material in the book about Northern wildlife. Meanwhile, leaving the bridge, I decided to spread that word around rather widely while I was in Nome, hoping it might reach the ears of any inclined to facetiousness at the expense of the Coast Guard.

OVER THE HILL

Wendy W. Fairey

I

The weather was hot and the terrain hilly as Grünli Tour #4218 set off after lunch from Gourdon, a village north of Toulouse, to which we had journeyed that morning by train. Dieter, the twenty-four-year-old Austrian van driver, had met us with the bikes, which we then tested out, complained about, adjusted. Water bottles got filled, worries voiced about the heat and the forty-one kilometer stretch that lay ahead for our first afternoon; everyone was nervous and expectant. Once in motion, however, even down that gently sloping first hill, I knew I was fine.

On the postcard I sent to my friend Miranda later that evening—a view of *"Rocamadour d'une falaise en haut"*—I noted that there were two age groups: the people in their twenties and thirties and those on the cusp of fifty, and two levels of ability: slower and faster. On the whole, the younger people were the faster riders, and the older ones the slower. And then there was me, facing fifty that very year and holding my own among the fleeter juniors. I tried to sound self-mocking; I know I was self-satisfied.

I will probably never again see Debbie, the thirty-three-year-old Canadian schoolteacher, Jennifer, the twenty-six-year-old television news program assistant from Washington, and tall, thin, bearded Mike, the twenty-nine-year-old engineer from Alexandria, Virginia. Yet in memory

I feel them alongside me. With something akin to intimacy, I know the sweat on their faces, the muscles on their legs, the set of their bodies. Leslie, on the other hand, seems distant—an indistinct figure at the far end of a long, dark tunnel.

It's sad to remember what good friends we were before the bike trip. First professorial colleagues, then confidantes, we used to meet for Sunday brunch in small, not-too-expensive restaurants with a bit of charm, usually in Chelsea or the Village. Leslie was an easy person for me to get along with because I always knew where she stood. If she was tired, irritated, happy, if she did or didn't want to talk, she told me right off. And that was that; the issues were clear. I thought of her as warmly and bluntly loyal.

Sometimes, it's true, she could be sharp. I haven't forgotten the time when, trying to be helpful, I extinguished the Sabbath candles on her dining room table at the end of a Friday night dinner. I didn't know you were supposed to let them burn out on their own.

"That's presumptuous," chided Leslie, after her initial outcry of incredulity and dismay.

The word *presumptuous* swirled in the air between us. As one might with a flashlight, I searched my soul to see if I could detect a shadowy corner of presumption. I couldn't offhand, but maybe Leslie knew better. I quickly relit the candles and hoped for Leslie's absolution.

I forgave Leslie for calling me presumptuous because I knew her concern was for Morris. It was he who loved the observance of the Sabbath, and Leslie was protective of his needs and pleasures. Morris was Leslie's mate, and at times he seemed almost her badge of honor or her cause. They had hooked up some years back at a three-day faculty development seminar on the subject of "Values in the Curriculum." Morris, a biologist who had written on ethics, was already afflicted with his degenerative arthritis, and he seemed to Leslie so courageous and impressive. They had gone to his office and made love on the floor, a piece of information that Leslie communicated very early in our friendship.

Leslie's confidences—boastful, exuberant, explicit—always left me uneasy, uncertain what to say to her. I thought hesitantly of my own adventures—some of *my* partners on the floor, and elsewhere, had not been men. "That gives you twice as much chance for a date on a Saturday night," said Leslie to me, more than once, doing her best to cheer and urge me on. I always laughed at the joke, and for the moment joined her in believing things that simple. But I always felt a little afterwave of depression. Really, Leslie didn't know the first thing about my perplexities. Sex was too complicated to be a subject for boasting. My boasting tended to be about my prowess at biking and tennis.

Leslie said that Morris was a *mensch,* and I believed her. Sitting next to him at Friday night dinners, I could feel the anchor, the comfort of his warmth. It wasn't that he said much. Illness and medications combined to slur his speech, and at least in company, he left most of the talking to Leslie, who, in any case, was always so effervescent, freely trading jokes and stories and opinions with her guests. Leslie candidly admitted that in some ways her situation with Morris suited her. It was not good, she said, that he was sick, but his condition did leave her lots of freedom to do things on her own—to go out to dinner with friends, to have our monthly women's poker night, even to travel. It was she who proposed the bike trip and passed along to me the brochure, "Europe Biking and Hiking," put out by a Swiss outfit called Grünli.

At first we were only humoring a fancy. In early morning phone calls—being morning people was another of our compatibilities—we reviewed the range of tours, from unchallenging Holland and "The Fabulous Loire Chateaux" (Category 1) to impossible "Switzerland's Alpine Grandeur" (Category 4). In between were "Fascinating Provence" and "Impressions of Tuscany" (Category 3). I remembered the hills around Siena and Florence, and we fixed on Category 2: "medium, a few hills. With a little bit of biking experience, it can be managed without any problems." Of the Category 2 trips to choose from, I was attracted to "Romantic Austria" or "A Hungarian Interlude," but Leslie had a strong preference for France. Finally we narrowed down the choice to Normandy, "graced by its wealth of serenity and culture," in a toss-up with the Dordogne, with its "flowing rivers, historic palaces and castles, medieval towns and villages, Stone-age grottos and caves," not to mention the "superb and delicate cuisine." Leslie and I read the descriptions aloud to each other over the phone, imagining ourselves among the apple orchards and gentle green hills of Normandy—but what if it did nothing but rain?—and, alternatively, in the Dordogne, visiting prehistoric caves and dining on *foie gras* and truffles.

Leslie had written an article on "Women of Prehistory," and was keen to visit the caves. We both liked the names of those medieval towns: Rocamadour, Loubressac, Beynac, Souillac, Les Eyzies de Taynac, Bergerac.

"Shall we put down the deposit?" I said.

"Yes," said Leslie, "let's do it."

For Leslie's birthday that spring I made her a card, a kind of cartoon, that showed two curly-headed bikers pedaling along a road—the slightly larger one was meant to be Leslie. "Leslie en Dordogne," read the caption. "*Bon anniversaire de ta copine de vélo*," read the greeting inside.

I looked forward to the bike trip, passionately looked forward to it. It was strange that I should feel this way, given my lifelong aversion to organized group activities. At nine I had gone to sleep-away camp and written desperate letters home until my mother came to rescue me a week before the camp officially ended. By then, I was beginning to adjust, but docilely I left anyway. The camp awarded me the archery prize *in absentia*, and I kept the brass trophy on a shelf in my bedroom beneath the few blue and red ribbons I had won in horse shows, and my framed certificate for outstanding penmanship. But I never went to camp, or anything like it, again. I didn't like moving with others in lock step; I didn't like feeling compelled.

The bike tour, though, seemed to offer a set of right relations with the world. Pedaling along the roads, gazing at the succeeding vistas, I could, I felt, be inward and solitary, yet with other people within range. Maybe someone would ride up beside me, but not, I imagined, for too long. As for the inns and the dinners, Leslie reassured me that *she* would talk to the others—she, if I liked, would talk for both of us, and I could be as quiet as I wished. As she offered me this option, I envisioned taking it and felt mousy. After all, maybe I would talk, too. But I wouldn't have to. Leslie was willing to buffer me.

"We could have gone twenty years," Leslie later said to me, after the sorry fact, as we met to talk over what had happened. We were sitting on a bench in Sheridan Square, the Union general in his oxidized dignity casting a shadow that fell just short of our place in the wan autumnal sunlight. "We could have gone twenty years without reaching the limits of our friendship."

The coming clash may have been predictable. The projected distances on the trip were twenty-five to forty miles daily, and I launched a training program that might have suited for the Tour de France. There I was each morning, carefully timing my 3.3 mile circuits of Prospect Park, pushing on the hills, extending my distances. Twice I went out to Long Island and rode thirty miles.

Leslie, meanwhile, did her sit-ups and mounted her exercycle half-an-hour daily in her apartment, pedaling to tapes of Sinead O'Connor. Once she rented a bike and took it to Central Park. But the weather was excessively hot and she didn't like the route to the park through the traffic and fumes of Sixth Avenue. "Remember," she said to me, "the trip is only a '2.' A 'little bit' of biking experience is all you need. That's what it says in the booklet."

Our friends in the poker game asked if we were looking forward to our trip. "Yes," I said. "But all I'm thinking about are the distances, the hills, the heat."

"And all I'm thinking about," said Leslie—before long we had settled into a little comedy routine—"are the inns, the other people on the tour, all that wonderful French food."

"Food? People?" said I. "What food? What people? I haven't given them a thought."

"Perhaps you'll meet someone," said Leslie to me privately.

"I seriously doubt it," I replied, then adding (maybe a touch too assertively), "and that's certainly not why I'm going."

Later, when we were on the train from Paris to Toulouse en route to meet up with the tour, it was remembering the banter at poker that led me to say what I did to the Air France pilot in our compartment. The pilot, a blandly attractive young man who welcomed the opportunity to practice his English, had chatted with us about our trip, his career, and the speed of our train, the TGV, on different rails. Then as Leslie was napping, stretched out on the seats across the aisle from the pilot and me, he turned to me with a new conversational gambit.

"Do you like French food?" he asked, carefully pronouncing each word as he flashed a winsome Gallic smile.

"I like it well enough," I replied. "But it's my friend who really likes it."

Afterwards Leslie, who had not been asleep, asked me why I had said that she liked French food more than I. Was it because she was fatter?

I quickly assessed Leslie's body—the square-shouldered torso, the more slender arms and legs. I hadn't intended an invidious comparison; I was just reaching for something to say. Yet as with the Sabbath candles, I felt at once guilty and aggrieved.

We had talked about competition before coming on the trip. "I don't want you making me feel bad at the end of the day if I've been slow and you fast," Leslie had declared. "As far as I'm concerned, it's not a race."

"Of course not," I had replied. "But I don't want you making me feel bad if I've chosen to push my hardest. That's what *I* like to do."

So Leslie and I struck an agreement. I could push, she could amble, and we'd meet at the end of each day's ride.

II

The swifter contingent was defined from the start, that very first hot afternoon. In tandem, or at least within sight of one another's bikes, Debbie, Jennifer, Mike and I rode past rolling fields of vines and sun-flowers—*"tournesols,"* say the French—and the occasional stone farm-house, as far as we knew the way, then waited together for Brigitte, the twenty-seven-year-old Swiss-German guide, to ride up and give us fur-ther directions. Later, Brigitte would tell us about being a guide. "First," she said in her lilting Swiss-German accent that, as you listened, soft-ened an impression of dourness, "you meet the people, shake their hands, get a face to go with a name. Then you see how they bike, who are the strong ones, who the slower. Then you hear their stories. It's the stories that make this job worth doing. I wouldn't still be doing it except for the stories."

I suppose we added to Brigitte's stock of stories, gave her a tale or two to tell another group of bikers as they lingered one night over their espressos, became a piece of her accumulated experience, the experi-ence that, as much as our deepening wrinkles, brings a sense of the weight of time. "I'm getting my first wrinkles," Brigitte said to me a few days later as we rode for a while side by side. "Tell me how you settled your life," she asked. Her boyfriend wanted to marry, but she wasn't sure. She knew I had two grown children.

"Well, I settled it," I answered, "but then it unsettled."

It was our first afternoon of biking and Brigitte had her hands full because the bikers in the rear were having trouble. "Wait here," she kept riding up to tell our contingent. We chafed at the disruption of our rhythm, and chafed even more when we were obliged to take several longer breaks to allow everyone to reassemble. Aside from Leslie, "everyone" included Isobel and Myrtle, a pair of middle-aged New York schoolteachers who, like Leslie and me, were friends back home and had signed up together for the trip. Myrtle taught high-school history and Isobel—spelled with an *o*, she told us, because her parents had felt she should have a beautiful, special name—taught junior high school physical education. Actually, Myrtle and Isobel had wanted to do "The Fabulous Loire Chateaux" (Category 1) but that tour was booked and Grünli had proposed the Dordogne as an alternative.

"I hope there aren't too many hills," Isobel had worried the previous evening in Toulouse, over *salade aux gésiers* (gizzards), a regional specialty, and lamb with a great deal of garlic.

"Don't worry, Isobel," Myrtle had answered. "If there are, you'll get off and walk."

"I guess I won't be last," Leslie had whispered to me, eyeing Myrtle.

"Aah, my thighs," now groaned Isobel, arriving at the spot where I sat in the shade of a cypress tree. "My lungs are okay, but aah, my thighs."

Myrtle was helped by her stolidness. When the hills were too much for her, she did as she had counseled Isobel—got off the bike and walked. "Just tell me the route and the name of our hotel. I'll get there," she said. "No need to wait for me." Fetching up our rear, Isobel and Myrtle found that they didn't like the van following behind them in "clean-up" position. It was noisy, they said, and it made them anxious. So Dieter was sent on to a point ahead.

I had my own thoughts about the van. That there even was one, carrying our suitcases from one inn to the next, offering an alternative form of transportation if we needed it, offended my sense of what a genuine challenge should be. It seemed like the boat that goes alongside the Channel swimmer, or the net under the tightrope. I disdained it as a hedge, almost a form of cheating. I liked it out of sight and mind.

Myrtle and Isobel may have been having no easy time of it, but the person having the most trouble was Leslie. "I think there's something wrong with me," she said, struggling on her bike up to the resting place.

As she sat down heavily beside me, her hands were shaking. "I don't think I can do it."

"Don't make any global decisions," I counseled, hoping a few right words might soothe her. "Go as slowly as you need to. And let's just take one day at a time." I patted her on the back before getting up to re-mount my bike.

Mike and I were the first to arrive at the little bar past the town square with the statue, where Brigitte had told us to stop. "This must be it," I said, feeling like an intrepid scout with the covered wagons coming on behind me. We took off our helmets, peeled off our biking gloves, and sat at an outside table waiting for the others to join us. I squirted the water remaining in my bottle over my head, then ordered and quickly downed two lemonades. The others were straggling in, first Jennifer and Debbie, then, one by one, the rest. With thirteen kilometers behind us and twenty-eight still to go, Isobel as well as Leslie now looked shaken, and Myrtle was more stolid than ever. It was at this point that the three of them decided to ride the remainder of the day's distance in the van. More hills lay ahead. A bit more difficult, said Brigitte, than what we'd done already. There'd be a couple of half-hour climbs. Myrtle, Isobel, and Leslie were complaining that the level of difficulty had been misrepresented. "The brochure says this is a '2'," they challenged Brigitte. And Isobel and Myrtle added that they had been told it was comparable to the Loire.

"Oh, yes?" responded Brigitte in her measured way, as if with a foreigner's difficulty catching the exact words. "I think in the European booklet it's going to be a '2-3.'" The tour was a new one and had not yet been advertised to Europeans.

"I'm going to write Grünli a letter," said Leslie darkly, as she and Myrtle and Isobel helped Dieter load their bikes into the back of the van.

Off they went, ahead of us, to Rocamadour. With the security represented by the van gone, I felt both exhilarated and a touch afraid. It was four o'clock. The sun beat down hard and the countryside was vibrant in its silence. With the slower bikers gone, Brigitte, taking the lead, picked up the pace. I had held strong over the first thirteen kilometers, but now the hills began to tire me. I realized I had started off too fast, not pacing myself for the whole day's distance. Confidence gave way to uncertainty as hills became longer and steeper and farmlands gave way to mountain scrub. Now I was regularly the last of the five bikers, arriving at the top of each hill winded and huffing and not taking long enough to rest for fear of getting left further behind. On the second of the half-hour climbs, I simply couldn't keep biking and had to get off and walk. Chills were shooting up my neck. I imagined just lying down and giving up altogether. It seemed I might die on the mountain. Struggling to overcome the panic, I got back on my bike and rode very slowly. The group was waiting for me at the top.

It was now seven o'clock and Brigitte told us that we still had an hour to go. Somehow I did it, a last, long stretch, keeping up pretty well, tired but not so afraid. Close to eight o'clock we stood on a bluff overlooking Rocamadour, which lay below us, way station to medieval pilgrims, jutting yellow-stoned out of the rock face just as in my post-card to Vivyan. We swept down an arc of road. I was careful to curb my speed—the descents scared me more than the climbs—and it took all my remnants of strength to keep an even pressure on the brakes. A small, final hill leading up to the town I did side by side with Debbie, pedaling in sync with her rhythm. As we put away our bikes in the garage of the Hotel Belle Vue, she offered to carry my saddlebag and water bottle. Perhaps it was just the emotionalism of weariness, but this seemed so tactfully kind, I wanted to cry.

Those who had ridden in the van were gathered for a drink in the hotel garden. "I'm fine now," said Leslie. "How was it?"

I announced that it had pushed me *"à la limite de mes forces."* My demeanor was calm as I concealed my secret pride. Leslie turned to Myrtle. "Do you see that?" she said. "It pushed *her* to the limit. This is certainly not a '2.'"

We had dinner in the garden restaurant. *Salade aux gésiers* yet again, *confit de canard*—we would eat a lot more duck before the week was out—and a wonderful raspberry charlotte for dessert. Still tremulous with fatigue, I sat quietly next to Leslie who had recovered her customary verve. Later as we lay in the dark in our narrow beds, three feet apart, we talked about the biking. Brigitte had more or less assured us that the second day would not be as demanding as the first. "I'm sure it will be easier for you," I said. "In any case you can go slow. And it's no disgrace if you log some of the distance in the van."

The next morning, though, for Leslie, brought no improvement. "There's got to be something wrong with me," she said as we came together for a morning coffee break. "I get winded on the least little hill." Her face was white and her hands were trembling. All I could think to suggest was that she should perhaps ride in the van and try biking again a little later. As it turned out, we had to quicken the pace in order to be on time for a visit to Les Gouffres de Padirac, renowned stalactite caves. Leslie, Isobel, and Myrtle all rode the second half of the morning in the van while the rest of us pressed forward under our own power.

The caves were impressive—a dark descent to a chilly nether world of giant stalactite columns, dripping and crystallizing over tens of thousands of years. Ferried in a punt on the underground river, we glided by La Grande Colonne, which at once dwarfed us and drew us into its grandeur. Back in the sunlight, we sat outside in a garden restaurant and ate *salade au Cabecou*, a round of warm goat cheese set in some lettuce leaves. The scene is vivid in my mind, for one remembers not only the moment of crisis. Memory clings to the undisrupted flow of time leading up to it.

The projected afternoon riding was short, a distance of only ten kilometers before we reached Loubressac—"a medieval town high above the Dordogne, adorned by its castle," said the Grünli brochure—and, more beckoning still, our next inn. Everyone now was biking, and I, along with the others who had ridden the whole distance, felt heavy-limbed. Leslie, though, had perked up. "You guys are slowing down now," she joked as she pedaled past me. "*I'm* fresh."

We were descending a long hill, with Leslie maybe a hundred yards behind me. I had just negotiated the right turn at the bottom when behind me I heard an ominous screeching and then crashing. I turned my head and saw Leslie and her bike on the road. As she later explained when she got back from the hospital and could tell the story, her feet had flown off the pedals. She got them back on, but then slid on the gravel making the turn.

A few seconds later we were clustered round her. Leslie lay on her back still wearing her helmet. Blood spread all over the road.

"Oh, my God, oh, my God," I heard myself repeating. The blood seemed to be gushing from Leslie's head and arm.

"It's not that bad," said Leslie, though it seemed bad enough to me with her lying so terribly still in that pool of blood in the bright summer sunlight.

I walked away, sat against a tree, and buried my head in my arms. "I can't carry her," I sobbed. At the coffee stop that morning Leslie had made a joke: "Let's tie a rope to your bike and you can pull me."

"I can't do that," I had retorted, smiling to cover up what for me was the horror of the thought of pulling, pulling, trying to pull Leslie up an endless hill.

"I can't carry her," I now sobbed aloud.

"Why should you even think that way?" said Myrtle, who now stood near me. "Pull yourself together. She needs you to be calm."

"Yes, yes," I said. "That's why I came up here so she wouldn't see me." I wiped my eyes and returned to Leslie's side. Brigitte was now kneeling beside Leslie, easing off her helmet and wrapping her bleeding arm with gauze. Jennifer was walking in circles in the road and seemed hysterical. "We've got to do something," she said. "We've got to get organized."

Occasional cars were passing, and a few had stopped. "Let's see if we can get a car to take her to the hospital," I suggested. A van ride would be so bumpy and uncomfortable. Jennifer and I talked to a young man who had stopped in a Peugeot. He was willing, he said, to go to the hospital at Saint Cere, ten kilometers away, if someone could tell him the route—he, too, was a tourist. I went back to Leslie and knelt at her uninjured side. Across from me, Brigitte was still working on the bandage. "You're going to the hospital," I told my friend.

"Okay," she said slowly," but I don't have to go alone, do I?"

"Of course not," I said. I looked up at Brigitte.

"One of us should go with her," she said. "Should it be you or me?"

"You," I said, hardly missing a beat.

"As long as it's someone," said Leslie.

And that for me is the moment, something like Lord Jim's moment on the *Patna* when he froze and proved a coward, that nothing ever can undo. Brigitte and I helped Leslie into the car; then the two of them were driven off. Dieter led the way in the van, and a sorry little band of bikers followed him the remaining five kilometers to Loubressac.

"Perhaps you want to ride in the van," Myrtle said to me, her eyes scanning my face.

"No," I answered tersely. "I'd rather bike."

III

I think I knew right away, even as I chose not to, that I should have gone with Leslie to the hospital. Normally we ask so little of our friends. Do we expect them to lend us ten thousand dollars? Or to drop everything and come right away if we're sad? And yet there are moments. Leslie described them as moments when the other person should come first.

Not that she seemed at first to know she hadn't. With three stitches in her forehead, ten in her arm, and a more serious injury to her knee which had swollen up with a large hematoma, she came back to us like a valiant, wounded soldier, and, together again in our room, the two of us looked up the French for bruises and stitches in my little pocket French-English dictionary.

"How do you say, 'I feel pain?'" asked Leslie. At the hospital she had said, *"Je sens douleur."*

"No, no," I laughed, though I felt just a touch impatient with her way of riding roughshod over the language. "It's *'j'ai mal.'"* Leslie said Brigitte had been terrific, the right person to go with her and how astute it was of me to know that. Brigitte had handled the whole business beautifully.

That night I washed Leslie's hair for her because she wasn't allowed to bathe, wiping the soap off her back with a warm washcloth. I felt tender towards her; we seemed close.

But later, months later, as we sat on the bench in Sheridan Square, we could remember only rupture and regrets.

"I reproach myself," I said, beginning with what seemed the lesser failure, "for not staying back and riding with you on the first day. Why did I have to be out front?"

"No, no, I had Myrtle," said Leslie. "I didn't expect you to do that."

"And I should have gone with you to the hospital," I said. "How could I not have gone with you? I'm very, very sorry."

"Yes," said Leslie. "I feel just terrible about that. You weren't there for me when I needed you."

"I was afraid. I didn't know the system," I proffered in explanation.

"But your good French," said Leslie.

"I was so tired and shaky myself," I said. "I wasn't sure I could help you."

"If it had been your daughter," said Leslie, "you would have pulled yourself together."

Miranda, whom I made my confidante in the long months of alienation from Leslie—the months of polite interchange, even laughter at poker, but of nothing warm left underneath—said she thought I was at once making too much and too little of what had happened. I nodded my head in agreement but remained puzzled. What would have been the golden mean, the just-right way to feel about it all?

Of course, Leslie and I both looked back to the accident through the memory of what came after, the disquieting week that followed. Leslie stayed with the tour. She seemed not even to consider calling it quits and going up to Paris, thinking, or at least voicing the hope, that she might be ready to bike again in a few days. To me this seemed wildly unrealistic. Certainly *I* considered her leaving, though I didn't know how to broach the subject. "Might you not be better off . . . ?" The self-regarding nature of such a query would have been as transparent to Leslie as it was to me.

In the days that followed the accident, Leslie felt less well. "I'm worse," she worried. "My leg hurts. The bruise is spreading." She rode each day in the van as Dieter's passenger while the rest of us biked, joining in at the stops at caves and castles and roadside cafes and in towns with the names that back home had beguiled us. It was in Souillac, I think, that my snoring made her cry; when, in turn, her sobs woke me up, I sat on her bed and held her hand. "Why don't you phone Morris," I suggested, "and tell him about the accident?" Leslie hadn't called Morris because she didn't want to worry him. Even now she didn't, and perhaps this made her look more to me than she might have otherwise. In Beynac Leslie snapped at me for using her bath towel, and I answered meekly that I had thought the doctor said she shouldn't get her leg wet. In Les Eyzies de Taynac I said nothing upon learning that she had used my bath towel as a bathmat, but then erupted at some later mild but insistent reproach. "Don't shout at me," I retorted. "I don't like it." And I stalked from the room for a midnight walk around the town.

"I lay there," said Leslie in Sheridan Square. "I lay there in my bed and felt so helpless. I couldn't run after you."

"But you were beating up on me," I said.

"But we weren't equal," said Leslie with great intensity.

"What do you mean 'we weren't equal'?" I asked. "You were you, injured and I was me, biking. What does any of that have to do with equality?"

Replaying in my own mind our words and feelings and actions, I have tended to defend myself on point A and counterattack on point B. By my reckoning I was nice to Leslie as often as I was distant or inconsiderate, and she, toward me, was repeatedly sharp, irritable, suspicious, resentful. I know, though, that I let her down, not just by failing to go with her to the hospital or by falling short in little acts of consideration; for example, Leslie said I could have offered to get her more aspirin.

I let her down in how I felt about her. Though I said nothing about the accident, I was stern about it in my thoughts. It was as if we belonged to a team that *she* had let down, and I was now a critic with no mercy. She hadn't practiced enough, was unprepared, had been a blunderer. I could see her flying down the hill with her feet flapping out from the pedals, not knowing the first thing about hills or turns or anything.

I was angry at her and grew to dislike her. Her jokes irritated. Her presence seemed to occupy all the space in our shared bedroom. I hated her when she complained how Dieter had failed to carry her bag or when she mocked the French doctor, so pompously proud, she said, of his English, who had extracted the blood from her knee before it turned to the consistency of "'am."

"Jambon?" she had asked him.

"Non, marmelade," he had replied.

"Ah, jam," had interpreted Leslie.

"Oui, j-ja-a-m," had said the doctor.

And my heart hardened against her, to a consistency thicker than jam. Riding by the van on my bike, I more than once kept my head averted, my eyes fixed on the road, so as not to have to catch her glance. She was like a dark shadow cutting across the sunlight. I wanted to pedal as far away as I could from her wounds, her weakness, her self-absorption, her flesh, to push up hills and swoop down into valleys, to accomplish with verve and grace each day's course, to be hardy and free.

One morning, I remember, it was raining hard, but we decided we would ride anyway and got out the bikes. I loved the whole business: of packing up the *sacoches*, the saddle bags, putting on gloves and helmet, unlocking the bikes, setting off. That day there was the added complication of the rain. Zipping up my yellow slicker, drawing its hood over the helmet, taking the gel seat covering off my saddle so it wouldn't get wet, I felt the rain not as an adversary but as part of the rhythm, the harmony. And then down we swooped, down a wonderful long hill, on into the Dordogne Valley. Soon we were riding along the tree-shaded road that bordered the river. The rain, now lighter, tingled cold on my legs, but my slicker kept my torso dry. We stopped at a little chapel, warmed ourselves with a cup of tea at the cafe across the street, and then pushed on, wending through fields of sunflowers. The sun was now struggling to come out, but the day remained cool and everyone was biking well. After a stretch of riding, Brigitte signaled to us to stop. She, Mike, and I climbed to a lookout, below which spread the valley, the river lacing through it, a deep green vista against the lifting clouds.

And absent from all that wide expanse was Leslie—Leslie to be connected to, Leslie to remember, Leslie from whom every day I tried to hide my exhilaration.

IV

"How was the bike tour?" asked forty-two-year-old Janice, our youngest member, at the first poker game of the fall. Glancing quickly at Leslie and then Miranda, I stayed silent, giving Leslie the chance to be the first to answer. Leslie laughed. "Oh, great," she said. "Do you know the joke, 'And aside from *that*, Mrs. Lincoln, how did you like the play?'"

By "that," Leslie explained to me on our park bench, she had meant the accident, and me. It stung to learn she had considered dropping out of poker because seeing me, she said, was painful. She thanked me quietly for my apology. Then when there seemed nothing more to say, at least that day, I remained on the bench and watched her walk away.

"I ate humble pie," I explained afterward to Miranda, "but it may not have been humble enough."

"What a clash of two large egos," said my daughter.

Leslie had said she was uncertain about our future as friends—we'd have to see. She phoned, though, the next day, leaving a message on my machine that our conversation had made a difference.

And two weeks later, warily hopeful, we got together for afternoon tea with Isobel and Myrtle. It was Myrtle who had suggested the reunion; we had proposed having tea. Isobel and Myrtle had never done tea before, and they eyed the little crustless sandwiches with suspicion as we sat wedged together at a rectangular table at Tea and Sympathy on Greenwich Avenue. Isobel was describing a faculty workshop at her school in which her assignment had been to write about a day, some day in the past year, when she felt happy with herself. "And you wanna know what I wrote about?" she said. "I wrote about the bike trip. And you wanna know why? Because it was an *accomplishment.*" Isobel had a way of isolating a word and unabashedly letting it shimmer.

I glanced at Leslie and felt afraid. But when Myrtle gave her a photograph of herself in wounded splendor—Leslie seated on the grass in her bathing suit showing off her bruised arm and forehead and leg—she gave her hearty laugh. That picture had been taken our last day of biking, the day before the tour disbanded, as we picnicked at a little lake. Leslie had not been feeling well, Isobel had persuaded her to swim, and Leslie, who loved swimming, had then felt "so much better." I remembered Isobel's self-satisfied challenge to me, "Could you have gotten her to do that?" And I had hugged to myself the guilty knowledge that, looking so to get away from Leslie, I would never even have thought to try.

"You know," said Isobel as we were walking away from the restaurant, Leslie in one direction and the rest of us, as it happened, in another, "I was right behind her and I saw the accident."

"Oh," I said. "Tell me about it. Leslie said her feet flew off the pedals."

"No," said Isobel. "But the pedals were going so fast, the gears weren't engaging. Then at the bottom of the hill she actually took her hands off the brakes. I couldn't believe it. She spurted forward just as she had to make the turn. She was wildly jiggling the handlebars"—Isobel clenched her fists and gyrated her hips in illustration—"I shouted at her, 'What are you doing?' And then it was too late. You know what she didn't understand? She didn't understand *momentum.* She was completely out of control."

As I now replay the scene in my mind, I see Leslie's feet on the pedals, not flying off them, and I see those pedals spinning faster and faster. I see her crouched over the handlebars, perhaps glimpsing me ahead as I make the turn. She releases the brakes, shoots forward, jiggles, starts to wobble. Everything is confused, chaotic, then violent. There is blood all over the road.

But what if then, turning around at the noise and apprehending Leslie's plight, I had rushed to her side and stayed there, without a moment's wavering? And when Brigitte had said, "One of us should go with her. Should it be you or me?" I had answered, without missing a beat, "Me."? What would have happened then?

I can see Leslie settled in the front seat of the Peugeot with me in the back seat right behind her. I am leaning forward, one of my hands on Leslie's shoulder in a gesture of reassurance. I chat a bit in French with the young driver, helping him to figure out the route. "Mille fois, merci," I thank him a half-hour later, as he deposits Leslie and me in front of the small provincial hospital in Saint Cere. Leslie hobbles along, leaning on my arm, as we make our way to the emergency room. "Mon amie a eu un accident de vélo," I explain to a tidy, young, female receptionist, who looks up in her quizzical French way at the two disheveled, middle-aged American women in biking clothes. We take our seats in a pleasant, if simply furnished waiting room. The walls are stucco, the floor cool stone. I am there for my friend. I admire her dignity, her fortitude in adversity. The wait to see the doctor is not long.

LEARNING THE ROPES

Betsy Aldrich Garland

I never intended to go all the way.

It was not in my nature to take that much risk, to compromise so much, to push myself to the limits. I was a "good" girl who played it safe, hiked with my feet on the ground, considered what people might think and seldom tested the boundaries. Now here I was being strapped into a seat harness and choosing a helmet. If the group had its way with me, they would cajole me high into the trees where I would find myself grasping a thin wire for dear life.

A child of protective middle-aged parents, I was raised more timid than gutsy. I took school work seriously enough to become a good—though not great—student. It never occurred to me to sign up for sports, and I looked forward to trips to the Cape with my mother for nothing more strenuous than shopping and beaching. It was not until my college years that I realized I was missing something: when I let my father and brother go mountain climbing without me, I did not know that backpacks and blisters have their own rewards. Although I dated in high school, my primary social life was a rather tame church youth group, and my classmates thought me shy—so much so that when I graduated, I received the award for being the "Quietest" in a class of several hundred.

Reading was my passion, and stories about nurses had shaped my decision to become a nurse. Although my application was accepted at both a local Ivy League school as well as a state university, I chose the latter. Not only did the less prestigious program offer a chance to live on campus and a more science-oriented bachelor's program, it also felt less overwhelming and threatening. Once, in freshman gym class, I was dribbling the ball down the field, heading right for the goal. I was out ahead and my team was cheering me on. At the last minute, I passed the ball. I was not ready for challenges and risks.

Nevertheless, for the first time I excelled academically and graduated first in my nursing class. At the completion of the five-year program, I moved back home with my parents and worked as a public health nurse in the agency in which I had been serving as a student intern. A year later, just as I turned twenty-four, I married. All of my friends were married; it was the expected thing to do. I would not have wanted to be "always a bridesmaid, never a bride."

On our honeymoon at my family's romantic cottage on a little island in New Hampshire's lakes region, my new husband spent all of his time on the beach, working on the property. I was assigned the role of watching from the cottage steps. Building a stone wall took precedence over building our relationship.

Because ours was not a particularly fulfilling marriage, I soon began to volunteer in the community in order to stretch my wings, find some support and add meaning to my life. Out of the house, I had a chance to grow. By the time I began to think about taking legal action, the atmosphere was so bad that, one night at dinner, my perceptive three-year-old daughter leaned over in her highchair, put her sticky little hand on my arm and said, "I know Daddy doesn't love you, Mommy, but I love you." Nevertheless, I struggled along, for better or worse, for twelve years.

When I finally divorced my husband in 1975, I felt free at last—but free to cry tears of exhaustion instead of tears of rage. With total responsibility for two young children, I needed a place to live, a job, child care and a schedule that would mesh with my work (if and when I found some) and their schooling.

That first summer, I worked in a small nursing home, nights, 11 P.M. to 7 A.M. The director gave me permission to bring my children to work with me, and they slept in the lounge while I made the rounds from room to room. We were so poor that I didn't have change for the laundromat, so if the patients were quiet, I also did our family laundry in the home's machine. And I longed for someone to bring me flowers.

My friends worried about me. A breakthrough came when one of them called and urged me to apply for a position as executive director of a small nonprofit agency. I did, and based on my years of experience as a volunteer, I was hired.

Although I was well suited to provide leadership to the agency, I had no office experience. It was a mysterious place. Buttons on the telephone took on a life of their own and cut people off. Cabinets—if one found the magic button to unlock them—swallowed file folders between the hanging files. The compensation, for both the board that had hired me and for myself, was that the paid work was surprisingly similar to the volunteer work I had been orchestrating from my kitchen table. I learned quickly. At first, the weekly newspaper column I wrote as part of my job took a full day, but after a year or so, only an hour. Gradually, I learned new skills and gained self-confidence. In a few years, I was a busy executive with a budget to balance, reports to write, a staff to supervise. The trophy I earned was a house in the suburbs, maple trees and a lawn to mow. On Saturdays, the children, golden retriever and I went hiking. We were settled in—in every way.

It was to this predictable life that the summons came almost a decade later. Counseling church camp for a week in western Rhode Island was not my choice. But I was on the camp board, and my friend, the director, was short a few volunteers. She talked me into it—just to be there, to supervise the younger counselors, to add a little oversight, to share my wisdom and experience. Little did I suspect that what I would undertake there would change my life.

All week, we were preparing the campers for the high ropes. We spent a morning on group initiatives, spotting each other as we crossed the wobble log, learning to work together to solve problems, using the groups' resources to get everyone over a beam lashed high between two trees. Even though I was old enough to be their mother, I was handed up and over in an explosion of group excitement. With so many hands reaching out for me, I felt weightless and free from ordinary constraints.

One afternoon we went orienteering with compass and map, trekking through mosquitoes and thick woods with the promise of a swim if we made it back to camp in time. I was sweaty in my jeans and tee shirt, sunburned where my hat had not protected my face, and footsore. Arthritis in my lower back was stiffening my walk. My air-conditioned office was becoming a dim memory.

Each evening was the day's reward. After hours of physical exertion, we trudged back to our campsite in the woods, hot, happy and tired— a family unit of sorts. And although we weren't through, we had only to gather wood, haul water and make supper over a campfire before we could rest. We all lingered in the firelight, reflecting on the adventures of the day, and tried to get some perspective on the serious business of being teenagers in a confusing world. As night deepened and the whipporwills began to call and the owls to hunt, we made ourselves as comfortable as we could in hammocks slung between two trees—all under the guise of building community, learning to trust, forming healthy relationships.

Late in the week, we were scheduled for the biggest challenge of them all: high ropes. Since I had a proposal to write and needed to spend several hours at my desk in the city, I planned an escape. There was nothing I could do to facilitate the afternoon's agenda. The trained ropes-staff would be there for the teenage campers. I slipped out of camp.

Returning several hours later, I wandered up to the ropes course to see how my campers were managing. We were in a lovely pine grove, fragrant with evergreen and carpeted with needles. Forty feet above us was the Postman's Walk: two cables, one above the other, strung between trees ten feet apart. Those who mastered that could take on the Burma Bridge, a loose rope concourse with rope "rails." The way down was the zip line—or a return back over the full course.

A few of the campers already had completed the ropes. Others were in the trees. One girl was sitting on a branch, crying, waiting for the courage to go on. The boys were trying to act macho, but their pale faces broadcast their fear. Everyone, at the very least, was expected to *try* the ropes, to test themselves in extreme conditions—although how far one went was a matter of personal decision.

"OK, Betsy, you're next," someone called. Thinking he was joking, I laughed. "There's no way I can climb that ladder!"

"Sure you can." The bigger boys were feeling empowered and insisted with missionary-like zeal, "We'll hold the ladder steady for you,

Betsy." Caution was my birthright, and reluctance, my middle name. I thought that I would take a few steps, and they would see that I was too old, too physically out of shape for this.

"How dangerous is this, really? I'm not very strong." I saw that Jack, the ropes director, belayed each climber. The rope on my seat harness went up through a pulley on the topmost cable and back down to the ground through Jack's harness.

"No problem!" he said. "If you fall, I just pull up on the line to catch you and then lower you to the ground."

Right, I thought, if Jack is paying attention. I had missed the dangling-in-mid-air, there's-nothing-to-worry-about demonstration while I was back at the office.

It was hot in the grove. OK, I decided, I'll fake it. I put one uncertain foot up on the first rung.

The boys showed me how to wrap my arms around the ladder, to hold on from behind, keeping the ladder close to my body. I inched up another couple of rungs. "That's the way, Betsy, keep it up," they said.

I didn't have a good excuse *not* to keep going, at least not one that would not have demoralized my campers. I climbed, sliding my arms up with each step.

Never expecting to go that far, I hadn't considered what I would do when I reached the top. The cables intersected with the ladder, one above my head about a foot or so; the other, near my feet.

"Now step out on the cable to your right," ordered Jack-the-Roper.

Silent prayers winged their way to heaven. "Where do I hold on?"

"Reach up and take hold of the cable above your head."

Slowly, with my heart pounding, I did as I was told. I moved off the ladder and onto the cables.

"That's it," Jack said helpfully from below. He stood alert, head up, legs braced, more confident of my safety than I, hands on the line connecting us. "Now turn around."

I was suspended forty feet in the air. The cable under my feet cut into my sneakers.

Jack called up, "Lean forward a little and pull on the cable above your head; that will help you to stop shaking."

With perspiration running down the back of my scalp, along my jaw line and dripping off my chin in a steady stream, I wondered if anyone noticed it was raining on the ground. My God, now what?

"Now walk along the cable to the tree."

The tree was a long way off. I tentatively moved my left foot an inch or two and then pulled my right one up beside it. Like a crab, I inched sideways, one baby step, then another, trailing my rope like an umbilical cord.

"You're lookin' good, Betsy—keep it up!" my campers encouraged.

Persistence pays off. After a very long time, I made it to the tree where I was welcomed by a staff person who invited me to step up on her knee so that I could throw my leg over the waiting branch. She hooked me into the tree safety system and freed the rope for the next climber. "Rest for a few minutes," she offered graciously. I leaned my head against the trunk and breathed. Now I knew why this was called the most-hugged tree on the grounds.

What was I doing here, high in this pine with its rough bark against my cheek and its beads of pitch gumming my hands? Having made it this far was more a surprise than an accomplishment. Was this a bad dream or a cruel trick? Had I, in a moment of being a good sport, allowed myself to be manipulated into this situation? Or had I myself chosen this high adventure?

Now it was beginning to get crowded in the air. Someone else was nearing the tree; I needed to move on to make room. The staffer hooked me into the bridge system, a new terror to be confronted and overcome. I took a step onto the ropes and sank about two feet.

"Push out on the rails," I was told.

To my surprise, doing so made the bridge firmer. I pushed my arms along, afraid to let go to advance my hands. The skin began to peel off the inside of my forearms, a small price to pay for life itself.

My concentration began to wane. Although I was getting tired, I had made it this far and the end of the course was in sight. I noticed that my cheering squad had disappeared; those who had been so encouraging of my ascent had abandoned me for others who were starting to climb. I was alone, high above everyone, stripped bare, vulnerable. Time stood still. There was neither past nor future, only sky and wind and texture, and the moment to which I held on with every nerve and muscle. I was there forever.

The sound of voices, familiar voices, brought me back to my plight.

Visiting church leaders had wandered up to watch the day's activities on the high ropes. "What is Betsy doing up there?" I heard one woman ask another. Good question, I thought, not knowing whether to be proud or embarrassed. High ropes are for campers, not for middle-aged women.

A new staffer hooked me into the tree system at the end of the course. There was a board nailed into the crotch of the tree where campers could sit. The only challenge left was to reach out, grasp the zip line and push off into space.

"Go whenever you're ready." Campers were waiting at the bottom to slow my one-hundred-fifty-foot slide to the ground.

After what I had just been through, this seemed easy. Nevertheless, I decided that, just like waiting on the end of the board to dive into cold water, I had better not think about it too long. I took a deep breath and a firm hold on the rope above my head, propelled myself out of the tree, spun around, and began my free-fall to solid ground. I had done it!

I was soaked with sweat and dizzy with excitement. My throat was dry, my knees weak. Someone took my picture. Someone else unhooked me and helped me off with my helmet. The ordeal—and I—were finished. Expecting, at my advanced age, that I would be allowed at least several hours to recover, I went and sat on the ground, until I realized I was needed to coax the boy behind me out of the tree. One by one, the campers were working their way through the system.

The counselors had been instructed that reflection on the exercise was as important as the exercise itself. "What was it like for you to be up there?" we asked when we were all seated in a big circle. "Did the support of the others help?" And even more importantly, "What did you learn about yourself?"

I sifted pine needles through my fingers. I had just had one of the most intense physical experiences of my lifetime. Only giving birth to my two children had demanded the same utter concentration, stamina and emotional control—before ropes. Now that my body was grounded, my spirit began to soar. I was, as my campers would say, "psyched!"

Because of that experience, I have learned to push against the limits. I have chosen, again and again, to discover what I can do, to expand my horizons, to achieve beyond my wildest imagination.

In mastering the high ropes, I knew, perhaps for the first time, that I could do whatever I needed to do to be true to my deepest self. Perhaps

I had strayed outside the norm by being one of the first clergy wives to file for divorce, but I had not understood the significance of what I had done then. I could buy flowers for myself, whenever I wanted them.

I learned then that I have a deep well of personal strength from which I can draw living water when needed. A year later, while working full-time, I enrolled in graduate school to earn the classical education I had missed in my nursing program. During my first semester on campus, I met a woman in the courtyard. "Aren't you Betsy Garland?" she asked. "I was a visitor to the camp on the day you climbed the high ropes." I remembered the people in the clearing. "You can do anything," she said. I knew it was true.

Life, in all its fullness, has tested me many times since. My father's unexpected death in an automobile accident not only stunned the family, it also meant my eighty-something-year-old mother now depended more heavily on me. Two staff members colluded, charging me with mismanagement in an unsuccessful attempt to usurp my leadership. Vacationing in Costa Rica, I was caught in the undertow and almost swept out to sea.

But over the years, I have learned to do what needs to be done, to focus on where I am going, to drink deeply. My experience in the air has helped me to become grounded, knowing how and when to hold on tightly, take one step at a time, trust the people around me, stay alert, do my best.

Now it is time to step out again, onto a thin wire.

My twenty years in the voluntary sector have been good years for me and for the agency. I have found the work both challenging and satisfying, and the program has thrived. When I took over in 1975, I was the only employee, the budget was $25,000 and our field of influence was very small. Since then, the organization has grown many times over. Hard work has built a program with a statewide presence and a national reputation. These have been productive years which have benefited countless people and agencies.

But times have changed. Hard work no longer brings the same rewards. The time has come for someone else to take the helm. And the time has come for me to explore new opportunities, develop new skills, pursue new dreams.

Shall I stay with the familiar? I sit by the fire, listening to the loons wailing across the lake and the wind moaning in the pines—and reflect. I have taken a few days' vacation and retreated to the island in New Hampshire. By nightfall, on the last day of my time apart, I am ready. It takes me about an hour to write my letter of resignation. Reading it over, I cry. I have three months.

Having been a single parent for twenty years in a low-to-moderate-paying job, I have almost no savings. At the same time, I have mortgage payments to meet, college loans coming due, cat food to buy, a daughter I am helping through graduate school. More importantly, I am fifty-six and have no immediate job prospects.

"Cool, Mom!" my thirty-year-old, high-ropes-accomplished son commented when I broke the news. Easy to say when one has a job, I thought.

I have stepped out onto another high wire. I am both excited and afraid: security seems an almost insurmountable distance away.

Yet I trust that I will arrive safely. I also believe that overlooked opportunities will surface and that my life, while changing, will be more freeing and fulfilling than ever. I believe in myself and my visions of new challenges and high achievements.

I am ready for almost anything. I have learned the ropes.

MY REENCHANTING GARDEN

Florence R. Krall

I've turned to permaculture. For a quarter of a century I have tilled soil and pulled weeds. But now on the advice of my good friend, Linda, who is an informed gardener and a wise woman, I am going to *stop digging*. This change in my approach to gardening came in response to a spring that brought me to the peak of frustration. After tilling one patch for the third time in an effort to rid it of weeds, and each time finding the regrowth more substantial than the last, I stood back with foot on spade, took a look around and asked myself, "What on Earth am I doing here?"

As is the case with the beginning of each gardening season, my expectations this spring exceeded possibilities. The results, after giving more than the usual attention and energy to the garden, were particularly disappointing. The carrots I planted repeatedly refused to germinate. Some creature gobbled up my spaghetti-squash plants as quickly as I planted them. I mistakenly planted bush instead of pole beans. Everything grew at a snail's pace. But the greatest problem was the infestation in the northeast quadrant by three tenacious weeds: one a kind of succulent that my neighbor used as a cover plant on a rock garden that somehow blew into my garden; another, field bindweed that spreads and takes hold above—and below—ground like some evil thing; and downy brome, whose spikelet matures into a stick-fast that won't let go of pants or socks, and whose scientific name, *Bromus tectorum*, is a splendid substitute for the expletives that have been heard arising from my "back forty." These unwanted plants took to the cool, wet spring that everyone agreed was unusually poor for gardens, as if the weather had been fashioned precisely for their genetic constitution.

Before proceeding with my garden narrative, I must digress a bit to provide context for readers who are authentic gardeners. The truth is I am an absentee gardener with an automatic sprinkling system. I, with my husband, live most of the growing season in the mountains of Wyoming, returning every month or so to our city home in Utah, where, at least until last year, my garden seemed to make it pretty much on its own. This essay, then, is about the garden at my home in Salt Lake City where the microclimate along the Wasatch Front provides excellent growing conditions for all types of vegetation, weeds included.

Since I claim a deep environmental leaning, I also feel compelled, before getting back to my garden, to add a disclaimer for owning two homes. Before I met my husband, Paul Shepard, I read his books which advocated owning only one home, preferably in the city, and leaving the countryside open for other creatures on our planet. I totally agreed, and still do, for ecological as well as pragmatic concerns: truthfully, I find one home more than I can manage. So in the early seventies, when I, a single mother, began teaching at the University of Utah, I chose a well-worn home of turn-of-the-century, prairie-style architecture in The Avenues, a neighborhood that has slowly improved through the years as older houses have gained in popularity. Not a very large house or especially elegant, my home, nonetheless, opens out wonderfully from one living space to another, bringing me satisfying feelings of spaciousness and freedom. The old house holds a quarter-century of memories, of celebrations of weddings and passages and pain, that come with growing up with children and getting older on one's own. It has been a good home, within walking distance of grocery, downtown and even a hospital, should I have to drag myself there. To my special delight, it is two short blocks from City Creek Canyon which leads through a park and up the canyon to the Wasatch Mountains, an ecotone between city and mountains that I have traced through the seasons and years since I moved in.

The lots in this section of The Avenues are narrow and long, and the houses sit close to each other at the front of them. The long, narrow back yards lead to a central open area in the middle of the block that once housed carriages but now serves as a place for garages and parked cars. For years from my kitchen, I have looked across and sometimes waved to my neighbors at work in theirs—I have outlived and outstayed several. This closeness to others, so unlike my childhood ranch home in the sagebrush country of Wyoming where an open horizon encircled me each day, surprisingly has never threatened my privacy. I have refused to put up curtains and blinds in my kitchen and bedroom to allow as much sky and sun to enter as possible. Often it is the changing quality of the light in the house that informs me of the scarlet sunset or the approaching steel-gray storm; it is then I run to an upstairs' window or to the front yard to observe the real thing.

A little over a decade ago, I met Paul Shepard, the author of the one-home ethic that I had adopted, and, in late life, we took to each other in a rather remarkable way, remarkable especially when I learned that he didn't practice what he preached. At that time he was teaching in California, and owned a cottage tucked away in a canyon in the San Gabriel Mountains as well as a cabin in Montana. We began commuting from his homes to my home as we formulated retirement plans. At the same time we rented a cabin in Wyoming on a piece of land close to my heart, my birthplace and excellent fly fishing, one of Paul's delights. After much discussion, we decided to buy a piece of land in Wyoming, build a cabin there, sell our city homes, gift his cabin in Montana and retire to Wyoming, all of which we proceeded to do in bits and pieces.

Plans change. Underlying our lives seems to be some constant thread drawn out of prehistory and our own biology, elaborated by our early experiences with place, kin and circumstance. The process of living and maintaining our personal identity, however, requires that we periodically select new paths for playing out the course of our lives which are shot through with adjustments and accommodations and, sometimes, dramatic shifts, like earthquakes that form new lakes, change the course of rivers and cause mountains to slip. Last year in that beautiful, early Wyoming fall, floating down the Green River lined with yellow cottonwoods with the Wind River Mountains as backdrop, the sound of geese and sandhill cranes migrating through, and moose peering at us unafraid as we floated cautiously by, our lives seemed very near perfect. But our plans for re-forming the rest of our lives were suddenly interrupted when Paul, a nonsmoker, checked on a persistent cough and was diagnosed with metastatic lung cancer.

All previous plans suspended, we moved back to our city home early in the fall and put our minds and hearts to healing and treating the malignant growth. The cold winter months almost took Paul with them, but as the sun approached the equinox, contrary to all predictions, he began a remarkable recovery. It was then that I became obsessed with my garden.

This city garden has a long history of people moving in and out, helping out or taking over, harvesting or just plain carrying off its fruits and vegetables, a sort of communal affair. Actually, when I first moved into the old house, there wasn't a garden. At that time the long, narrow lot that is my back yard was divided in half by a high lattice fence covered in early summer with a cascading array of diminutive pink tea roses and velvety-white and deep-maroon blossoms. Near the house, a huge English walnut tree dominated one side of the yard and an ancient cherry tree, the other. The lawn was surrounded by beds of periwinkle, ivy and lily-of-the-valley. Enormous maple trees in my neighbor's yard kept the back yard shady and cool. At first I planted pots of impatiens, begonias and lobelia and let it go at that. Occasionally I would venture beyond the lattice fence into the back section where I stored things in an old garage. At such times I would take a minute to look around and dream of ways to bring order to the chaos.

The area beyond the lattice fence was a netherworld, a place gone wild that had apparently been a dumping ground for cinders and refuse back in the days when they burned coal in the house. This narrative, then, is about that area beyond the lattice fence, that wild dumping place and its genesis into my garden, a vegetable garden interspersed with a few flowers, mostly edible, thrown in for aesthetics.

One day, a neighbor who lived on the corner and had no back yard asked if I'd mind if he planted a garden in the area beyond the fence. It seemed like a good idea. Little did I anticipate the far-reaching consequences of this good idea, like others that have come to me suddenly in my lifetime, such as remarrying or building a second home.

My neighbor was mild-mannered, and I knew his wife as a participant in one of my environmental education workshops. He seemed to be someone I could trust. What could I lose? He began with a small section, tilling the soil and planting. The first set of seeds sprouted and then immediately shriveled and died, as if the soil were sterile or toxic. He took a sample for analysis, the report indicating that wood chips were needed to balance the pH. Being a carpenter, he brought in sacks of sawdust and began composting. He kept at it for several years, and each harvest we marveled at the dramatic improvement in productivity. Then he and his wife moved to a small rural community where he would restore old homes, and they would raise their children away from the city.

It was then that I halfheartedly fell into gardening. During the ensuing years I have recruited, bribed, cajoled and manipulated friends, relatives and house sitters to help with or take over the garden. For most of those years, Jason and Meredith, my two oldest grandchildren who until recently lived nearby, helped me dig and plant. Now as I work the soil, I can see again their grubby, chubby children's hands and their utter concentration as they carefully planted seeds. I always favored their help because they seemed to have a special relationship with the garden divas who are supposed to inhabit the wild peripheries of gardens and help seeds to sprout and plants to grow.

Along the way I have also hired two "gardeners," both of whom have accepted only limited involvement with the kitchen garden, their self-defined duties confining them to the front and back yards with lawns to mow and shrubs to trim. I first met Mr. Paxton when I looked over the fence into my elderly neighbor's yard one day and discovered a still-more-elderly gentleman on his hands and knees grubbing away in the flower beds. I forthwith recruited him into doing some work for me.

Mr. Paxton had distorted hearing. When I spoke to him, he always looked into the top of the walnut tree as if I were a bird on some high branch chirping at him. Besides altering his perception of the direction of sounds, his hearing defect also prevented him from following directions, or so it seemed. I soon found that the only way to work with him was to give him free rein. He loved to mow the lawn, separate tulips and irises, trim the roses and gather walnuts in the fall, but he totally ignored my kitchen garden. He came to the door occasionally with a slip of paper in trembling hands on which he had recorded his hours and for which I paid him twice the going rate. I figured at his age he deserved getting paid a little extra, even if it was for having his own way. Mr. Paxton has gone where good gardeners go and has been replaced by Tom, a handsome young man with an engaging smile who only works with machines; that is, he mows, trims and blows. Other than adding clippings to my compost heap and occasionally trimming a few tree branches, he, too, prefers to stay out of my garden.

My involvement with the garden has escalated each year due as much to my proprietary and reclusive attitudes as to necessity. My children and grandchildren have moved one by one from the city, and now I find myself, in this twilight time, living peacefully with Paul in the old, "family" house and working the garden in solitude.

Through the years, time and my own intrusions have wrought profound changes in my garden, but until this spring, I had not stopped to understand what was happening. At first, the changes seemed to be improvements. The lattice fence fell down and the old garage collapsed in a snowstorm one spring, and I had them hauled off along with the huge rocks that kept emerging as I tilled and tamed more and more of the wild area. This opened the entire back yard to view so I was forced to do something about the unsightly mess.

Slowly I have added plants that have changed the constitution of the garden imperceptibly yet irreversibly. I planted grapevines, apricot, cherry, apple, peach and plum trees and raspberry and blackberry bushes, all of which, each year, require more space and create more shade. I started a perennial-herb garden of rhubarb, chives, sage, parsley, sweet marjoram, dill, thyme, tarragon, fennel, garlic, lemon grass, mint and horseradish, each year replacing chamomile, rosemary, basil and such plants that won't regrow or reseed. At times when I have been on leave or traveling and have totally neglected the garden, I have returned to find one or another of these fine herbs gone completely out of control. One year, much to Paul's delight, we returned to find a whole section of my garden covered with horseradish, which he relishes freshly grated. In a phone conversation with his friend, Daniel, who is the kind of gardener who grows twenty varieties of potatoes, as many kinds of to-matoes and all sorts of unusual things, he mentioned we had a garden full of horseradish. On the other end of the line, Daniel asked in bewil-derment, "What in the world do you do with a garden full of horserad-ish?" I now have the answer to that question. You dig up every sprout of it for three or four consecutive years until you have contained it once more to a small, designated area.

Amid the perennials, each year I plant, by seed or set, the ordinary vegetables that have become family favorites: sugar peas, carrots, beans, chard, peppers, eggplant, beets, onions, sometimes corn, all varieties of squash and nasturtiums for spicy addition to salads. I have tried to grow everything organically, and, although not a Mormon, I have followed the advice of Brigham Young who admonished his followers to plant enough for insects and other creatures as well as for themselves. The plan seemed to work fairly well; that is, until we decided to build a cabin in Wyoming. It was then we installed the sprinkling system.

That spring I was teaching, and we stayed at our city home longer than usual. Every spare moment, I worked in my garden with gusto. It was a rainy, cold spring. In my eagerness, I began planting too early. Some plants frosted. Seeds rotted in the cold rain. I replanted, finally at the right time, one blessed morning when the back yard quivered as I stepped into it and then rose in a cloud of painted ladies that were migrating through. My son gave me blue-corn seed, grown from origi-nal Anasazi corn; ceremonial, he said, that a friend had found in a pot in an Indian ruin and had been dated at eight hundred years before the present. As I placed the tiny, shriveled kernels in the earth, I could not imagine anything much coming of them.

I began the sprout watch. Soon seedlings appeared. I pulled weeds and dug shoots of recalcitrant herbs. Tom added clippings from other lawns, sprinkling them here and there among the plants and in the compost where snails, never overabundant before, emerged and rasped the marigolds, supposed to repel insects, to spindly stalks. When I went out to check the garden each day, their slimy trails glistened in the morn-ing sun. The bean sprouts were chewed back and the mustard greens riddled with holes. Would anything survive?

Then the corn sprouted. Each day I counted more erect, vital shoots that grew at unprecedented rates. When it was time to return to the mountains of Wyoming, I reluctantly set the sprinkling system and left my garden to follow its own course until I returned to harvest its gifts. That first summer of automatic sprinkling, my plants responded to the extra water with such enthusiasm that each time I returned, I found an enchanted garden. By the end of June the corn reached as high as my thighs. By midsummer it towered six feet above me, bearing huge plump cobs of blue corn. I stood in my corn patch looking up through tassels to the blue sky, pollen sprinkling down on my hair. The tiny kernels and the Goddess Earth had brought me close to her gods: Sun God, Corn God, Green God. I felt their energy, mighty yet short-lived.

As summer and fall progressed, the garden grew more out of control, producing fruit in unprecedented places. Vines trailed over the fences to my neighbors' yards. Mesmerized, their cats prowled under tomatoes intertwined with raspberries. Hubbard squash hung from the apricot tree. At night raccoons from City Creek feasted on cucumbers that had climbed the apple tree. After these visits to the city and garden, I returned to the mountains that resonated with wildness, loaded with produce to last until our next visit. Life blossoms in unforeseen places, out of control, without our intervention, I told myself. We are the benefactors of this sacred exuberance, I chirped. But unbeknown to me, underneath this wonderful productivity, weeds were taking hold, using up nutrients.

The weeds steadily spread and took over my garden. Last spring I decided I would have it out with them. I was vicious. I dug up every weed that appeared. Whereas before I would ignore the snails or tie them in a plastic bag and put them in the garbage to die a slow death of suffocation out of sight and mind, this year I crushed every snail I encountered with my big, green, English garden boots. A less violent death, I rationalized. Each time I returned to my city home, the weeds had reemerged. I dug them out and upon my next return, they were back in full force. Finally I took out one whole section where weeds, onions, garlic and shallots had grown in the tangle. I covered the section with black plastic, went back to Wyoming and called Linda for advice. Stop digging, she advised. Obviously, whatever I was doing wasn't working. She suggested I try permaculture cultivation: spread newspapers over the weedy area, cover with manure and then with straw. Keep wet and repeat more layers as needed. Next spring leave everything as is and just pull away the compost from the place you wish to plant. No tilling. No digging. No weeding. It seemed too good to be true.

I proceeded with this plan throughout the fall, adding leaves and loads of manure brought to me by another good friend, Liz, from her farm, together with tubs of day lilies that she thinned from her borders. I mulched the entire garden, and now as I wait for the snow to melt, I formulate further plans: I'll move my herbs to the shade under the fruit trees, some of which I may have to cut in order to open the area to more light. I will transplant the irises that are overgrown and losing their bloom into a huge bank where, like Martha Stewart, I will smile through a profusion of blossoms looking as if I know exactly what I am doing. I will thin the raspberry patch and give the excess to Liz. I'll cut back on watering and perhaps convert to soakers in the garden. And as I can afford it, I will replace the lawn in front and back yards with cover and native plants that won't require as much water and care. I might even forget about squashing snails.

In retrospect the garden wasn't a total loss this year. I returned to our cabin after each visit with loads of basil for pesto and salads, green beans and chard, squash and cucumbers, peppers and tomatoes, rhubarb for pies, succulent garlic for *bagna cauda* for dipping French bread and thyme for stuffing under the skin of chickens before baking. There were even vegetables for our good neighbors, Tracy and David. In the fall, back in the city, I was busy canning applesauce, tomatoes and green-tomato relish, grape jelly and jam and raspberry jam until the frost came. The flowers I planted in the spring continued to bloom, the fox-glove in beautiful, long stalks of pink flowers speckled at their centers. And I found a special gift in a corner, a tiny daisy with delicate little flowers that came from who-knows-where. Such discoveries and de-lights lifted my spirits and gave me faith to continue my gardening enterprise, albeit more cautiously and more thoughtfully.

When friends find me in the garden, my face flushed and smudged with dirt, typical queries from them are, "You really enjoy gardening, don't you?" or "Isn't gardening healing?" My quick response has always been, "It is very hard work."

It *is* very hard work. At the end of the day, soaking my aching muscles in a bubbly, steamy bath in the big old bathtub supported with lion's claws, I reflect on gardening. I think of other gardens, fading and blooming with the season, that I have passed on my walks through the neighborhood. One in particular has attracted me through the years, an old-fashioned flower garden tended by a very old woman. One day as I passed, she seemed almost too feeble to get up from her kneeling position. With her head bent in concentration, she steadfastly weeded and thinned with such determination, as if it were her last chance. A few weeks later, there was a "For Sale" sign and no trace of her. Had she died in her garden still digging away as if her life depended on it? Often, since then, submerged in bubbles, I wonder if I might end that way. I could come up missing, and no one would think of looking in the garden. I'd be grown over in a couple of weeks. Later when my house was sold and new occupants moved in, they would discover my bones in their back yard.

Besides sore muscles and death fantasies, tilling the soil brings many delightful discoveries. My garden is like an archaeological dig, artifacts surfacing from middens of the past: a porcelain doll's arm, a rusty nail, pieces of Wedgwood china, part of an old lamp, purple and green glass, a delicate teacup handle, a lump of coal, a bronze door handle, cinders and boulders of pure milky quartz, granite or the sandstone that was quarried for the foundations for the first homes in the city. As I dig, I imagine the household that produced these castoffs, and I feel some deep affinity for those past residents whose home I now occupy. I stack the shards in little piles here and there, thinking of what to do with them but never coming to any conclusion, and in the end, letting them recycle to be dug up again another year.

Gardening is also good for remembering. The kinesthetic feeling of an act repeated through the years, the smell and feel and heft of the soil, draws up memories long buried. I remember the garden on the sheep ranch in Wyoming where I was raised and where, from an early age, I was involved with the rest of my family in planting, weeding and harvesting a garden that must have covered an acre. After spring tilling, the planting was completed primarily by my mother who wanted it done precisely. She trusted us with bean and pea seeds, something we would not lose track of like the precious, fine radish and lettuce seeds. After the planting she checked each day and rejoiced in the first sprouts that appeared miraculously. When the plants were tall and distinct enough to distinguish from the weeds that had sprouted in profusion, we began weeding. Then my father hoed and built up rows and ditches so that the garden could be irrigated. The weeding-hoeing-irrigating cycle was repeated every few weeks throughout early summer. The garden, planted late in May, was productive by early July when we harvested lettuce, peas and radishes, and in full swing by haying time with beans, carrots, beets, turnips, onions, parsley and chard. Peas and new potatoes, creamed turnips with parsley, thick, white chard stalks dipped in batter and fried, beet greens and green beans and new carrots pulled from the ground, crisp and sweet and gritty. The words themselves draw up tastes on my tongue.

My garden is also the harvest, not just the event of picking ripened fruits and vegetables, but marvelous revelations along the way, transitions from bud to blossom to fruit, clutches of potatoes unearthed, swollen roots pulled from their moorings. Harvesting brings its own kind of memories, of hard but gratifying work on the ranch, of cleaning vegetables for meals each day and of storing beets, turnips, carrots and potatoes in the root cellar. And as rhubarb, apricot, cherry and apple pies and jars of apricot jam and chutney, zucchini relish, raspberry jam, grape juice, tomatoes and apple sauce take their places on my kitchen counters, I return to that ranch kitchen in the fall—filled with steaming jars of canned fruit, jams and jellies made from produce bought by the bushel from a peddler and canned by my mother for the long winter months ahead.

If you are a grazer and nibbler as I am, gardens, during their blossoming, are a gastronomic delight. As the season progresses, as well as at certain times of the day, there are special treats in store. Juices sucked from plump, ripe tomatoes warmed by the sun. Raspberries bathed in dew in the cool of early morning. Sweet grapes with a cast of yeast after the first frost. Nasturtium leaves, buds and flowers popped into my mouth whenever I pass their way. Crisp, cold carrots surviving the winter and pulled as the snow leaves. In all truth, it is probably my taste for fresh fruits and vegetables, as much as anything, that keeps me plugging away at this gardening enterprise.

Although I hate to admit it, my friends are right. Gardening is healing. Perhaps, more accurately and more personally, I come to terms with myself as I muck around out there in my garden. In the spring I had to fight the weeds, chop them down, squash the snails, get my anger out. But now I have mellowed. Watching Paul, I have learned. He is getting stronger each day, helping himself in every possible way with meditation, nutrients, acceptance of prayers, as well as traditional medicine. He has gained strength and restored his health in many ways. He is a better man, a better writer, a better father, a better husband, a dearer person to all his friends than ever before. He faces his mortality and stands against his odds with the power of a giant. He does not rail against the conditions of his existence. As Montaigne suggested, he has learned to endure what he cannot avoid and has made peace with what he cannot alter. At the same time he sees new promise and hope in each day. Paul inspires me. I am ready, now that the anger is gone, to take a more harmonious route, ever cautious, however, that the bloom of productivity and abundance may mask disease.

Perhaps I was too greedy. I was looking for that paradisiacal garden, free from work, without weeds and pests. Its sudden fall, and mine, reminded me of the tenuous line between health and disease and made me ashamed of my mindlessness. Restoration will take time. I know there are more weeds to pull, but I won't lose faith. Perhaps eventually I can learn to live at peace with weeds and snails that, hopefully, will dwell benignly in a healthy surround restored to balance.

My garden isn't my whole life, but each spring it is a new beginning. I'll continue to work hard at it, for I identify and define myself as much by the symbols of my work and pleasure as by my words. Much more than what I see when I survey it, my garden is the source of my self-understanding, a mirror and metaphor for my existence. In answer to my original question, "What on earth am I doing here?" I can now reply. I am taking stock of things, testing the soil and myself. At my fingertips, my garden encourages me to question the reality of reality. In some small way, it draws me closer to nature with its expanding possibilities and unfathomable mysteries—and undeniable limitations.

SWIMMING PAST SEVENTY

Ruth Harriet Jacobs

At the end of August with fall breathing on summer, I am the first morning swimmer at Craigville Beach on a cool Massachusetts day. Because I am seventy-one and the wind is cold, the young lifeguard huddled in her sweatshirt says, "Good for you," as I head into the water. Her voice is patronizing, as if I were a child. She has no way of knowing I rarely miss my daily swim, whatever the weather, and that swimming is vital to this week's attendance at the Craigville Conference Center's Cape Cod Writers' Conference.

> _One August week each year_
> _I write white wicker poems_
> _on a porch over the ocean_
> _My swimming stroke sets_
> _the poem's meter_
>
> _Wave after wave of poems_
> _drown out the gulls_
> _I praise novices' poems_
> _they praise mine back_
> _at meals we devour poems_
> _Talking poets' talk_
> _we litter famous names_

like shells on the beach
seized to keep forever
or crushed contemptuously

We beachwalk at sunset
toward clarifying truth
expressing our dreams
toward that perfect word
toward publication and fame

Under the summer sun
we burst and burn with poems
nobody reads newspapers
nobody calls work or home
one August week each year

As the shivering lifeguard carefully watches her old-woman swimmer, I wonder what her attitude toward me would be if only she knew how tame this swim is. Unlike now when I am a registered guest at Craigville, I have taken many others where I am not entitled to swim.

I think back four months to early May when I swam without lifeguard, illegally, at the Wellesley College lake, frigid in the cool New England spring. This was my first outdoor swim of the year, and I was exhilarated by the exercise, fresh air and leafing trees around Lake Waban. I was also feeling quite superior, because, seven decades old, I plunged right in, unlike the two young Wellesley students standing on the dock, seeking the courage to get wet. Perhaps they were afraid of campus police. I knew they would not put *me* in jail for swimming.

The students finally jumped in and screamed, "It's cold!" and in a minute they ran out to their towels and clothes. I continued to swim, warmed by swimmer's high. This was the beginning of my daily outdoor regimen continuing until late October. Most of my swims are at the college's lake or the town pond, but now and then, I go to saltwater to commune with the ocean and ocean birds. On Cape Cod, many of my ocean swims are stolen. That only increases my enjoyment.

As I swim this August day at Craigville, I have an imaginary conversation with the lifeguard that I know would shock her. I confess to her the high adventures I have finding and crashing choice swimming spots from a glitzy hotel in Bar Harbor, Maine, to the supposedly well-guarded Boca Raton Hotel and Country Club in Florida and the classy Biltmore Hotel in Phoenix, Arizona, with its gorgeous outdoor pool designed by architect Frank Lloyd Wright.

I imagine saying to the lifeguard that actually some of my special beaches on her Cape Cod in Massachusetts are restricted to residents or hotel guests or have very high parking fees. None of this inhibits me, as I swim early in the morning or early evening after the money collectors or the inspectors of car stickers leave. I park at the beach club of an expensive Cape Cod hotel as if I belonged there and use its beach house with hot showers after my swim, and this during peak summer months. Nobody suspects that a gray-haired septuagenarian is a beach crasher. I am surprised that the "beach police" are not looking for me, as I publicly confessed to this in my book, *Be An Outrageous Older Woman: A R.A.S.P., Remarkable Aging Smart Person.*

A few readers questioned the ethics of using private beaches, but my conviction is that lakes, rivers and oceans should be for everyone to enjoy. In addition, the more expensive the beach, the fewer people swim. They are just there to gossip, tan, show off their bathing suits and figures and to keep their hair dry. Besides, I give the place class and stir up the stagnant waters.

Mostly I cannot afford, when paying my own way, to stay at hotels with swimming pools, so I stay at a youth hostel or el cheapo motel and swim at the best hotel in town. It is easy to walk in at my age if you act as if you belong there. I've never been stopped. As I lift a swim, I can understand the thrill that kleptomaniacs must get. I feel self-righteous, because if I don't swim I get stiff and cranky and can't effectively give the workshops and talks I do around the country to help elders and elder service providers. Of course, when my way is paid, I stay at hotels with good swimming pools, so I figure it all evens out on the hotel swimming scale.

Probably I would shock the young lifeguard if I told her about my swimming-free escapades. Or she might think I was bragging if I told her how, on Anna Maria Island off Bradenton, Florida, all the timid people stayed in the warm motel pool while I alone swam in the coolish January ocean, sister to the fish.

I must add, so as not to alarm, that when I am the sole swimmer, I do not go out over my head in case I get the rare cramp. I do not take chances with my life. When I was ten, I almost drowned in an ocean swim. That near fatality did not stop me from swimming, but it made me cautious. I urge caution on others.

Another thing I am cautious about on my legal and illegal swims is always to have a notebook and pen handy on shore, so I can rush out of the water to write a title, line or even a whole poem given me by the universe and the swimming process. I have stood on shore shivering with the excitement of creation and the cold, as I record these gifts of air and water, rocks, trees, sand, birds, waves.

For me, swimming is not a social event. Mostly I swim alone, reaching my soul as I stroke rhythmically and long. I don't get bored as I vary my strokes: Australian crawl, sidestroke, backstroke and breaststroke. Mountain ponds are my favorite places to swim; they have transposed me from the mundane to the profound. I meditate, pray, recite others' loved poems, as well as compose my own poems while swimming.

One glorious June, when I was a resident of the Edna St. Vincent Millay artists' retreat, Steepletop, the swimming pool Millay originally created in the cellar hole of an old building was not filled, because the mountain-stream water used was too cold for most people. So I scoured the area and found other places to swim where I could have mountain views. My legacy to future residents was to leave directions for how to find these holy swimming holes. I like to think artists are looking at the mountains while stroking and are inspired by the views and water.

Now, as I swim at Craigville, I remember my long swimming history and all the tales I could tell that lifeguard, who thinks it cute and brave that an old lady can swim on a windy, cold day. For example, at midlife, when there was a terrible crisis in my life, I was unable to relax to sleep. A wise psychiatrist, who knew better than to prescribe pills readily, asked me what I did for exercise. I told her I loved to swim and did so in good months but couldn't in the winter. She pointed out that indoor swimming pools were better than not swimming at all.

Like many patients, I was a "yes but" person. I said, "Doctor, but I don't like chlorine and swimming between walls."

"The chlorine won't kill you and you need the exercise for your anxiety and tension," she said.

Her pushing me into being a pool user in bad weather was probably worth more than all our hours of talking. However, I can't blame her for my crashing of hotel swimming pools when I am out of town and unable to use the pools at the colleges where I am affiliated.

Had I not had the release of swimming, I do not know how I could have gotten through the death of a child, the death of a marriage and the death of some dreams. The physical act of swimming, especially of swimming in nature, mobilizes endorphins in the body that raise our spirits. True, other forms of exercise will also contribute to our mental as well as physical health. But there is, I believe, a spiritual quality to being immersed in the elements in a rhythmic way. To be swimming at sunrise or sunset, or with a mist over the waters, truly brings us in tune with the universe.

Oh, we who swim past the age of seventy are outrageous and courageous. Our limbs are flexible; our spirits soar. While the young sun on the beach, we know the ecstasy of water. When we have a bit of trouble walking, we can still feel powerful as we skim over the waters. We feel more complete than canoeists and other boaters who are only on top of the water, not *in* it. And, of course, we despise motorboaters who pollute with gasoline and noise.

A swimmer must also be an environmentalist. You cannot love to swim in lakes, rivers and oceans without working to end the pollution that drains into them. If I want future generations to enjoy swimming outdoors, I must support projects and causes that insure this, such as the Environmental Defense Fund and the North American Lake Management Society at a national level, and my local groups, such as the Charles River Watershed Association. There are local groups all over the country.

I have also worked to convert other people to swimming. It is a gentle exercise, safe for all and especially good for my age peers. It often dismays me how hard it is to get women to put on bathing suits. They often feel that it is disgraceful not to have a perfect size-six body or to have such marks of age as enlarged leg veins, wrinkles or brown spots. I am obese and spotted, but I get so much benefit and joy from swimming that I don't care who looks at me in a bathing suit. In fact, I often have to dress and undress at the shore. Though I am reasonably careful to cover myself with a large towel when changing, I am sure my abundance of flesh shows now and then.

But while swimming outdoors, I do cover my face with sun block to prevent skin cancer, and I swim early morning or late in the day as advised by my dermatologist. Actually, I worry about the young Cape lifeguard and others who fail to use and renew sun block in this age of diminishing ozone layers. In my imaginary conversation with the life-guard, and in actuality afterwards, I remind her to use sun block. She makes a dubious face, probably thinking me a nagging old woman. Yet I thank her graciously for watching me swim and leave to go to my poetry-writing class.

Perhaps I will write a poem about beach crashing and shock the rest of the poets, or at least make them laugh. Maybe I will persuade some who have not yet come to swim at this beach by telling how swimming fosters creativity. I can be a nautical nag.

I plan to swim and crash past seventy, past eighty and however long I am here, before I swim in that great ocean in the heavens. Swimming is about the only place left where they can't reach you on the phone to interrupt your rhythmic, healing thoughts and dialogue with yourself and the universe. There are more species of fish than land creatures. Swimmers survive.

The Agony and the Ecstasy

Ginny NiCarthy

The time had come for Elizabeth and me to mount our camels. They lay on the ground, apparently docile, awaiting their burdens. I looked at hers. Then I looked at mine, closely: a humped back and knobby knees bulging out from legs so absurdly elongated they necessitated an equally protracted neck to reach the ground for food. At the end of that neck was a head with one of the uglier faces I'd ever encountered: fierce-looking eyes, ears borrowed from a small dog and lips that flapped open awkwardly. Is there any season in which a camel's coat isn't matted and moth-eaten? Clearly the creature was invented while Dr. Seuss stood in for God. A rope looped through my camel's nostrils did nothing to enhance its appearance. But none of these attributes was its own fault, and I recalled a spring day at the zoo when camels amused me, cavorting in ungainly efforts to have sex. So they could be fun to observe, and if my mount treated me with respect I would try to develop a kindly attitude toward it. Perhaps its unwillingness to shake away small flies walking around its eyes indicated a patient, loving disposition, not sloth as I'd first assumed.

Elizabeth began to mount her camel. With a furious braying it sprayed spittle from a gaping mouth. It bared cruel-looking teeth the size of elephant tusks that were coated with a garden of slimy fungus, then frenetically jerked its head back and forth and began to push up its rear end. But Elizabeth wasn't on its back yet, and was jolted to one side before our guide, Salmadon, helped her back onto solid ground. The camel appeared outraged, and resisted Salmadon's efforts to calm it. Elizabeth stoically waited to try again.

"I sure wouldn't get on that creature," I said to her. But she ignored me while our guide finally subdued the animal's wrath.

"I think he's dangerous," I said. "We don't have to do this."

But Elizabeth is stubborn, tough, not prone to back off from a little risk, once started—pretty much like me, in fact. That was a major reason we traveled well together. More than once, excited about an adventure or too proud to quit, I had taken on ridiculous challenges. But for a moment there, in M'Hamid, Morocco, I glimpsed our situation objectively. It appeared idiotic to ride for a full day into the Moroccan desert on a loutish, ferociously resentful creature. Nevertheless, Elizabeth mounted, the animal succumbed to its subservient role and I watched it raise its hindquarters, slowly this time, as Elizabeth leaned back to gain equilibrium. Then it unfolded its front legs, legs that looked only tentatively connected to its shoulders, and raised its torso, bringing it even with the rear. Elizabeth grinned triumphantly.

As a child, I had puzzled over my mother's anxiety when I leaned over a second-story wall. I was fearless. Not until I was well into my forties did I experience vertigo, but once started, it flourished year by year. I need not even be far off the ground for my nervous system to quiver in anticipation of plunging into the void. I'd been surprised at that reaction just a year earlier, in Guatemala, as I contemplated arcing my leg from the ground up and over the back of a horse. I suddenly perceived the animal as unconscionably tall. I hadn't remembered how high horses stood. And once mounted—after several false starts—I felt uneasy about my ability to remain in the saddle, especially when he insisted on galloping. At age twelve, I had loved to ride, and was disappointed only that I wasn't permitted to gallop all the time. What had happened in the intervening flash of time, the fifty-five years? Whatever it was, after the Guatemala ride, I had vowed it would be my last trip on a four-legged animal.

But now, my camel seemed receptive to serving me, had graciously laid down his body for me to mount. I could say "his" now, since we were finally properly introduced, and I learned his name was Muhammed. I shrugged. This would not be the first time I broke a promise to myself, and I flung my leg over the animal's back. I told myself it was not really as wide as the Nile, which in any case is not so wide as rivers go. Then Muhammed hiked up his rear end, and there I sat, precarious as a china teacup on a suddenly up-ended sideboard, as if I were about to slide right along the slope of his body over his shoulders and down his nose. Instinctively, I leaned back. Then he laboriously unbent his front legs, placing his forefeet on the ground, first the left—tilt—then the right.

My mount was up, his body leveled out. Calling upon long-dormant habits, my feet reached for stirrups but met only air, and my calves dangled, rag-doll style. Nevertheless, I stayed aloft, and was able to sit up straight in the saddle, behind Muhammed's hump. That definitely called for kudos, I thought, then laughed. I was feeling cocky for having merely positioned myself at the start, and hours of riding the unwielding creature lay ahead. I took courage from the thought that I'd never have such a chance again. Put differently, since I'd reached the allegedly wise age of sixty-seven, prudence might save me from repeating the experience.

I had eagerly sought adventure in the Moroccan Sahara partly because I *was* sixty-seven. My physically active days are numbered. I'm among the fortunate in having an old body that still functions well. But I shouldn't push my luck. I'd better do what I can, while I can. For nearly forty years I had yearned to travel in North Africa. I had longed to hear *muezzins* cast their deep, powerful voices into the air, netting the faithful, towing them in to prayer; to see dark eyes peer from the folds of delicately embroidered saffron-colored scarves; to gaze at secretive openings—the eyes of buildings—cut high in the walls of adobe homes.

With Elizabeth, twenty-five years my junior, I had explored Cairo and drifted down the Nile for a couple of days and nights on a traditional *falucca*. Elizabeth and I had known each other for over twenty years, but had never before traveled together, and our compatibility astonished us both. Then, alone, I wandered through western Turkey—and beginning my trail of broken promises to myself—had ridden a horse in Petra, Jordan, through spectacular ruins. My last stop was Morocco, as I was determined to experience the desert as well as the usual tourist stops. Elizabeth met me in Casablanca.

I had recently given up my psychotherapy practice, and found myself with little money but oodles of uncommitted time. Despite her taste for adventure, Elizabeth's law practice allowed limited vacation days, so she would accompany me only to the exotic market towns of Fez and Marrakesh. No time for the desert, she said, stiffening her spine with the reminder that she could not have it all. I had accepted that and planned to go alone after she left. But as we traveled east toward the town of Quarzazate, we could almost smell the Sahara. Like setters sensing quarry, we felt our noses twitch.

"I want to go with you," Elizabeth suddenly announced.

"Great," I said, and we hired a cab. It wasn't a long drive across the middle of the country. I knew little about our destination, except that I would finally be in the true desert.

So there we were, taking off from the village of M'Hamid, about eighty kilometers west of Algeria. M'Hamid is far enough from the urban track that it has no electricity. A new hotel had opened a year earlier, making a total of two, and doubling the tourist capacity to about twenty. We arrived at sunset and immediately encountered Salmadon, a twenty-one-year-old guide, well spoken in English and apparently knowledgeable. Like most of his professional colleagues, he possessed the essential trait of charm. He had a sweet look, a boyish smile and smooth, dark skin. He wore a turban and *djellaba*, the traditional North African man's ankle-length shirt, and spoke in softly persuasive tones. He said he was the only guide working in the area, and that we had two choices: a Land Rover to the highest dunes, which would take half a day, or a camel to the lower ones for the entire day. I didn't like the idea of a Land Rover defiling the romance of this mysterious territory. But all day on a camel? I hoped Elizabeth wouldn't be that crazy. I certainly didn't plan to be.

A little history belongs here. In Egypt—before Elizabeth joined me— I had ridden a camel to the Giza pyramids. Though a mercifully short jaunt, it had reminded me of how, in aerobics class, I'd admired the agility of women who could do the splits. I hadn't come close, managing only to stretch my legs into a narrow V. So in Giza, after a short ride with thighs at a ninety-degree angle—a sort of forced split—I had once more promised myself, "Never again."

I explained all that to Elizabeth, who had never ridden a camel. Trying to be fair, I described just how miserable we would be on the creatures, and then asked her what she wanted to do.

"The Land Rover is expensive," she said. "And anyway, we're in the desert. We should be on camels." Her desire reflected exactly the romance I had imagined I wanted. I had craved to be in the dunes, but had thought little about how I'd get there. Recognizing that gleam of excitement in Elizabeth's eyes as similar to my own when I wanted to do something out of the way, something a little exotic, I agreed, even while telling myself I'd once more lost my wits. Perhaps my easy acquiescence had something to do with my own absurd sense that I could handle anything my forty-two-year-old friend could—if not as well, at least in some sort of way. "Some sort of way" turned out to be precisely right.

At last we were ready to begin our trip, with Salmadon leading Elizabeth's camel; his assistant, Hussain, guiding mine. Hussain looked nearly as old as I, though mostly I saw only the back of his head, swaddled in a black turban above a white *djellaba*. A third animal carried supplies. As we began to move out, I casually asked, "Do we have lots of water?"

Salmadon stopped. "Oh, yes," he said, "we're getting it just now. Please give us the money." I had the distinct impression our guide would not have remembered it if I hadn't reminded him. About then, a rational person might have begun to worry, or simply have withdrawn from the enterprise. First, a balky camel, then forgetfulness about water for a full day in the desert. Furthermore, after struggling out of our beds at first light, as instructed by Salmadon, we had waited an hour-and-a-half, with no word of when he would arrive. I had suppressed my irritation at the delay. I've become generally adept at flexing with cultures alien to me. But getting up in the middle of the night—anytime before nine—strained my composure. When it turned out to have been unnecessary, that was really pushing it.

However, as we waited, we were well entertained by Abduhl, a strikingly tall man with black eyes and a deeply furrowed face: another guide. So Salmadon had not been our only alternative after all! Abduhl was enamored of Elizabeth's scarf, which she'd purchased in Egypt to make her acceptably modest during visits to mosques. Of soft violet-blue rayon, it seemed to us undistinguished, yet Abduhl insisted he must have it for his mother. He would trade Elizabeth for another item, he said, and spirited her away into his home to look over his wares. I thought it might be the last I saw of her, but she reappeared with a bare head and a silver box, and soon, Salmadon arrived as well. He said he'd been delayed by the midnight escape of his camel, and had spent hours tracking him down in the desert. It was my animal that had run loose half the night, and I wished Elizabeth's had stolen some extra exercise to calm it, as well.

My legs did not begin to seriously ache for a half-hour or so, or I was too distracted by the tension of making my way over sandy knolls to notice. Up was fine, and Hussain led the animal at an easy pace. But descending even a slight slope potentiated my vertigo. Knowing that Hussain didn't understand English, I admonished him each time, "Take it easy!" "Slow down!" Each time Salmadon, in dulcet tones, murmured, "Slowly-slowly, slowly-slowly," and Hussain shortened his stride. Still, I leaned back as far as I could. I felt that the camel's front end was on one trip, its rear end and I on another, with little connection between the two. When he paused, head to ground, for leisurely munching on low growth, the slant-board angle unnerved me. I envisioned toppling over his head and being trampled by his big feet. I told myself that was a silly fear. As it turned out, it wasn't completely unwarranted.

We plodded across the sand, up and down small hillocks, and the village receded into the background. Broken only by occasional scrawny bushes, sand stretched before us, finally swelling into high mounds in the distance. Shadows from the still-low sun accentuated graceful contours. I began to relax a little—until, that is, my thighs cried out as if stretched on a rack. I raised my knees, but without a place to rest my feet, that position didn't last long. Ahead of me, sitting solidly on her now-compliant, lumbering animal, Elizabeth looked content. Throughout our trip she had worn a baseball cap, and now, for further sun protection, she had covered it with my Egyptian cotton scarf. It billowed behind her, as if, I thought, she were Lawrence himself. At other times she and Salmadon, in his loose gown of bird's-egg blue and transparent blue headdress, reminded me of the Holy Family on the way to Bethlehem. Donkeys, I reflected, envious of Mary, have narrow backs and short legs.

Just as I began to wonder how much longer my legs would hold out, our leaders stopped the camels and announced that we would have tea. The idea struck me as incongruous with our surroundings, but anything could happen here, and I half expected a silver tea set to appear from the saddlebags. Flexing my legs on the ground was a heavenly experience. So was relaxing on warm sand, while the menfolk gathered more scraps of brush to add to what they'd picked up along the way. We watched them heat the water. I make that sound simple. It was a long process, building and tending the fire, then waiting for water to heat. But I was not checking my watch. Time drifted, boundless in the desert. Our tea was served—alas, not in china cups—but in short sturdy glasses, the same sort we'd been offered time and again in North African cities. We sipped eagerly; basked in the hot sun; gazed at blue, blue sky and sand in every direction; indulged our pleasure in the affable men who waited on us. Most important, I lounged on a blanket *on the ground.*

All too soon our comfort came to an end, and we were exhorted to mount the camels. As we went forward, I told myself to take it easy, that my tensed muscles exacerbated the ache in my thighs. I managed a little better and an hour or so later, huge mounds of smooth, silky-looking sand loomed ahead. As they grew larger, my discomfort faded, replaced by awe.

We stopped at the foot of several high dunes, looking up to admire their swirls and curves. It was time for lunch, and our camels lay down for us to dismount. Salmadon was solicitous toward Elizabeth, and flirtatious. She has a marvelous capacity for joy, and here in the desert she grinned and grinned. Her strawberry blond hair, blue eyes, tall stature and broad shoulders must have struck him as exotic.

I thought nothing about Hussain's attitude toward me until I tried to get off the camel, and found I could not move my leg. I was only a couple of feet from the ground; the creature was lying down. But my right leg, which I had to raise a few inches to get over the camel's back, was immobile. My leg had lost contact with my brain, and order it though I might, I could not get it to move. Hussain put his arms around me, ostensibly to heave me off the animal. He had done that at our stop for tea, but had taken the opportunity to pat my pancake breasts. I hadn't thought of that old phrase *cop a feel* in years, but it fit. Hussain's skin was dark, and as incised with grooves as a weathered door. The black scarf wound around his head and his bushy moustache gave him a brooding, melancholy appearance when in repose. But at the thrill of touching my breasts, he had giggled with a rich and pure joy. My embryonic righteous indignation had instantly fizzled. It was all so silly, and his smile resembled a ten-year-old's. I had judged Hussain to be about fifty, but he said he was thirty-five. I was twice his age and Elizabeth, twice the age of Salmadon.

I had pointed out to Hussain that I was old enough to be his mother. He and Salmadon were shocked. Salmadon mimicked his mother, roughly my age, walking, bent nearly in half. We had seen many old women who stooped that way, resembling American women of eighty or ninety. The women worked like beasts in the raging sun all their lives and endured too many pregnancies. They certainly weren't going off on desert jaunts for the pure excitement of it. To the eyes of our companions I had sprung from a species different from that of their mothers and grandmothers.

I was still wondering how I would disembark from the camel. I didn't want to encourage Hussain's opportunism, so when he reached for my breasts again, I hollered, "No! Lift my foot!" Puzzled at first, he followed Salmadon's directions and went around to the other side of the camel. He gingerly lifted my leg over the camel's back, while Salmadon and Elizabeth stood by grinning. Standing upright presented my next challenge. When I tried to straighten my legs, I thought, this is how the burdened, old Moroccan women must feel. My back leaned forward at a forty-five-degree angle. My knees seemed as knobby now as the camel's, and it took me a few minutes to flex them into working order. We had arrived at the half-way point. I began to wonder how I would endure the same degree of agony on the way back, but the vista of high dunes in every direction lulled me into serenity.

Salmadon and Hussain built another fire, and I resisted the urge to help forage for wood. I was busy, still trying out my knees and ogling the landscape. The fire crackled and we sipped tea. Then Salmadon got the idea that Elizabeth and I should try on his head scarf. He unwound the filmy cloth, handed an end to Elizabeth and stretched it out like a huge, gauzy tablecloth. Together, they folded it into a long strip. Then he wound it around her head, let some of it fall in a graceful cowl around her neck, pulled it over her forehead, up over her nose, and let the rest drape over her shoulders and almost to the ground. She resembled a blue-eyed Moroccan madonna.

Next it was my turn, and Hussain did the same for me. I looked like, well, I don't know what. Not a madonna, certainly. The pictures show an old woman with an arrogant tilt to her head—a stance comically inappropriate for the veil of a Moroccan woman. Salmadon swiped my hat and put it on his nappy hair. He wore jeans under the *djellaba*, and I realized with a little shock that if he exchanged his soft, red leather slippers for running shoes, he could fit right into an urban U.S. environment. Hussain's jeans and running shoes peeked from beneath his *djellaba*. I snatched my hat back and slapped it on top of my headdress. We laughed at the incongruous mix of Eastern and Western garb. All of this was great fun, but I was hungry, and it seemed like hours before they put on the meal to cook.

My legs had recovered, so I wandered away from our group until I could see nothing in any direction but the contours of the dunes. I trudged upward. The day was pleasantly warm and the air felt still. But every now and then a breeze formed a sudden, ominous, dark cloud across the sand and brushed away its surface. The undulations mesmerized me. Bulges became concave; sculpted ridges drifted into flowing drapes. I heard nothing but silence as I watched sand subtly shift, as if by an unseen hand. I was grateful I hadn't been born into this terrain, yet I reveled in the mystery and a titillating touch of anxiety, as I envisioned the contours of the world transformed before my eyes. I tried to picture living an entire life in the midst of such fluid space. Imagine waking up to find everything a different shape from when you went to sleep—not just once, as some people have waked to the wreckage of flood or earthquake, but night after night.

Salmadon's family lived a two-day camel ride from the village, and I wondered how he found his way without stable guidelines—none visible to my eye, anyway. Though very much a desert creature, he was surprisingly knowledgeable about the Western world. When he had work, he slept in a Bedouin hut he had built on the hotel roof, thus spanning disparate worlds. Even more remarkable to me, his brother was studying medicine in Switzerland. How, after growing up in a desert culture, virtually unchanged for centuries, does he make his way through a European landscape?

From the crest of the dune, I slowly slid down, and at our fire, found my three companions sitting close together, smoking *kief.* Earlier, Salmadon had made a great to-do about never using drugs and disapproving them; I asked him how that attitude squared with the deep drags of *kief* he was taking. He insisted this was different, not really a drug, not a serious one, and he didn't do it often. He passed the cigarette on to Elizabeth, and then to Hussain. I joined them and soon felt a bit lightheaded. I wished we were going to stay the night, wished I could smoke myself into an even more altered state under the wide sky. But I resisted taking much, since I was already afraid of plunging right off the camel.

Riding that horse in Guatemala two years earlier, I had never felt quite sure I was in the middle of the saddle, or, if there, whether I could stay. No one else on that trip had the same trouble, but they ranged in age from twenty-five to forty. On the camel I had a similar feeling of dis-ease, and wondered whether unstable equilibrium is another sign of aging about which no one had warned me. Untrumpeted aging symptoms have begun to multiply in me: loss of memory, leaky bladder, impaired parking ability and even faulty spelling—this last, something I'd only recently added to my list. Why does no one alert us to these manifestations? Now I have to add shaky equilibrium—on a horse or camel, anyway.

At last, lunch. Salmadon had cooked a superbly tasty *tajine,* a stew composed of carrots and potatoes, and including, this time, some sort of meat, mutton, I supposed. I eschewed the meat, since I'd already given notice that I'm a vegetarian. The four of us leaned over and dug into the pot, tearing off pieces of fabulous flat bread to use as scoop and spoon. The vegetables tasted scrumptious, whether from the spices or the waiting or the atmosphere, I'm not sure. We gobbled up the food like starving waifs, speaking little, but making *mmm mm* sounds and smiling a lot to each other. The end of the meal would mean getting on the beast again, so I chose to concentrate on the delectable present. I enjoyed the wait. The men washed the dishes with sand, while Elizabeth and I climbed a dune again to gaze out at undulating space.

By this time, mounting the camel unnerved me less than either staying on it or dismounting. As we turned toward M'Hamid, my legs felt better for a while, then worse. I envied Elizabeth, who was slightly high. As she rode along, ecstatic, she flung her arms and legs wide, looking utterly nonchalant and free. I would have liked to do the same, especially to move my legs. But I was too insecure to trust I'd stay on top of the camel if I let my calves stop clutching its sides. The tension I felt exacerbated my aches. With a great effort of concentration and deep breathing I gained some relief, but soon tightened up again. I held onto the front of the saddle like a child on her first pony ride. I recalled times I'd held a leg stretch as long as possible, just to prolong a kind of excruciating pleasure. Riding the camel, my thighs felt as if I'd held that position for hours.

Discomfort evolved into pain, and I wondered what would happen if I couldn't continue. I didn't see any taxis handy. I kept silently urging myself, "Five more minutes, five more minutes." Every now and then Hussain would turn around and say with a smile, "Is good?" I managed to push the words "Good" or "Yes" through clenched teeth. For a while it amused me to say, *"Coolshee mizzevin,"* meaning, "It's fine." But eventually Hussain's incessant inquires began to annoy me. I felt neither *coolshee* nor fine. His question reminded me of jokes that start, "Was it good for you?" after a clumsy, insensitive man fails to satisfy. Finally, I answered, "No. Not good." Surely he must know. But each time he asked and heard the same answer he acted equally astonished.

Hussain suddenly stopped, and handed me the puny rope that served as a rein, an unprecedented move. He disappeared behind me. I did not like being in charge of the beast, and had visions of him galloping across the desert with me hanging off his neck, desperately clinging to the saddle, legs dragging on the sand. I had not the faintest idea of how to control him. I wanted to know what was going on behind my back, but I was afraid to try turning the animal around. My arthritic neck wouldn't permit me to twist enough to see behind me without turning my whole torso, and I felt too unstable up there to do even that. I heard Salmadon and Hussain solicitously asking Elizabeth if she was really all right, and her insistence that she was fine. By the time I was able to inch my head around a little, I saw that the camels were now grazing, and my three companions lolled on the sand smoking Parliament cigarettes—as I remained, helpless, on my steed. I did not know how to get him to lie down so I could escape.

"What's going on?" I shouted, not graciously.

"Do you want to rest or go on?" Salmadon asked, casually.

"I don't care which, but make up your mind! I don't like being isolated up here, while you all sit around smoking!" I spoke indignantly, as if smoking were the most heinous of crimes. "If we're going on, it has to be right now," I added. I had driven myself to keep going, keep going, and now I feared that once I dismounted I might not ever get back on the camel. My fury stemmed from feeling somewhat like Fay Wray, perched on top of the Empire State Building by King Kong. We could stay there until the dunes disappeared unless someone helped me down. Hussain got the point, left the others and lured Muhammed to the ground. Hussain again lifted my paralyzed leg, provoking my friends to a round of convulsive laughter.

Then I learned that Elizabeth had fallen off the camel; my fears hadn't been crazy after all. I just hadn't expected it to happen to Elizabeth, who had looked so stable. She and Salmadon had stopped, and when the camel lowered its front half to the ground, she hadn't paid sufficient attention and had rolled right over his head. For a moment her scarf had caught under one of his feet, and she had visions of being stomped. However, Salmadon had moved in to rescue her.

When I learned of Elizabeth's accident I felt mortified about being ill-tempered. She insisted she was fine, that she hadn't even been frightened, and had no compunction about remounting her camel. Once reassured that she was all right, what galled me was that her legs didn't bother her much. How was that possible? Another disparity between the relatively young and the old?

All too soon it was time to begin again. I looked at that animal, felt my thighs tremble, and knew I would not ride him the rest of the way. "How far is it to the village?" I asked.

"Not far." Oh, yes, I'd heard that one before.

"How many minutes?" I knew this was a silly question since these men attended to the sun and moon, not watches. But sophisticated Salmadon came up with an answer, and however arbitrarily arrived at, it satisfied me. His pretended estimate: thirty minutes. Since I was finished riding, it didn't matter. I would simply have to walk all night if necessary. The air had grown cool. The sun, now low, created sinuous ripples of shadow on sand.

Our little parade began again. Elizabeth appeared serene. The men walked at a good clip, trying, I felt sure, to beat the sun. We walked and we walked and we walked. Hiking, even though faster than my preferred pace, felt good. And I was not about to make anyone slow down for me. Anything they could do, I could do—*some kind of way.* Now Hussain's refrain changed. Every few minutes he asked if I didn't want to get on the camel again. With each step I became more certain I did not. The ride had been well worth the agony—once. I tried not to look at my watch. I knew the alleged half-hour had passed. The village was still not in sight.

The sun lowered, painting brilliant red striations across a nearly royal-blue sky. Then a luminous half-moon and profuse mantle of stars gave us light. As we traveled, I gaped at the sky, entranced by its chameleon ways. Again, I forgot my body. As we neared the village, it was clearly nighttime, and still the sky did not turn ebony. Finally adobe buildings stood in inky silhouettes against the midnight-blue dome above. I was buoyant. Reentering M'Hamid felt as secure as coming home. Unaccountably, my thighs were healed. My spirits soared.

I bade Hussain good night. Elizabeth explained to Salmadon that, no, she would not go with him to his roof tent, "just to talk." Salmadon's shoulders dropped as he padded upstairs alone. We had known the two men for about twelve hours. Our experience with them had created a bond, and as we parted, I already missed them. Elizabeth and I took candles and settled into our welcome beds.

At five o'clock in the morning we struggled to pack by candlelight and ran for the bus leaving town. We had only a couple of companions, men who slipped immediately into sleep, heads nodding under the peaked, monk-type hoods of their wool *djellabas.* We envied their cozy garments, but soon perked up when the bus stopped. In a small, dark hut we found strong coffee and doughnuts dipped in fat right before our eyes, and handed to us on a string: the best doughnuts I ever ate.

"My legs don't even hurt," I said, smiling my surprise.

"Mine don't either," Elizabeth said. "This is the best trip ever."

"Yes," I said, "pain and all, I'm thrilled that we did it. Even that we rode the camels instead of taking the Land Rover."

"But no more four-legged rides, right?" she asked, confident of the answer.

"You got it." I bit into my doughnut, looked around at the passengers who had arrived to join us on the bus, now staring at us aliens dropped into their world. I couldn't remember ever feeling quite so good.

"You know, Elizabeth," I said, before I realized what would come out of my mouth. "There's a place in India, Rajasthan, I think, where you can take a camel ride into the desert for a week—"

Elizabeth's eyes were wide with astonishment.

"Wait," I said. "The best part of all: they have stirrups! It would be luxurious, after this."

Her eyes glittered and I knew they mirrored the light in my own.

ECSTASY AND TERROR

Harriet Laine

I will always feel like a beginner no matter how long I do this, this riding, this obsession of mine to be on the back of a horse, feeling the movement under me, moving that movement, attempting connection with each step. Maybe it started when I was a kid, hating parental restrictions, longing for freedom. I grew up in suburbia, no place for a real horse. When I was very young, maybe four or so, I fantasized being a vegetable lady, since the only horse I knew belonged to the vegetable man, who used a horse-drawn wagon to sell his fresh cauliflower and cucumbers. By the time I was five or six, I wanted to be a cowgirl and enthusiastically galloped alongside my mother; she, wheeling my sister in her carriage, me, constantly reminding her not to step on my horse. I did not see myself so much rescuing blond beauties in distress or stealing sacks of gold coin from the bank, but just galloping along, open and free.

I loved Black Beauty but I didn't collect horse dolls or read every horse book ever written. And other than the picture of me taken when I was about two, sitting on a pony's back and looking somewhat amazed to be there, I have no memory of ever being on a horse until I was twelve. It was summer, and my family and I had gone on vacation out West. Somehow, my father managed to meet the local sheriff (who did not wear a sheriff's star over his heart), and the next thing I knew I was being placed on a horse's back, as part of a Fourth of July parade. In my awkwardness and haste to get on my steed, I tore my totally inappropriate woolen slacks, and held tightly to the pommel of the saddle the entire time we walked along. But oh, what a thrill! There I was, amongst real cowboys who wore boots with jingling spurs and big cowboy hats. I fancied myself as one of them, even as they struggled to help me dismount.

Distracted by hormones and boys during the remainder of my teenage years, I did not think about riding so much, although I did go trail riding a few times with some friends. Again, I was thrilled just to be sitting there as the horse walked along, and although I continued to fantasize about moving at a gallop, I was secretly relieved that only as we approached the barn on our way back did the horse ever move faster than a walk. I did not know I had any part in the decision. It was all up to the horse to take me how and where it chose.

I was about thirty and on vacation in Nova Scotia before the next riding experience came my way. Foolishly, I lied about my abilities and managed to convince a young woman that I could handle a quiet horse on my own. This horse clearly knew what an idiot I was and ran through the woods with me as though we were part of a Hollywood chase scene, branches and burrs whipping over me like so many mad hornets. Although I stayed on, the rapid beating of my heart, the scratches and bruises over my face, arms and legs (not to mention the serious reprimand I received from the guide), left such an impression that it was years before I tried riding again. Yet, if you had asked me during this time to list my favorite activities, riding would still have been at the top of the list. The fantasy—the idea that I could move with total freedom, the need to feel this freedom from the back of a horse—remained strong. The thought of riding was like an insistent tomcat brushing up against me, demanding to be fed, being brushed away—only to return.

I was in my late thirties when I rode again. By this time, I had moved to the country and met someone who actually owned her own horse. She and I bartered: lessons on her recalcitrant mare in exchange for firewood. It was hard work for me and my chain saw, and Penny bucked me off the first chance she got. I was too intimidated (and too sore) to get back on; once again, riding returned to the familiar, comfortable world of fantasy. Easy for me to let myself enjoy it there; in the real world, I began to feel that riding was something I could not have. It was something that belonged to others.

So I more or less forgot about riding until maybe ten years ago, when I was in my mid-forties and a barn opened up nearby. My riding fantasies once again stimulated, I suppressed all previous doubts and fears and, with a beginner's openness, immediately signed up for instruction. One of the barn's earliest customers, I still remember the huge smile on my face during that entire first lesson, a lesson that consisted of going around and around in small circles at a walk, not under my own power, but being led on a long rope, a lead-line. It didn't matter. I was on a horse. And hooked. Back as soon as I could find the money, my one lesson a week quickly moved to two. I volunteered to muck out stalls in my spare time just so I could hang out with those in the know, those people whose vocabulary included words such as *forehand* and *hocks* and who clearly knew the difference between a halter and a bridle. How I envied them their knowledge and their abilities. The more time I spent at the barn, however, the more I realized how little I knew, and the more I began to wonder what I was doing. How many times I left a lesson in tears, frustrated by my inability to do what was asked of me. "Heels down," I would hear my trainer command. Where *were* my heels, for God's sake? I couldn't seem to locate them. My body and mind would not come together; each acted independently; my brain needed to repeat a command several times before my body responded, if it responded at all. But some other element mixed in with the tears and awkwardness I felt, some other feeling pulled at me, not letting me give up: the need to connect, to be intimate with this extraordinary animal. I understood this the day I learned to canter.

I will never forget that day, or Spike, the first horse that found my heart. A palomino gelding who knew how to strut and liked to buck you off on the landing side of a jump, he opened my soul to the magic that drew me toward horses. He taught me about connections, how it is possible to communicate through touch alone—the kinesthetic sense, it has been called. I delicately pressed my leg against Spike's side, some dynamic force passed between us and we cantered. Our bodies connected, and our breathing shared a rhythm: Yeats's dancer and the dance. This connection, this conjunction of spirits, left me marveling; even now, ten years later, the exhilaration of that first canter continues to thrill me, the very idea that I can connect like that with another animal. Extraordinary.

But it was hard. I grew up thinking of myself as graceful, elegant even. I moved my body with ease and freedom. I loved to dance and was good at it. It never occurred to me that I would not be a good rider, and that I would have to work so hard to be relaxed and comfortable on a horse's back. But it has been hard work all along, and it continues to be hard work. I am not a natural rider, and I am a slow learner. I am tentative when I need to be firm. I frequently lack courage and conviction. It is easy for me to panic and let my horse take over. I compare myself with those who started riding at the same time and are so much further along. They look better; they jump higher fences with greater equanimity; they handle more horse than I do; they take greater risks. Always, I stand against them, judging my performance and seeing only failure. Always, I put myself on the outside. I ignore compliments and am pierced by minor criticisms. Yet I persist, for it is also true that absolutely nothing else gives me the thrill or the joy of sitting on my horse's back, feeling the rhythm of breath and step under me, trying to match it with my own. And so, despite my slow learning and self-judging attitude, all I have to do is smell the sweetness of the barn and everything else disappears. I am focused, clear, in the moment as nowhere else in my life. Like making love, I am attentive, charged, alive.

After a while, even two lessons a week were not enough, and I moved to share boarding. Pretending to ownership, I bought bits and blankets, first for Tripoli, then Coco, Abby and Chausette. Owning a horse was clearly beyond both my financial and emotional capabilities. That was something other people did, not me. Instead, I rode this succession of animals, trying to let each give me something of what I needed and wanted. I managed to avoid falling really in love, steeling myself against the inevitable time when the sharing of a horse with someone else, the owner, would no longer work out.

Finally, though, I allowed myself to fulfill a dream. What did it mean to do so? Last year, at age fifty-three, I bought my first horse, an experience fraught with psychological issues, fears and insecurities. Jargon of the nineties rang in my head about "giving myself permission" and "caring for the child within"; so much about self-worth came up. Not feeling competent to make this purchase on my own, I enlisted the help of my trainer. Horses were brought to the barn for me to try. I was not even allowed to ride the first horse that came. I wasn't good enough, was all I could think. I was an old lady who needed an old lady's horse, not a spooky-eyed ball of dappled-gray fire bucking around the ring. OK. So the second horse came. Sweet. Calm. Gentle. Safe. All the wrong adjectives. I could only think that this was what I was supposed to have— this—this placid gelding who would no doubt take good care of me in the woods, but would never make my heart beat. No passion. No magic. I was supposed to settle; after all, isn't that who I was? The other people at the barn all seemed to have fancy horses that strutted and pranced, extended their trots and made beautiful arcs over jumps. Where was this horse of mine? Did I have a choice? I fought that old battle: what did I want, what did I deserve, what were my choices?

Then I fell in love. Just as had been predicted by other horse owners, the very first time I sat on her and felt the length of her stride, I knew I wanted her. All caution gone, all questions answered, I put my arms around her neck and hoped that someday she would recognize me, nicker at my approach. A shimmering bay mare with a white blaze running down her face and what is called a kind eye, I named her Nairobi, for the dark, mysterious adventure of life. Today, when I brush her and feel her warmth, my soul, too, is fed and warmed. I get lost in her heat and smell. They comfort me, making the world safe and secure, even if just for the moment.

I hoped for courage with Nairobi: the courage to let go and relax. I said I rode because I loved it. Yet it was hard for me to experience this thing called fun. One woman I knew took the jumps and laughed, regardless of mistakes or consequences, saying there was no more fun an adult could have. I took the jumps with my heart pounding, shoulders crunched, breath and body held tightly, waiting for disaster.

Soon after I began taking riding lessons, I saw an ad for a riding vacation in Scotland. What an extraordinary idea! I had always wanted to go to Scotland and immediately sent for the brochure. Could I do such a trip? I asked my trainer. The pictures looked lush, most inviting, and they also showed people sitting most poorly in the saddle. Well, I could sit better in the saddle than those folks, so why not? Why not, indeed! Only now, after years of experience, can I see how crazy that first trip was. Led by a teenage boy whose idea of fun was to gallop down hills as fast as a horse could go, we leaped over thyme-scented ditches and flew across mountains freckled with sheep. I barely saw any of the countryside; we moved too fast. I fell three times in one week and do not know to this day how I survived some of those gallops over thyme. But there was as much ecstasy as there was terror in that ride. A powerful sense of freedom, some glimmer of what it would feel like to fly, filled me during these gallops. I wanted more—and I began to want to seek it in unfamiliar landscapes.

Now, I have traveled a fair amount on horseback. I have been chased by crocodiles in Botswana, have felt like Lawrence of Arabia in a sandstorm in India, have lost myself in the fragrance of eucalyptus in Australia. Although my insecurities about riding are still present, and I feel constantly measured against all the other very excellent riders on a trip, no one can take away the thrill: the other animals, the smell of heat and earth, the vastness of land and sky. I pretend to a freedom that is not really mine; it is a gift of the animal under me, upon whose back I impose my weight for hours at a time. Always, these trips teach me: to stretch, to find solace in the kindness of a horse, to be quiet and listen to the sound of hoof beats against rock, in water, through sand; to learn the earth's red clay, brown mud, pink sand; to know sagebrush, fig trees, heat, zebra dung; to be caressed by the wind, an embrace of life, of strength, of something deep in my soul. These trips show me my limits: there are days of long rides, of eight or nine hours in the saddle when I think I will not make it to camp; I am too old, too soft, too timid; what in hell am I doing here, anyway, in the middle of Africa, Asia, Australia? I should be back in the comfort and security of the ring, on a familiar horse, where all is more predictable. But something else pushes up at me, and even as I am feeling I can't go on, I am thinking about where to go next, what part of the world, what new kind of horse, what different smells and flowers and animals and light and people, and I go on.

My most recent trip through northern Kenya was the hardest. We were creating a route as we rode, knowing our ultimate destination but having only a rough sense of how we could get there, riding through desert scrub, across the savannah, the relentless sun our constant companion. Never totally comfortable in hot weather, I developed heat stroke, with chills, fever and a weakness that left me unable to keep up with the group. I wandered the savannah, an endless sea of dancing, blond grasses, by myself, tears streaming down my face at every mirage of trees. I watched the group far ahead of me as they gamboled with a herd of giraffe. I no longer cared if I ever saw a giraffe again or if the lion we had heard the night before was following close behind; all I wanted was to stop, to reach some cover. Just one tree. We rode for ten hours without a break in that unbearable heat. When we finally did stop, my body could not, its muscles trembling in endless contractions. Lacking all control over my pathetically weak body, I had to be helped off my horse. Would I do it again? Of course. Like any other pain, it has lessened with distance, and I remember instead all the brilliant-colored birds, the rhinoceros, the baby elephants.

Why is riding so important to me? What does it give me? Something that's mine, that no one can take away. Although I fantasize riding the trails with my girlfriend at my side, I think, really, I don't want that. I am afraid I would give up my pleasure to her, that somehow it would make me less confident, as though her accomplishments would drain me of mine. Riding has taught me (and continues to teach me) courage, patience, determination. I constantly marvel at the power of a message communicated, it seems by breath alone, between horse and rider. I find this experience to be a profound one. But more than all of this is the sense of freedom, of flying, of being so very focused in the moment. There is nothing else, no one else, just the now. It is my drug of choice, my addiction—this intensity, this centering. Riding has become my meditation, a time simultaneously out of my life and the deepest part of my life.

For sure, not all of my riding is like this. There is also the quiet ambling through the woods when I sing a little sustaining song for us both as we cross a shallow brook. There are just the two of us, my horse and me, greeting this world of twenty shades of green, and I feel connected then to the earth, and at peace. Then there are my trips. They can be scary, and there is always a moment when I wonder what I've done and how I'll get through it. What if I can't handle the strange horse, the length of the day? How will my knees hold out? What if we go too fast and I fall off? (But that has happened already, I tell myself.) Still judging myself against others, I wonder if other riders will find me acceptable. But then afterward, I forget about the scary part and remember the exotic, the adventuresome, the thrill and chill, and I am ready and eager to go again.

Why do I ride? There is for me the pure exhilaration of going over a jump, flying through the air. It is a kind of dance, of movement in space, a rhythm of movement that excites and thrills me. Still I ride on a breath between ecstasy and terror. Maybe it will always be there for me. Maybe that is why I ride.

How do I describe this passion? If I do, will I lose it? Will I understand something on another level and then not be able to engage in the same way? I certainly hope not. Riding takes me out of the routine of my life, allowing me distance, softening the edges. Riding sustains me: helplessly watching my brother die of AIDS, I frequently raced from the hospital to the barn, finding solace in the heat of a horse's breath. The day he died, I rode with all the fury in me, tears and exhaustion ultimately forcing me to stop. I think of a childhood story I loved, *Harold and the Purple Crayon*, about a boy who drew a world to his liking and then stepped into it. Harold has his purple crayon, and I have my bay mare. But Harold went back to his bed; does that mean I have to come back, too? Back to what? I try to learn, to remain open to new experience, to let go. Possibility and potential are really what life is all about. And the courage to act. Riding is my metaphor.

Four months ago, I was diagnosed with terminal cancer. For the first two of those months, I lay in my bed, too sick to do much more than get to the bathroom. I concentrated on remembering the smell of Nairobi, the rhythm of her trot, how we take a jump. Slowly the pain dissipated, and I began to be able to do more. I began to be able to think about riding again. The first time I got back on my horse, I was reminded that the earth is not flat. I needed a person on the ground on either side of me, supporting my poorly balanced and weakened body. I had to get off after just a few steps. But a few days later, I was back, and this time managed to sustain three or four minutes of a walk, repeating my very first lead-line lesson, smile and all, before having to dismount. Now I am riding with almost full body strength. Curiously, I am riding better than ever. Somehow the fear is gone, the lack of confidence replaced with a sense of security in my body. Maybe it has nothing to do with cancer; maybe it is that my horse of six months and I are beginning to know and trust one another. I am listening to her; she tells me what she needs, and I say OK. I tell her what I want, and she gives it to me willingly. I let go and relax. We are having a good time. I am having fun. For the first time in my life, I am enjoying the moment while it is happening, not having to wait until it is over and I can review it from a safe distance. If cancer has given me this gift, then I am eternally grateful, for it is a gift of magic. And I have learned to fly.

Harriet Laine died in November, 1995.
A portion of this essay was read at her funeral service.

HOT FLASHES FROM THAILAND

Alice Kent Stephens

I was fifty when I went to Thailand to work as a missionary teaching English as a Second Language to Thai of different ages. I was a fat little old lady in a land where I knew neither the customs nor the language. I soon melted down that fat, but I never did learn the language well enough to have a serious conversation. I worked at a church and nursery school in Nonthaburi, a small town north of Bangkok.

I lived in a room on the third floor above the nursery school. I had a bed, a word processor brought from the States, a desk, a small filing cabinet and a neat, little stand-up fake closet bought at the market. As time went by, I added to that. I had my own bathroom with a bucket and hose for clothes and showers. I pooped in a hole on a platform with one foot marked on each side, and used the bucket for washing off. (All the toilets were like that in Thailand, unless you went to one of the classy hotels in downtown Bangkok.) I didn't mind. Before I got my own room, I lived with the boss and his wife and family: that was hard. They often stayed up very late and I would have to come crashing through a business meeting to get from my bedroom to the bathroom. Nobody could understand why anyone would want to be alone, but when a room became available on the third floor of the nursery-school building, they let me take it. My room on the second floor had been on the street side. Now I had a window and a door to open and shut. I could hear the crickets and see the rain and smell the earth. It was my own little home. I worked very hard, and it was especially nice to fall into bed with the sound of rain, upstairs, away from people.

I arrived in Bangkok by airplane in the late afternoon. I was coming from Indonesia where I had been surfing with my two youngest sons: that is; I surfed on my belly and they surfed on boards. We had hugged and prayed at the airport, then went off in different directions. They were going back to California and I was off on my grand missionary adventure. I was met by a group from the Nonthaburi Church. I grew to know and love each one of them, but at that moment they were beautiful smiling strangers, giving me flowers and a white, fuzzy, Jackie Kennedy-type hat.

Sahat was the head of the school and the church. He was there with his two children, Solomon and Esther. His wife, Surang, was at home with the newly born Stephen. Upin was the secretary and missionary of the church. She was my guide and gave me my orders that first month in Thailand. Gik, Nah, Oi, and Ying were sisters and leaders of the youth group and the camps. Nah became my Thai teacher until I went to language school. Chy was head of the youth group. Pratuan and Gae were two of the nursery-school teachers. These Thai and others I met later were to be my teachers and students, my brothers and sisters for two years.

There was much to be done in preparing for the school and doing visitation. We went out to meet the families of the students in many areas of the town. They were very excited that an American had come to teach English and wanted to meet her. At the time I was the only Westerner in the area.

One day four of us went into the jungle. It was monsoon season, so the ground was wet and slippery. Gae and Nah and Upin went on ahead. In the heat and the dark-brown, dark-green of the jungle they were fluttering bits of color, like butterflies, dancing on ahead of me. They were so sure of foot, so graceful in the heat. I puffed along behind them, soon happily lost in the pleasure of new sensations. It was very hot, even though we were protected from the sun's rays in the jungle by huge leaves. The sun did not penetrate except in tiny places where a dot or streak of light could be seen. I was dressed in what I thought was appropriate missionary, older-lady wear: a heavy, long-sleeved, pink-and-white striped dress with a long, full skirt that bobbed along around and about me. Surang had given me a pink umbrella to use in the heat. I had it up and opened, more to help balance myself than to protect from the rays of the sun. There was something whimsical and funny about this fat, absurdly dressed, oldish lady in the jungle, and the parasol put the exclamation mark on the image! Time stopped. It was as if I were both in my body and out of it. I was in this incredible heat bobbing about clumsily, more like Aunt Clara than Mary Poppins. The jungle was infinite. The time was eternal. The colors contrasted perfectly. There were no sounds except for the happy babbling of my friends ahead. For that moment in time, I was alone, observing the scene.

And then I screamed. The foreign sound vibrated in the jungle. In front of me, stretched out across the path, was a huge snake. I had never seen such a big snake before. All I remember was that it was brown and definitely not part of my color scheme. There was a stunned silence. All eyes were on me (except for the poor snake's; he was dead).

The young women came back rustling and bustling and chattering to each other. They were surprised. The jungle was full of large snakes: snakes lying on the thick branches; snakes hanging from the trees; snakes resting in the underbrush. The jungle was their home. I just had not seen them. This was close to my first week in Thailand, and the Thai did not know how to relate to me any better than I knew how to relate to them. We got to someone's house where they clucked over me and put me near a window and turned on a fan and brought me some water. Needless to say, I recovered, but for many months that pink dress and the dead snake would be cause for much humor.

I liked teaching the older teens best. Children five to sixteen were very shy and cautious about things like rules of grammar. Adults were sedate and stuck in the rules of proper behavior. The kids in the middle were more adventurous, asked a lot of questions and were able to laugh at themselves and with others. We had a text. I used what Thai I had, and they used their English. I taught three classes of young adults; tutored two older men; taught nursery-school age silly rhymes, songs and dances; and assisted the Thai teacher in drills of pronunciation for both the adults and the five-to-sixteen-year-old group. The classes were of three months' duration, and then we all went to camp at the beach for a week. The camps were a wonderful break between semesters.

I also had a lot to learn about language myself and went to language school every day. I went to school in downtown Bangkok, and in order to get there, had to catch a bus before six in the morning. I walked to the place where the buses stopped. It was dark, but the humidity was already in the nineties and the temperature soon would be. The trees were alive with crickets. They would sing and chortle and stomp about until sunrise and then they would be still. Animals appeared dead on the street, as they clung to what coolness they could on the earth. People became testy, and the normally gracious Thai would scowl at the bus stop. It was always a battle to get a seat because it was a long way into the big city and no one got up for anyone, unless they were monks or infirm and old. Spring and early summer are when the heat wore down the kindest of natures. The trees hung in waiting. The bus drivers growled. The mosquitoes swarmed. It felt as if it would never rain again.

Then one night, the sky filled with clouds. There was a roar of thunder, and lightning split the heavens with an orange blaze. Rudyard Kipling's "wild elephants" were marching across the night sky. It had turned a dark black-green. Fourth of July spectaculars pale in comparison to the heavenly display and symphony of the monsoon storm that night. I ran outside, cheering the bellowing thunder and dancing to the glory of the infinite streaks of orange. I felt as wild as the sky and as relieved as the parched earth. The monsoon breaks open the whining yet silent spirit and brings out a roar of relief and rejoicing.

Surang called me in. It was foolish to go out into all that electricity, but I wanted to celebrate, too. I went upstairs and lay in bed and cheered and sang until I faded out in exhaustion.

(About a month later I tried to take pictures, because I didn't trust myself and knew I would not be believed. Who would believe the sky could be so black and green!? Was the lightning orange because the sky was that amazing color, or was the sky that color to balance the brilliance of the orange streaks of light? The pictures didn't turn out. I guess you have to have special lenses and other kind of lighting. A picture may be worth a thousand words, but a picture is only a shadow of the glory seen and experienced. Like the dark-green jungle and pink dress with parasol, it doesn't matter. It is in my heart with such intensity that proofs or pictures could never describe it.)

My Thai got good enough to take me out in ever-expanding circles from the nursery school and church. At first I walked, then rode the buses. I spent a lot of time lost on buses at first, but gradually I was able to use the system. My second year out, I even went by bus to Sukothai, the ancient capital of Thailand, to explore the ruins by myself with a Thai speaking guide. My guide was the *samlor* (bicycle-taxi) driver. He pedaled along a flat, dusty road. There were some straggly trees, some small hotels and eateries, but, other than that, the road was bare. And then, right there before my own eyes was the old Sukhothai wall, and beyond it a city of ruins: a kingdom from the thirteenth century. The *samlor* driver talked with me, but, truth to tell, I didn't understand much of what he was saying. I just walked and stared, and then walked some more. There is a sense of presence in ruins, even when they are out in the bare-flat ground. " . . . And this was the palace for the queen, and this was the third moat built to protect from the ravaging Cambodians . . . " Words meant little. They floated over my head. It was the presence of a kingdom and the presence of a culture which turned me and made me want to stay and stare. I left promising myself that I would go out in search of more archaeological treasure.

Later that same year, Sahat took me on an archaeological tour way back into the jungle, by outboard motorboat this time, to explore the old temples. He translated for me. Like Angkor Wat in Cambodia, these temples have become a part of the jungle. Rough bits of stone lie on the floor. Rows of beheaded, statued monks reveal the horror of the Thai-Cambodian wars. Behind the web of vine and tree sits a serene Buddha. Despite the heat and rain, wooden temples still stand, hidden deep in the dark of the jungle.

Central Thailand is beautiful country, very different from the United States. It is so hot and so green, except for the rice fields, which can be the most extraordinary yellow. If you take a train south "on the road from Mandalay," these colors all rush past you until sunset. Sunset in Southeast Asia takes a lifetime. The chattering in the train may not stop. The train certainly doesn't. But time appears to stop dead. Colors rush one upon the other—reds and golds and oranges—until the whole sky is filled. The sun becomes a bright red ball, and sinks majestically into the land, or the waters. The reflection of all this color is in every eyeglass, every body of water and every possible place it can fit itself. For at this moment the eternity of time and the everyday world unite together.

When I went to the king's sixtieth-birthday celebration in Bangkok, it was another extravaganza of color. This time the whole city was decked out in yellow, the color of the king. There was no traffic, only people and lights. Strings of little yellow lights hung over the streets and in the trees. It was very crowded and hard to find a place to sit while waiting for the fireworks to begin. I found a place by one of the canals between two young families. I worried about what I was going to do with my feet, but the young women told me it was all right to stick them out. One thing I had learned while traveling in Thailand was to be careful how you point your feet. Thai sit with their feet underneath them. I can't do that, especially not for a long time. They are almost universally a kind and forgiving people, but you have to make sure you watch your feet. To show the bottom of your bare foot to someone is akin to the rudest of our gestures. One time, two women inadvertently made the gesture to a large statue of Buddha and were summarily kicked out of the country! I was very grateful that I could stick my feet out, as there was a long wait for the fireworks. Thai people are not in a hurry. One of their favorite expressions is *"My Ben Ry,"* akin to our "Relax."

After the celebration, I made my way home. There were only a few Thai getting off the bus at Nonthaburi. I walked along the road. The stars were out and the night eerily quiet in contrast to the roar of the fireworks downtown. It had been a glorious, explosive collection of yellow bursts and cascades against a perfectly clear, dark night sky. I thought of my first class for the nursery schoolers down at the big sandbox. I had taught them how to make a birthday cake, decorate it with candles and stand around singing, "Happy birthday, dear King." When Surang found out, she was afraid I would be booted out of Thailand. The king is very close to a god to these people. Several foreigners had been kicked out for *lèse majesté*. To make the king someone you had a birthday cake for, and sang "Happy Birthday" to, was gross disrespect of his person. Of course, no one had understood a thing I was doing. They had just enjoyed this silly old woman.

I laughed to myself. How extraordinary it was to be in this beautiful land, and how extraordinary to be able to meet such lovely people. By this time I had walked all the way to the Chao Phrya River and was suddenly overcome with a longing to cheer and shout and dance about and hug and give high-fives. No one hugs or yells, even when celebrating the birth of their king. The Thai bow their greetings and speak softly. They are taught to be polite and quiet. This is not to say they are a bunch of grumpy folk who find no pleasure in life. Often they live together with grandparents and married brothers or sisters with their children. They are taught that if you are going to be in the same room with the whole family, you need to learn to be gracious and quiet and careful of spreading any kind of infection.

I sat down and watched the night lights dance across the great, dark expanse of the river, letting the memories of the dark jungle and that outrageous pink dress, the monsoons and sunsets, filter through the longing. I went back to my room. There were things to be done. I walked back to the nursery-school building. The heavy metal gate was down, but I knew Surang and Sahat would be awake and able to open the door for me. They hardly ever slept, and with three children, the midnight hours were the only ones when together they could make the plans for the nursery school, the camps, the English school and the church.

I rang and Surang came down from their apartment on the second floor. She had been watching the celebration on television and was full of the excitement of the big night in Thailand. We talked for a bit, and then I made my way through the nursery school to the third floor. I put a pot of water on my hot plate to boil while I hosed off and changed into my night clothes. Dressed, I got out my cup and spoon, and my instant coffee and the sweet milk from my refrigerator. By then the water had boiled enough to be safe, and I indulged myself with a cup of coffee.

I thought back on how I had learned to say *sweet milk:* one tone meant breast milk; another, evaporated milk in a can. I laughed to myself as I remembered the shock and then the smile of the little old lady when I asked if she had breast milk. My brain kept reminding me: plans to be written, papers to be corrected, report to be done. But my heart and my soul were quiet. I sat down on the bed, propped up against the wall with a pillow and drank the coffee. How often I had leaned up against this wall and listened to the rain. It would come in sheets against the window, banging insistently at the pane and rattling against the tin roof. I would awake to the sound of it; the rain washed down into the weary soul and brought relief from the heat. There wasn't always the high drama of a great roar of thunder. Sometimes I would awake at night to just the sound of the downpour or even a gentle rain. I loved to get caught in the rains. I remembered helping unload the camp gear from a bus in the middle of a storm. It was fun to get just drenched with water: count to twenty and, on good days, you were a puddle. But I was homesick. I loved the job and the people, but I wanted to go home and be loud. I looked over at my wall covered with 11" x 14" pictures from home: my family, my church family and my house. Gradually new pictures had been added to the montage: my church family here in Thailand, my students and my friends.

My children and my mom had encouraged me to go out and be a missionary—something I had wanted to do for several years. But when my mother became very sick, I decided to come home. I was just starting my third monsoon season in Thailand. The people I worked with fully understood. They are raised to care for the elderly in the family. Some would even ask me what I was doing in Thailand when my family was in California. They did not understand that children leave at eighteen as adults who want their own space and freedom, and come back only for family celebrations. Even with some excellent material and a bright class, my students could not understand the "John Wayne" philosophy of independence, toughness and competition. Their culture embodies dependence with love and a responsibility for others. They don't seem to need to cry out for more space. They are respectful of each other even in very crowded conditions and can't imagine wanting to live by themselves. They wonder why older people live alone in America, and why children leave home so soon. "Aren't you lonely?" they would ask. I was lonely, but I was lonely in my little room above the nursery school. I wanted to go home. My mama was sick, my youngest son was graduating from U.C. Santa Barbara, my eldest and his lovely wife were going to have their first baby. I was ready to go home and be youngest daughter and grandma.

So I left Thailand as I had come, from the airport. This time, I was stronger in my body and in my faith in God. Instead of being the fat stranger, I was fifty pounds lighter and surrounded by dear friends. I was embraced by Thai flower leis. Instead of bearing gifts for strangers, I had gifts for my family. I was on my way home. To be in Thailand was to be in jungles and monsoons, sunsets and ruins. For me, it truly meant being in an "otherness." We bowed and prayed, then went off in different directions. I returned to my "other" world with all the razzmatazz extravagance of expression and choice; they, to theirs in all its gentle quietude and simplicity.

CAPTAIN MOM'S
CARIBBEAN JOY RIDE

Jean Hand Triol

The plane drifted over brilliant blue ocean and a chain of dark-green islands rimmed with white surf and sand. I leaned closer to the wind-etched glass. A sailboat miles out to sea looked like a white bird skimming the waves. I wondered about the people, the sailors. Were they part of the fraternity of island cruisers my sister had written about in a letter last Christmas?

I smiled at the thought of Bette as captain of a thirty-eight-foot sail-boat crewed by her two kids, a neighbor's son and a cat. All of us were a little shaken when, after her husband's sudden, tragic death last year, she put aside grief and anxieties and sold most of their possessions to finance this private dream. Noel had talked about buying a boat and cruising the Caribbean, maybe taking early retirement. With him gone, the Morgan 38 and the purse for the cruise were now the sum total of everything she owned in the world. They were gifts to herself and their children, gifts of healing and a chance at renewed life. She named the boat *Cadeau*.

Bette Jane of large heart and spirit was bound for adventure; bound and determined. Had she been a child of the privileged class, perhaps she wouldn't have found the strength or courage to take on such a challenge virtually alone, but she was not. Self-reliant and well tested by life, she was a woman who accepted no obstacle once her mind was clearly set on a goal, something worth doing. I knew she had prepared well for the trip by reading books, taking navigation courses from the coast guard and, after she bought the boat, taking practice day sails in the bay with an old, salty captain. She questioned experienced Caribbean cruisers. Advised to carry a gun, she bought one and learned to use it.

I had gone to Galveston Bay early last fall just before departure time to see them and the boat, and enjoyed watching and listening as my younger sister confidently gathered supplies and information. While buying provisions and outfitting the boat she talked to shopkeepers, sail makers and most anyone who was willing. I felt reassured. Now on the way south to join them in Jamaica to sail one leg of the journey, I dozed and dreamed in the warm April sunlight, the tensions of the last three months on a new and very difficult job temporarily at bay.

Disembarking at the airport in Montego Bay, the dreamy mood vanished. There were hard stares and guards in khaki uniforms with guns. Dark-skinned men and women crowded into the baggage area, dragging sleepy, protesting children. Passengers busied themselves hauling bags off the belt and making their way through customs' lines. Finally passing the immigration desk, I looked around hopefully. Nowhere— they weren't here. Outside there was a crowd of silent people standing, facing the concrete veranda where I stood. I perceived a vague hostility and felt chilled and disappointed. A row of battered taxis stood at the curb. With no friendly face or greeting to soften my first impression of Jamaica, I chose a cab and gave the driver the name of the hotel. This wasn't a good start.

My three small bags were stacked in a corner, as I paced the dingy hotel lobby with its worn upholstery and faded carpets. Some ancient, dusty flypaper stirred under creaky ceiling fans. The place looked as if it had last seen prosperity fifteen or twenty years ago.

Where was Bette? Did we both understand the time and meeting place? Tension and fear grew more acute as several hours passed. My vision blurred with tears and sweat in the oppressive, humid air. They're lost at sea. Oh God, I'll never see them again! I agonized.

Partly angry at feeling abandoned and partly crazy with imagined fears, I paced back and forth, incapable of seeking relief or assistance. The desk clerk was well aware of me, his not-at-all-friendly customer. Forewarned by a travel agent that Jamaicans disliked tourists and were often surly, even dangerous, I had entered his world abruptly, with a noticeable chip on my shoulder. Although I knew that getting worked up was the worst possible approach to gaining any sympathy or cooperation, I persisted, stubbornly refusing to register. His eyes followed me as I paced.

"Are there any messages for me yet?" I asked for the third time in the past hour.

The clerk smiled slightly and said, "Hey. Your friend will come. No problem." That annoying expression. When *they* say no problem, it means that there is one. I registered—both to escape the lobby and to help ensure that messages were saved for me.

My room was hot and bright. It looked clean, but there was no phone and the doors didn't lock, a chain but no key. I unpacked a few things, changed to cooler, more comfortable clothing and then left, carrying my valuables with me. After checking at the desk for a message again, I left the hotel, intending to take a walk. It was almost five o'clock in the afternoon.

A cab pulled into the courtyard and stopped abruptly at the hotel entrance. Someone waved. Perhaps resignation to being alone had engendered a self-absorbed mood so deep that it took a moment to comprehend—they were here! I felt lightheaded as joy and relief spun me around. Four very familiar people piled out of the cab.

Warm greetings and a feeling of belonging worked instantly to mend the spirit. All was fine and as it should be in Montego Bay. "Isn't this a lovely place? Let's rent a cab and see more of the island tomorrow," said Bette.

"Yes, wonderful," I answered, meaning it. My niece, sunny, laughing Nicole, eighteen, embraced me.

"How was your trip, AB? Were you worried?"

"A little worried, but no matter, no matter at all. You're here!" AB is short for Aunt Bean, a pet name bestowed on me some years ago by my nephew Peter, now twenty-two, tall and tan. With an added air of self-confidence since I last saw him, he gave me a gentle hug. And David, too, grown in a few months' time from boy to man, beamed his welcome. He had stayed with the crew since Galveston Bay and was now one of the family. The boys, captivated by the thought of a real shower and beds with enough room to spread out, stayed with me in the hotel room that night.

Cadeau was moored at the new yacht club about a mile from the hotel. I moved aboard the next morning. She was beautiful to look at: white with clean lines, gold lettering on the transom, forest-green cushions, and matching bimini on deck. Teak woodwork glowed a rich golden-brown. The large wheel near the stern glistened in the sun as she rocked gently with the swells. I carried my gear below. Free space in a cabinet or corner was tough to find; the cabin was packed tight. It would be a little cramped sleeping five people while we were ashore. Traveling at sea, though, not more than four would sleep at once; at least one member of the crew was out on three-hour watches day and night. There was a tiny head with a shower and a small galley with stove and icebox.

Bette looked happy and relaxed as she showed me around. "Captain Mom," the kids liked to call her. Excited voices all spoke at once. I was immensely impressed and pleased. Peter had personally rewired all the circuits and redone the plumbing since I last inspected her. The boat had also run afoul of a reef and spent a month-and-a-half in dry dock getting repaired, under his watchful direction. As a result of that misadventure, however, we had to wait for an important shipment, a Global Positioning System (or GPS for short) before we could leave the island of Jamaica. We decided to use the time stocking up and doing some sightseeing.

"And some snorkeling, too?" I asked.

"You bet! There are some nice reefs in the bay just off the beach. Did you bring your bathing suit?" asked Nicole.

"I came prepared. Watch out for Jeanie in her yellow polka dot bikini!" I teased. This was wishful thinking only. My serviceable blue-skirted affair, much more flattering to a matronly figure, had seen me through many lap miles at the Y pool back home.

Later that day during a relaxed tour with a friendly cab driver, we followed a section of Jamaica's coastal road, then explored unpaved byways. The driver enthusiastically shared stories about celebrities with homes in Jamaica. At the end of a long dusty road we peered through the fence of Johnny and June Carter Cash's hillside house, while a suspicious resident caretaker stared back. At a deserted, ramshackle mansion our driver related some gruesome history about turn-of-the-century murder and madness among the white folk.

"Lights sometimes flicker in the windows late at night," he added softly, almost in a whisper, perhaps wishing not to disturb whatever might be sleeping there. Our imaginations were captivated by the story and the storyteller. The violent history of Jamaica has shaped a rich culture over many generations. The past may have grown dim, but it is not forgotten.

Back in town, uniformed school children, handsome women in bright, flowing dresses and chatting, bicycling, laughing people filled the streets. Musical island accents with not a trace of menace mixed with street sounds and rang all around us in a delightful cacophony. Strange: the people seemed so different from the day before at the airport.

In the town marketplace we bought fresh bread and bargained for goods. I was thinking of handing over fifty dollars for a large beautiful woven basket when Nicole stopped me. "No, no, AB—don't pay that. Much too much." I stepped back and gave her the stage. Soon she had several vendors trailing her, the price rapidly falling as she shook her head convincingly and walked away. After much hand-wringing and sighing, a twenty-dollar sales price was agreed upon.

The woman muttered, "How can I live if you make me give away my baskets?" But later when we passed the same women standing with a group of other vendors, she nodded and said to Nicole, smiling, "Hey, you're good."

Nicole had bargained like a native, and her skill was recognized and openly praised. I considered the lesson. Troubling ourselves to learn the values and mores in countries we visit makes it so much easier to understand and like each other. How different from yesterday, I thought, remembering the way I had acted, and feeling somewhat chagrined.

Bette and Noel believed in diversity and immersed themselves and their family in other cultures. They weren't ones to wrap their children in cotton, but rather exposed them to life and to people different from themselves. How wise and courageous for parents to allow children to experience and develop their own sensibilities and strengths rather than to shelter them from the world and its troubles. At fifty-one, I was beginning to suspect that I needed to relearn the importance of that attitude, to resensitize myself to other people and cultures. I wondered why this was so much more of a struggle now than it used to be. Perhaps I was just out of practice.

Cadeau and crew had sailed many miles through the Caribbean since

I had last seen them. I wanted to hear all about it, every detail. Bette and I carried our snorkeling gear onto an almost-deserted beach and found two lounge chairs nestled in the sand. A very fat, painfully pink man lay in the sun about twenty-five yards away. There, over a glass of wine cooler in the shade of a group of coconut palms, Bette began the saga of their journey.

From Texas they had traversed the inland waterway to New Orleans, through southern Mississippi to Gulfport, across the Gulf of Mexico to Fort Meyers, then on to the Florida Keys. This was the time to practice navigation skills and learn the ways of the sea. Bette spoke of exotic places and adventures, interesting islanders and fellow sailors. As they cruised from port to port, they kept meeting the same boats and people, and made friends, helped each other and became bound together, a mobile community. At Key Largo, they gassed up before crossing the Gulf Stream to the Bahamas. That was the first journey across open sea.

I marveled at Bette's courage. I admired her face as she spoke. She had dark hair, just beginning to show some gray, soft brown eyes and skin tanned from days at the helm. A strong woman, her beauty flowed from an inner peace, a deep core untouched no matter how rough life got. I wished our parents could have lived long enough to see her and what she was doing and feel the pride that I did. Loving her more than I had ever realized I could, I listened, fascinated, as she continued the story.

"Even though I was pretty confident that Pete and I hadn't made any navigational errors, I was relieved when we sighted land, the first since leaving the Florida Keys. The Bahamas are hard to miss, though, since they are a string of about three thousand coral islands, stretching north to south," she said. "The waters of the Grand Banks are shallow and treacherous for yachts. While there, we had to keep a lookout posted at the bow all the time we were underway, to watch for unexpected coral heads."

Bimini, Nassau, Long Island. They spent a week slowly making their way south, exploring islands such as deserted Sand Key, pure, clean white sand on one side and littered with floating plastic trash from ocean-dumped garbage on the other. One island was inhabited by thousands of iguanas two to three feet long, creatures bizarre and interesting enough to merit a chapter in the voyages of Sinbad and Ulysses. Rum Key was a sparsely populated island with one saloon and few houses.

"I treasure the memory of a black woman I met on Rum Key. We found we had lived amazingly parallel lives. A whole lifetime of friendship was shared in the space of a few hours together."

The sea was rough in the aftermath of a storm. The travelers were headed south toward the Virgin Islands. Bette would normally have waited for the heavy weather to pass, but time was growing short. She felt compelled to move on.

"Nicole finished fall quarter at college and was flying to Saint Thomas to meet us. I was getting very anxious waiting out that weather, and attempted a night crossing against my better judgment. I didn't want her waiting alone," she explained.

The sea heaved and the night was dark; there were no stars or moonlight. A second person was stationed on deck as lookout, but the navigator believed they were sailing a safe course free of obstacles. No one realized until too late that they were drifting off that course, the work of strong wind and currents.

The lookout went below to check the charts. David, at the helm, grew apprehensive. He could hear waves breaking. It sounded like surf pounding on a beach. But he couldn't see anything. Suddenly—rocks! No time to turn away.

"Nooo!" he yelled. Then there was a jarring crunch. The captain leaped out of her bunk onto the deck followed by crew. The boat hit three times before miraculously lifting itself free from a reef.

"I said to myself, this is the end, the end of this trip. But I didn't really fear for our lives. I could make out land close by," Bette continued. "In retrospect, though, I don't know what would have happened if the boat had broken up. Providence was with us that night. It didn't happen. She passed safely over the reef."

The crew quickly hauled down sails and started the motor. When the boat seemed clear of the reef, they stopped to check the damage. Peter gathered courage and slipped beneath the black, churning water. He ran his hands over the hull. Four punctures, two ragged, but the hull seemed otherwise sound. *Cadeau* was wounded, but they kept her afloat with the bilge pump running, circling the area till dawn, to avoid running into another reef.

I shuddered imagining the horror of that long night. Waves lifting and crashing, the boat slowly taking on water, invisible, deadly reefs threatening; it had to have been a nightmare straight from hell. But they had coped with it all. They survived the Bermuda Triangle, despite having encountered one of the two most deadly perils that threaten Caribbean cruisers: reefs and pirates.

"We didn't know where we were at the time, but managed to find our way back to some good landmarks after daylight. We discovered that we had hit the reef right off Crooked Island," Bette added. The crash happened before they bought the GPS. "Another cruiser escorted us from there to a safe harbor in the Turks and Caicos Islands. That's the southern tip of the Bahamas." Much to Bette's relief, she was able to contact her daughter before she left school, and the family was reunited there, instead of Saint Thomas.

Captain Mom and her crew stayed in the Turks and Caicos about six weeks during the Christmas festival while *Cadeau* got patched up. Meanwhile, the family wasn't permitted to feel bored or isolated. Fellow cruisers offered sympathy, advice and non-stop partying. Islanders were attentive, extending hospitality and including them in Christmas festivities.

Under Peter's critical eye, native craftsmen fixed the badly scarred keel and knocked out and patched the holes and a large soft spot in the fiberglass hull. The yacht slowly became seaworthy again.

"Sometimes I feel guilty that I'm allowing Peter to take on so much of the responsibility. I rely on him very heavily," Bette said.

"Don't worry," I responded. "He's obviously thriving on it." It was midafternoon, and the sand on the beach was a bit cooler now.

"Excuse me, but do you have the time?" We noticed that the pink gentleman had moved down the beach to where we were sitting. He was not wearing a watch—or anything else.

"Uh, yes, it's three-fifteen. Beautiful day, isn't it?" We didn't quite know where to look. This was evidently a nude beach, and we were overdressed. It seemed the perfect time to retire for our swim.

Gathering our snorkeling gear, we walked across the sand into the waves and swam to an incredible reef barely fifty yards from shore. Looking through our masks deep into the water, we swam above the reef and encountered a marine wonderland: brilliant fish of every color and size, abundant calcified plant forms in the shapes of brains, antlers and fans. But I couldn't help imagining what it would be like to run a boat into such a massive coral structure. I tried not to touch its menacing sharp surfaces.

The evening before departure was full of music, not the traditional calypso, but reggae: wild, colorful and very loud. There was no partying tonight for *Cadeau's* captain and crew, though. We had to bunk down early. The new GPS had arrived. Captain Mom notified customs officials at the airport of our intended departure time. *Cadeau* was cleared, stocked with fuel and provisions and ready to cruise. Next stop: Georgetown, Grand Cayman.

Five days had passed since my arrival, and time was short. I was taking a risk leaving Jamaica so late, since I would barely have time to catch the plane back to Montego Bay for my return flight home, in two days. Bette thought we could make it. I wasn't going to be cheated out of the adventure.

We were up before dawn. David tuned the radio, checking on the National Weather Service off-shore forecast. Channel 16, the coast-guard station, was always open under sail to listen for distress calls from other ships and messages from shore to ship. I made everything secure in the cabin as Captain Mom and Peter plotted the course. They studied the chart for currents, depths and major obstacles on the sea bottom, such as reefs, rocks and wrecks.

"All hands on deck!"

As the sky brightened at the edges, the crew performed their assigned tasks. My stomach and head felt light; I was giddy with suppressed excitement. The motor purred.

"Get ready to cast off. Fenders on board. David, spot the channel markers."

We pulled slowly away from land moving out of the harbor into the ocean. The adventure was beginning again—and I was part of it!

Once we passed the harbor checkpoint, it was time to put up the sails and kill the diesel engine. Captain Mom stood at the helm. "Take off the sail cover and raise the main! Nicole, get ready to unfurl the jib. Pete, give me my bearing and keep up the charting."

The captain estimated that this would be an eighteen-hour crossing. We were due to reach Grand Cayman at about four in the morning. The breeze, gentle but steady, caught and filled the white sails. *Cadeau* passed out of the bay and met the ocean swells. What a wonderful, beautiful, terrifying feeling.

Later that morning Peter explained how the GPS worked. A hand-held device that looked like a calculator, it received signals from high-altitude satellites and pinpointed geographic position; hence its name, Global Positioning System. This device has revolutionized navigation on land, sea and air. Now any fool who is able to read a chart can learn to navigate. Position can be pinpointed from just about any spot on the planet Earth to within a few hundred feet.

Lazing on the deck after lunch, well fed and content, I watched the sea and Peter at the helm.

"Look over there, AB! Watch over the starboard bow and you'll see some flying fish." There were fish, each about a foot or two long, leaping out of the water and gliding twenty-five to fifty feet through the air.

"Mom was at the wheel and got hit in the chest by one in the middle of the night—just about scared her to death. Found thirty on the deck in the morning," he added.

Later that afternoon, a school of five dolphins spotted the boat and formed a lively escort, putting on a marvelous show: synchronized swimming three abreast, obviously having a wonderful time. Dolphins follow and perform around boats, apparently just for the joy of it. The kids tried to reach out and touch them when they swam close to the boat, but the dolphins didn't permit it. They always managed to stay a hair's breadth away from reaching fingertips.

At about two-thirty, a U.S. Coast Guard ship appeared off the port bow. It was moving fast. *Cadeau* had been boarded by the USCG off the coast of Venezuela last month. They were checking for drugs, a very dangerous job. The thought nagged at me that it could be quite dangerous for pleasure cruisers, too, should they come across these bad actors, these modern-day pirates, somewhere far out at sea. I tried not to think about it, but sometimes employed our mother's lucky charm: preventive worrying. While still back home, I had invested plenty of energy worrying on my sister's behalf. The coast guard didn't appear to be interested in us this time.

Meals at sea weren't fancy—wine and cheese, or peanut butter and jelly, a few sweet, black olives and bread—but our hunger from the work and salt air made any food satisfying. Our dining room, carpeted by sea and decked with sky tinted by the setting sun, was a cathedral. We sat together in silence for a moment.

Peanut-butter-and-jelly sandwiches brought back memories of growing up. During the early forties our family, together with an elderly aunt, lived in an apartment in Trenton: three adults and four children crammed into four very small rooms and a bath. There was no privacy, and no money. Sometimes Daddy would get fed up and just take off—but never alone. He'd pile us into his black Ford and just go. It made Ma crazy, but she'd pile in, too. He had some money in his pocket, I guess, enough for gas, a loaf of bread and a jar of jelly. He'd just head out with no plan, running from unbelievable pressures, until he found some peace somehow, then turn back toward Trenton again. Once we found ourselves way down south in Georgia, sleeping on the ground in a field, with no blankets. That was a record for just getting up and going, even for Daddy.

Darkness fell as I prepared to take my turn at night watch. Everyone else hit the sack. I was alone, eyes riveted to the compass, white knuckles gripping the wheel. This ship was considerably larger, with more sail, than I was used to, but the wind was light, and I began to enjoy the solitude and sense of adventure. I gradually relaxed.

A small brown bird landed on the rail by my right shoulder. "Where did you come from so far out to sea, little bird?"

The sea grew rougher, but the sky stayed clear with no clouds and layer upon layer of stars. With no earthly landmarks to restrain it, the boat transformed into a spaceship that I piloted through the Milky Way that night. Deep, deep into the universe we traveled, to the moon and on, to galaxies light years away from Earth. Far off in the distance appeared a faint light on the horizon, a light from another ship, and the sails and the sounds of the night sea materialized again, and suddenly we returned to Earth.

Fantasies. Bette and I played for hours, sometimes days in that small apartment, acting out our stories. Next to building blocks, or perhaps the living-room sofa, our most treasured prop was Mother's wooden clothes dryer. It folded down into rectangular compartments just the size of two small boats. My dolls carefully arranged in one side and Bette's in the other, our imaginations carried us away on danger-filled journeys over the ocean. We'd talk for the dolls, and sometimes tears would fill my eyes. Being the oldest and most assertive sister, I'd usually take the lead. One time I gave Bette a cue and she didn't respond.

"Bette, Lucky Ducky falls overboard now," I had prompted.

I looked up at my sister. Eyes big and round, mouth partly open, she was totally enthralled. That story was an all-time great.

Seven years after those imaginary voyages, Daddy, more prosperous in his construction business and with more leisure time at his disposal, handcrafted our first sailboat, a Comet named *B Gay*. New Jersey's Barnegat Bay was where we had our first real sailing adventures and acquired our love of sailing. That clothes dryer, though, may have been *Cadeau's* first true prototype. I believe Daddy would relate to the compelling motivation behind Bette's cruise today. Mother, maybe not as well, but I know she wouldn't have wanted to miss it.

Sleepy, I found the last hour of my watch long: rising and falling, large waves growing larger. The small bird rested on the rail, another living, breathing creature.

Relief: Bette appeared on deck. After a few sleepy words, I went below to bed, to sleep on a rough, very rough, sea. Seasick for the first time in my life, I missed the bucket. Everything moved, rolled; nothing was still. But Bette was there. "That's love, sister, when you can do that for me," I whispered.

Out on deck, in the fresh air, the constant motion became tolerable. Bette was again at the wheel, and no one else was up yet. I relaxed. The breeze and sounds of the boat moving through the water soothed. We talked. What is there about a boat that makes talk flow so easily? We always found this to be true.

We spoke about how our relationships had changed over the years. Our family hadn't been overly demonstrative while we were growing up. There was a time when I would have rather choked than tell either sister I loved her, yet once when little Ruthie, our youngest sister, was lost for a while on a beach, I remember sobbing in anguish. I learned how much I really did care, and knowing that, I liked myself better. After we began to raise families, we were out of each other's lives. Peace Corps families, Bette and Noel lived in India, and Ruthie and Rich in Venezuela. Then we were on different coasts. Later, Bette's family spent almost three years in Yaounde, Cameroon, where Noel, a medical doctor, started a clinic.

Now, in our fifties, it's so much easier to show warmth and affection, with no embarrassment. We've weathered illness, death, unspeakable emotional trauma: our brother drowned at age twenty-five; both parents were killed by cancer seven years later. Bette spent five years helping her husband recover from a debilitating stroke suffered in his mid-forties. Her role and her personality changed during that time: from follower to leader, decision maker. His fatal traffic accident just as he was about to resume a professional life was especially cruel.

"Bette, I want to tell you how much I admire as well as love you. You're a person I'd choose for a friend, even if you weren't my sister. You mean so much to me. I've never known another person who comes even close to having your fortitude and courage."

"What do you mean? I'm no one special. But *you*, Jeanie, you've achieved so many good things in your life." She smiled, saluting me with her eyes.

"No one special. My sister thinks she's no one special." I shook my head, then reached over and squeezed her hand. In forty-eight years her character hadn't changed very much. Honest, good and unassuming, she had always underrated her own accomplishments. Had I, as self-important big sister, ever belittled or made her feel inferior? Eyes welling, I silently begged forgiveness.

The small brown bird left sometime before dawn.

The sea grew still. Rows of lights slowly moved by: street lights and houses. We were to the lee of Grand Cayman Island. At the helm again, I tacked *Cadeau* back and forth at the harbor entrance for an hour-and-a-half, waiting. We needed enough daylight to see the channel markers and find the way safely into the harbor. The eastern sky gradually lightened. Peter started the motor.

"Lower the sails!" ordered the captain. "We're going in."

We entered Georgetown harbor at daybreak with several other boats that had arrived during the night. *Cadeau* was dwarfed by a commercial cruise ship that reminded us of the famous *Love Boat* and a large, private yacht with a rather forbidding look, a Mercedes and a helicopter secured on her deck. We approached the immigration pier and stopped to wait next to two other sailboats closer to our size.

"David, hoist the Q flag." The nautical Q flag means *quarantine*, with which all boats are labeled until they are boarded by immigration and checked. It was six o'clock Monday morning.

Georgetown awakened, as the rising sun caught the tops of high buildings painting them brilliant gold. The boat lay almost motionless in the morning still, as we did our chores and ate breakfast. I changed clothes and packed bags ready to go. Captain Mom radioed the port authorities. They'd open at eight o'clock, she was told. That would give us two-and-a-half hours to clear the harbor checkpoint and get me to the airport in plenty of time. By eight-fifteen, eight-thirty, though, nothing was happening.

Our captain radioed again and explained the situation. Our boat was given priority. Still nothing happened. There was no other choice but to wait. I remembered Montego Bay, thinking how a few short days ago this delay, with a plane to catch, would have been just about unbearable. Now I was only amused that the world wasn't operating according to my schedule. An hour later we were called to the dock and boarded by immigration.

An official asked to see the captain of the ship. "A woman? A woman captain? Really, madam. Most unusual!" He erupted into chuckles, considering it most amazing and amusing when he finally accepted the situation.

Getting back to serious business, they confiscated the pistol, to be returned when the boat departed, and collected a harbor fee. This included a "tip" for themselves. Bette had explained that the tip is customary in every Caribbean port she had entered. You have to accept it as one of the local customs; otherwise it spoils the fun. Yes, I supposed I'd already learned that lesson in Jamaica.

We anchored in the harbor, this time far out of the way of commercial traffic lanes. It had taken over two hours to clear customs and anchor. It was ten-ten now, twenty minutes before the scheduled departure time of the one daily flight to Montego Bay.

"What do you think?"

"I'm afraid it's impossible. I'm sorry."

The morning sun was growing warmer. I lay stretched out on a deck cushion. David was writing in his trip log, and Peter was below changing clothes, leisurely preparing to go ashore. Nicole composed a postcard to a friend, while Bette, seated next to me, shaded her eyes as she casually checked the harbor for familiar boats. Snorkeling gear and swimming fins lay around us in disarray, ready for action.

At ten-forty I watched a plane slowly rise and circle over Georgetown. My face relaxed into a wide grin.

"You know what I think, guys?" I said. "No problem."

WRITING THE WIND

Nan Watkins

for Ellen

As long as I can remember, I have been attracted to windy places and have been excited about taking a trip, no matter how small. A passion for the journey is what led me to walk the streets of Casablanca, to camp on the North Rim of the Grand Canyon, to watch the sun rise over the Himalayas high above the Kathmandu Valley. I remember the excitement of the windy places of my girlhood vacations on the beaches of Barnegat Bay and Nantucket, and the thrill of raising a homemade American flag on the windy edge of the Rhone Glacier on the Fourth of July. This passion also led me, at sixteen, to cross the Atlantic on an old student ship, standing for hours on the deck in the wind.

Now I was setting out on another trip, this time to Ireland and Wales. My affinity for Celtic civilizations was calling me again, and I was off to explore the west coast of Ireland and to return to Wales, the land of my ancestors. I wanted to find people still living in simplicity from the land and the sea. And I wanted to pursue my lifelong affair with the wind.

For someone who loves wind, Ireland and Wales are the right places to be. Situated on islands in the North Atlantic, they receive the brunt of the winds coming across the whole expanse of ocean. In both countries I was attracted to the coastlines where the winds howled along the beaches and cliffs, and I stood wrapped in a zipped-up coat, with scarf flying and cap snug on my head against the June and July weather.

When I landed at the airport in Dublin, I was greeted by the cheerful smile of Joan O'Flynn. Joan, whose blond hair shone above her lavender jacket, was an Irish friend I had come to know back home in North Carolina. I arrived on a "soft day," she told me, humid with a gray drizzle in the air. Within ten minutes we were driving toward Dublin, where we were soon swallowed up in the traffic of daily life. My spirit quickened to be back in James Joyce's town, and before the day was over, I had walked to Joyce's birthplace a few blocks from Joan's house. We spent the evening in the Ferryman's Pub on the Liffey, drinking Guinness and listening to local musicians sing and play late into the night.

Early the next morning, the two of us left Dublin in Joan's car and headed west to the coast and County Clare. After a quick side trip and pilgrimage over the border of County Galway to the town of Gort and Thoor Ballylee, the site of Yeats's legendary tower, we finally reached our destination: the Burren. The name means "Great Rock." It is a large, desolate stretch of bare limestone, a plateau occupying a vast area in north Clare and strewn with hundreds of stone forts and megalithic tombs. Joan had told me about the place before we arrived, quoting Cromwell's lieutenant-general's description: "Savage land, yielding neither water enough to drown a man, nor a tree to hang him, nor soil enough to bury him." I couldn't help noticing that this wasteland of rock was carefully defined by stone walls, as if it had been, at one time, valuable grazing land. Joan said the walls were an example of government relief during the Great Potato Famine of the 1840s. During those desperate days, starving citizens were given employment, building unneeded stone walls and roads leading nowhere in exchange for a pittance of rations. As for Joan, she came to see the great array of wildflowers that bloomed in the fissures and deep cracks of the Burren.

Taking advice from a local woman, we followed "the green road," an unpaved lane named for the green grass that had grown up in the center, and we bounced along in Joan's Vauxhall until we thought the transmission would fall out. Finally, we came to a halt by an old stone croft at a curve in the road that by now was totally green. I got out of the car and started to walk. I wanted to see what lay ahead. A few hundred yards down the path, I came upon a protected valley that was carpeted with a brilliant display of wildflowers. The diffuse light coming through the clouds only deepened the color of the flowers. A tall wall made of gray limestone and riddled with dark caves enclosed the opposite side of the valley. I felt I was in a secret place, an Irish Brigadoon. The silence rang in my ears. In the quiet, not a soul was to be seen in this landscape outside of time.

After a while Joan joined me, and slowly, we hiked the length of the valley in silence. We dodged fresh sheep droppings and saw tufts of wool hanging on branches of hawthorn, but no sheep. I wanted to press on and find the sheep that could survive in this inhospitable landscape. Oddly, there were none in the valley below. As we climbed higher and higher, we ascended into the wind until we pulled ourselves up on a peak of rough rock that allowed us to see across the broad valley beyond. All along the horizon, there was gray limestone, luminescent under the silver light filtering through the clouds. By now the wind was fierce, so strong that as I leaned into it, it supported my body against the pull of gravity from the ground. We sat in our own silence, surrounded by the roar of the wind, surveying the seemingly infinite sweep of rock that ran out to greet the horizon. When we finally got up to go, I saw something move out of the corner of my eye. There were sheep in the distance, blending into the rocky landscape, nuzzling nosefirst into the rock crevices for shoots of grass and wildflowers. No shepherd, just rock and sheep free to forage—and howling wind pushing the gray clouds across the sky.

In the next days, the two of us made our way up the Irish coast, stopping on a wild stretch of beach while Joan dunked herself in the freezing, stormy North Atlantic, and later, pausing in Galway to take in a lively champagne reception for an art opening. Our little car persevered over the narrowest of single-lane roads up into County Mayo, which Joan declared the most beautiful county in Ireland. Our destination was the home of Michael Joe and Alice, a retired couple related to Joan. We found them snug and sheltered from the wind in their small home on "the Hill" in Corraun, a community of a few houses overlooking the incredibly beautiful Clew Bay. Alice had a midday meal ready for us when we arrived, and we ate in the kitchen around a slow-burning peat fire, peat which she and Michael Joe had cut and dried a few weeks before.

After lunch, Michael Joe took me out back and showed me the

remains of the original stone croft where he had been born and raised along with his seven brothers and sisters. He uses the stone building now as a work shed in which he keeps all the tools and paraphernalia he needs to maintain his sheep and do his fishing in his *currach*. He took me to the local dock and showed me a haul of giant crabs and sea urchins that, as I watched, he cleaned out with a sharp knife and set on his stone wall to dry. He pointed to a solitary tower standing on the opposite shore of Achill Island. He said it was the stronghold of Grace O'Malley, a pirate who sailed the waters of the west coast pillaging towns and vessels, and then bringing her booty to keep protected in the tower.

That afternoon, when everyone else elected to sit by the fire and watch the soccer match between England and Ireland on TV, I chose to take a walk on the stretch of beach not far from the dock where Michael Joe's *currach* bobbed up and down in the waves. Of course there was wind. It was a rare, brilliant day of sun, showing off the deep colors of the Irish coast at its best. Across the cobalt-blue water of Clew Bay I could see Croagh Patrick crowned with its halo of clouds. I sat on the edge of a high dune and watched the myriad facets of sunlight sparkling on the water. I tried to collect my thoughts. It was difficult to center down; my body had been in motion so much of the time. My senses had been assaulted, though pleasantly, with so many new experiences, and it was hard to concentrate with that infernal wind roaring in my ears, coming at me from behind. What I need is a quiet place out of the wind, I thought. I moved forward and stepped down under the grassy ridge of the dune onto the warm sand. By sliding down a little further, I discovered that the wind shot over my head, providing me with a haven of warmth and stillness on the leeward side of the shore. I lay back and relaxed, watching singular clouds change shape as they moved by overhead. In these clouds I saw my life parading across the sky: first a child, then a wife-mother, then a woman walking on her own.

If too many men, I said to myself, spend their lives fighting battles for turf and dominion over rival clans, too many women spend too much of their lives defining themselves in relation to others. In my case, I lived my childhood in my passion for music. I played the piano four hours a day and raced across windy beaches. Looking back, that's what I remember. Then I burst out of my first family into the world, defining myself as musician, adventurer. When I married, I slipped into the family I would help create and became wife and mother for nearly thirty years. But I could feel a shift even as I was making my vows on my wedding day. When the veil was lifted, I felt I had lost my liberty. My attempt to maintain my individual freedom within family life became a daily struggle. Like so many wives and mothers before me, I gradually sacrificed my own will for what I thought was the good of the family. I knew something was wrong, but I couldn't grasp how to right it.

In order to give my life meaning, I defined myself as both heart and anchor of my family. It was inconceivable to me then, that we—husband, wife, son, daughter—could break apart. But after many years, the inconceivable happened, not once, but twice. In the black of a winter night, the phone woke us from sleep. It was a stranger calling to tell us our son was dead of cardiac arrhythmia. He had been lying on a sofa watching the eleven o'clock news with a friend, when his heart, inexplicably, stopped beating. Peter was just twenty-two, standing tall and handsome on the crest of his manhood, and now a strange doctor was saying he did not exist. Never, never, have I felt so helpless, so useless. And, oh, I had not been there to comfort him in his dying as I had been present to hold him in my arms at his birth. For a long time I was drawn into the darkness of that black night. My body grew so exhausted from the strain of the loss that I felt I was a hundred years old. Every minute I was afraid my daughter would die, and I lost all desire to live myself. Then gradually, but also rather quickly, the rest of the family I had worked so hard to build fell apart. The cord that once had bound my husband and me together grew taut, then snapped. Our daughter, stunned and confused, went her own, tentative way.

Abruptly I found myself living alone in a little white house with a porch, overlooking a long, grassy lawn and the Smoky Mountains beyond. My moments of peace came when I drank my tea each afternoon on the porch, pouring it from a china teapot which my mother had given me just before she died. I sat out on that porch in all kinds of weather, taking the necessary and long-overdue moments for myself in contemplation of where I had been, and gathering strength to move on.

During that time, I took control of my life. It seems second nature to me now. I am no longer married but live in a no-less-holy alliance. I live with a sovereign man and enjoy my own sovereignty as a woman—finally.

The solitary and hypnotic clouds passing by overhead in the midday sky had become a bank of gray mist. Turning my head, I saw a yellow wildflower bobbing in the wind. It made me think of Joseph Campbell, how he held up a daisy, and with a broad smile, asked, "Meaning? People want life to have meaning? Does this flower ask, 'What is the meaning of life?' No! It just blooms. It just *is!*" And that's the way I see my life now. Just being; no questions asked about the meaning.

When we bid thanks and farewell to Michael Joe and Alice the following morning, I could hear Joan getting directions for the seaweed baths. "Just what we need to relax," Joan said. It was to be our final day in the west of Ireland. We headed inland through Mayo and over to County Sligo on yet another windy day. We found Kilcullen's Bath House on a slice of the most enticing Atlantic beach we had seen on the trip. We wasted no time in entering the midnineteenth-century establishment, and within minutes, we each found ourselves in a private room equipped with a long, claw-footed enamel bathtub and a wooden box in the corner, hissing steam. The tub was filled with warm seawater and a mound of seaweed; the Turkish bath had a round hole so that my head was free to breathe the cool air, while the rest of my body sat in the steaming box. The routine was to begin in the box, then lounge in the bath, finally standing and pulling the cord to release a shower of ice-cold seawater—then begin the whole process over again. There was no time limit. We could repeat the routine as often as we liked and stay as long as we wanted.

It is hard to describe the feeling I had lying in that warm tub of seaweed with the wind howling outside on the other side of the window. The oils from the boiled seaweed coated my body in a rich, satin smoothness I had never felt before. The seaweed itself was downright sensual. I lay back and floated easily in the warm saltwater. This was all I needed to be happy. And no one was knocking on the door telling me it was time to go. When I tried to sit up, my hair was so drenched with the heavy oil that I could barely pull myself upright. Each round of steam, bath and shower was more pleasureful than the last, until my body had relaxed to the point of weightlessness. All it took was pure physical pleasure and no deadline to put me in a state of quiet bliss.

Finally I toweled myself dry and joined Joan in the bright solarium for tea and cakes. I was in such a state when we drove off that I left my favorite sweater hanging there on the chair. Ireland is a small island, and by the next evening, I was on a ferry named *Felicity*, being blown by the west wind across the Irish Sea to Wales.

When my Welsh friends Wil and Rosemary Rees greeted me at the Fishguard Dock, they were all smiles. We picked up our conversation of two years before as easily as if it had been yesterday. Wil, the perennial teacher, had planned a tour for me on the way home, and he wasted no time giving directions for Rosemary to drive us to the site of the best-preserved dolmen in Wales. Pentre Ifan, meaning "Village of Ifan," is the remains of a megalithic burial site. It has been standing for some five thousand years in a windblown field, not far from Crymych. Sheep grazed lazily around the striking structure of great, standing stones, one huge stone resting like a tabletop on the other three.

It is impossible to stand before these ancient monuments without slowing down. It is a staggering thought to imagine your ancestral peoples walking these same fields many thousands of years ago. It is humbling. And all that remains of their presence are these standing stones, the skeletal gateway to the aboveground burial chamber filled with ashes that had long since vanished. What would remain behind of my life?

We headed back home to Laugharne, the seaside town nestled in a valley out of the west wind, on the south coast of Wales. It is famous for its Norman castle and the Boat House that served as the last home of Dylan Thomas. This place is so much like home to me that each time I leave it, I feel as if I am ripping my own roots out of the soil. I first came to Laugharne when I was twenty, with my sister, to see for myself where the legendary Welsh poet had lived. Then I returned two years ago to visit the land of my ancestors and live with Wil and Rosemary in their bungalow for six weeks. Now I had come back again, attracted by the simple way of life in the Welsh town that lives side by side with the rhythm of the tidal river Taf. Every six hours the waters of the Celtic Sea and Carmarthen Bay pour into the riverbed of the Taf, flooding its banks, and every other six hours the waters recede and flow back out to sea. This whole miracle is accomplished by the moon, that sphere of silver light, that muse, which rises and sets to the music of its own rhythm, over both river and town.

Eager to show me their beloved Wales, Wil and Rosemary suggested we visit Saint David's, the town on the west coast of Pembrokeshire that was home to its namesake patron saint of Wales. This place had a special appeal for me, because I felt I was connected to Saint David. Back home in the mountains of North Carolina, I play the organ in an old wooden church that was built a century ago by a Welshman from Saint David's. He not only named the new church after his native parish but surrounded it with seedlings he had brought with him from Wales.

We set out for Saint David's on the west coast with a picnic basket of Welsh cakes and tea, along with warm jackets to shield us from the wind. I was taken by surprise to find the handsome cathedral down in a hollow instead of standing proudly on a hill. "It was built here so the Vikings couldn't see it from their ships," Wil told me. We toured the massive stone church. It reminded me of the Cathedral at Brecon where my father's people had worshipped, and where I had once been given the key to the great organ so I could play my own music on Welsh soil.

It didn't take us long to head for the shoreline where the Atlantic was crashing on the dark cliffs. I wanted to hike a stretch of the Southwest Peninsula Coast Path, a rugged 515-mile coastal trail, the longest footpath in Britain. Here the path circled the town of Saint David's precariously high above the sea. The grassy slopes were covered in wildflowers, and the gorse, blooming its sturdy, mustard yellow, grew right up to the edge of the cliff.

I was determined to hike on the path up the coast and pressed on alone. The going was slow because of the severity of the wind, and because I stopped often to breathe the salt air. After over an hour of walking along the cliffs, I came upon the ruins of a monastery for nuns, some fifteen hundred years old, where it was said Saint David's mother had been in charge. Wil had told me to look for the holy spring, and I found it in a small grotto of hardy bushes. Thirsty, I bent down to drink. Could this water be more holy than other water? I wondered. Weren't all things from this earth sacred?

When I rejoined Wil and Rosemary, they were setting out the tea on a blanket. We sat close to the cliff edge and enjoyed the constant rhythm of the waves. We all laughed as the wind kept blowing our hair in our faces. The tea and the Welsh cakes never tasted better.

I spent the remainder of my days in Laugharne walking Sir John's

Hill, climbing the ruins of Laugharne Castle and happily eating Rosemary's sponges with my afternoon tea. I drank Buckleys at the Brown's where Dylan Thomas used to drink and play cards with his friends. And one evening the three of us, joined by friends, ate a great Laugharne meal of cockles from the river, laver bread made from local seaweed, and nettle soup from the weeds in fields nearby. After we finished the dessert of Wil's fresh fruit salad, we watched the high tide overflowing the green banks. The river had swollen to cover the entire valley and looked more like a lake than a river. Rosemary turned to me and asked if I would like to walk across the river to the other side. "We could do it tomorrow," she said, "at low tide." She consulted her tide table, and we made a date to leave the house at one o'clock in the afternoon the next day.

I love taking walks with Rosemary. She is a fifth-generation native of Laugharne and knows the town and its long history by heart. Everywhere we go, she tells me stories from her childhood about the local people, the "Larnies," as she calls them. She remembers Dylan and Caitlan Thomas when they lived with their three children in the Boat House. She tells me stories of her grandfather and uncle who were sea captains, how her grandfather lost his left arm in an accident at sea. She takes me over stiles, across potato fields and on dirt paths through woods to a hidden little church in Llandawk. When we push the church door open, we hear the hum of a thousand bees buzzing against dusty cobwebbed windowpanes. To the left of the simple altar she shows me the marble coffin of Margaret de Brian, who died in the thirteenth century. She was sister to the lord of the great castle in Laugharne, and somehow ended up here in this forgotten church.

We are headed out to cross the river Taf, walking down our steep driveway, down Gosport Street and across the Frist Square. We walk the cinder path below the castle and continue on the red rocks that serve as foundation for the Boat House and the old Ferry House next door. Because of the strength of its tidal currents, no one swims in the Taf these days. Rosemary remembers seeing her best friend, age ten, sucked into the current off the jetty where they were swimming as children, and drown. So she has deep respect for the power of the river.

We slip out of our sandals and begin walking over the damp sand and mounds of seaweed drying in the sun. It is low tide, and what had been underwater last evening is now sandy river bottom exposed to the sun. The wind picks up as we walk along the shore, next to the deepest channel of the river that always contains fresh water, flowing down from its source in the hills. Rosemary leads me out onto a plateau of warm sand that we walk over until we come to the river at its shallowest point. There, we cross fresh warm water, feeling the tug of the current on our legs. We walk across slippery black mud, and Rosemary tells me its story: it is called "slime" and is a mixture of river mud and coal dust from the freighters that used to come up the river to deliver coal. The Larnies would gather the slime in baskets, mold it into balls and let it dry briefly, before poking a hole through it with a stick. These slime balls were excellent slow-burning fuel for the fires. They would glow hot all night long so that the women would still have a fire to start cooking breakfast when they woke in the morning.

As we walk on, I gather cockle and mussel and razorfish shells. We walk past the Scar, a point thrusting out into the river where it makes a turn to the left around the base of Sir John's Hill. Rosemary says the Scar is always covered with seaweed and looks the same today as it did when she was a child. We stop to look at the sand that harbors the cockle beds, where air bubbles come to the surface, then walk on to a line of fishermen's stakes, standing upright in the sand. Across the river channel is the Ginst, a windy stretch of strand where thousands of rabbits inhabit the grassy dunes, yet another place where Rosemary ran as a child. We stand and survey the huge expanse of open sand, the riverbed, marveling at how broad it actually is. We look across to the medieval town and see it from a completely different perspective. Then, watching the placement of the sun, Rose says we had better turn back, so we'll have plenty of time to cross the river before the tide comes in. We turn around and walk back closer along the river channel. Finally, we reach the crossing point, and legs tired, we fall into the warm water, letting it wash over us, clothes and all. We can't help laughing; it feels so much like being children again. Rose tells me she hasn't taken this walk in years, and that it is bringing back all sorts of memories for her.

We sit in our own spots in the rushing water, sinking into the sandy bottom as the force of the wind and water pushes against our backs. While Rose becomes lost in the memories of her childhood, I am thinking that the river is like a feminine force, flowing softly, yet firmly, around me. I can easily identify with the flowing motion, always moving on, yet definable in its own right. It is constantly in a state of change. Motion is its very essence. I love liquid and swimming and water. I think of the river Liffey carrying the woman's name Anna, and wonder if the Taf has a feminine first name, too.

In a time when it is not always popular to praise the feminine, I can say I love being a woman. I think of coming into my own, belatedly, but nonetheless vibrantly: of being myself, and doing what I desire to do. I think of the sheer thrill, now, of composing my own music, performing and recording it. "Windblown Watkins," the reviewer said of the photo on the cover of my first solo album. That photo was taken right here: in the sands by the river Taf.

I consider the women I have known in my life. I think of Gail who used to say, "I have to get out of the house. I can't stand being alone with my own thoughts." I never feel like that. I love my own thoughts. I think of Mona and Shanti, two beautiful sisters I visited in Nepal, how they lead their lives of grace as wives and mothers in an ancient country where women are trying to find a place for themselves in the modern world. I think of Rani living in Lagos, Nigeria. She's caught in a corrupt society where nothing works, and bribery and brutality are the order of the day. "I'm so tired of the fight, of the constant haggling," she says. I think of Les who is struggling with the nightmare of Parkinson's disease. "I have to dance with it or I'll go mad," she tells me. "I am dying." "We are all dying," I say. And that makes me think of Renate, so beautiful, talented, sensitive, kind. The deepest conversations I have ever had with a woman were with her. But Renate was dying of leukemia in Germany while I was innocently writing her cheerful letters from North Carolina. When I received the black-bordered card in the mail announcing her death, I couldn't believe it. I hadn't even had the chance to say good-bye, to wish her farewell, to tell her I loved her.

I was sinking deep into the sandy river bottom now. The water was approaching my neck. I looked over at Rosemary, and she was getting up out of the water. We shook ourselves off, like dogs after a cool bath, and laughed at the sight we would make walking back through town. We returned to the red rocks and dry seaweed beneath the Boat House. As we sat down to clean our feet and put our sandals back on, I heard the sound of waves forming in the river channel. It was the tide coming in. "We're just in time," Rose said. The salt water from the sea was meeting the fresh water from the hills and trying to overpower it. Of course it was succeeding, and each minute it progressed a little further up the channel. The sea was flowing into the river and making it overflow its banks. We stood awhile and watched. The wind and the sun were slowly drying our clothes. When we reached home, we looked back toward the river. The broad sands we had walked were once again covered with water.

That evening, my last in Wales, as I walked alone by the river in the slow-setting sunlight, I could hear the sound of the water birds' cries punctuating the steady drone of the wind. Nature's music, I thought, and I remembered the "singing fence" on the Isle of Skye from a previous trip I had taken to Scotland. It was a fence of metal pipes at the edge of a cliff high above the sea, and when the wild wind blew through the pipes, it produced a music as haunting as the pipes of Pan. For a moment, my heart leaped, knowing that on this journey my body, too, like that magic metal fence, had become an instrument of the wind.

I'm back home now in North Carolina at the old farmhouse with the tin roof that has stood more than a century on these sixty acres. It is raining softly. "A soft day," as Joan O'Flynn would say. Sitting outside on the porch, I listen to the whir of the hummingbirds' wings as they fly in for their early-morning feed. It is my son's birthday today. He would have been twenty-nine if he had lived. I'll go to my local Saint David's Church and play his favorite Bach on the organ, the way I used to bake him his favorite angel food cake. The music will fill the old wooden church, and the sound will flow out the tall, open windows and be carried by the wind of the Southern Appalachians toward heaven, just as the wind carries Buddhist prayers written on colored silk flags up over the Himalayas to God. The wind is my winged messenger to all those I have loved, and to those who have left this earth before me.

For a lifetime, I have carried on a magnificent affair with the wind. Everywhere I have gone and been, the wind has greeted and dismissed me, pushing me ahead to new places and people, to new vistas and plateaus, like those reached inside, where the wind fills my spirit like a sail.

Journey to the Sea

Evelyn Wolfson

For over a quarter of a century I have stolen solace from the quiet calm of a pond in front of my house. I am happiest outdoors. Had my husband and children been willing, I'd have set up housekeeping by the pond.

Local lore has it that Indians camped on the banks of the pond and probably planted corn all over what is now my neighborhood. To me, the best part of the story is that after the corn was planted, they paddled off to the sea to spend the summer by the shore.

For years, I daydreamed about an Indian-style trip to the coast. If Indians camped on the pond, they probably canoed through a narrow outlet that courses through dense marshlands before it opens into the Sudbury River. I'd made a game out of finding the river through the marshlands with my children and, over the years, we had paddled up and down much of the river. I only imagined a trip to the sea.

In another life, I am sure I was Native American. And if spirit is a qualifier, I am one today. Wherever I go I visualize Indian campsites. I create pictures in my mind of how they lived, ate, dressed and traveled.

When my children were young, they helped me build a wigwam, collect edible plants, make a corn grinder by burning and scraping a pine log and sew mats out of cattail leaves. Our projects and my research taught me so much about the flora and fauna of New England I became a teaching specialist in environmental education. My programs were a great success because children would study anything that had an Indian connection. And what better way for them to learn about their environment than to study the material culture of New England's natives?

Slowly, the years brought more time at the pond. My children grew up and moved away and dreaming turned to planning. Paddling to the sea intrigued my naturalist friends who understood, and even shared, my Indian spirit. Ann, the youngest, is an environmental lawyer whose well-proportioned body belies her muscular physique. Karen, the group's historian, is the most fragile. She has a bad back and bum ankle. But without her overwhelming attention to detail, our trips would be far less successful. Betty, an occupational therapist, wears sensible clothing: rubber-soled boots, all-wool sweaters and flannel shirts—all in extra large.

Some of my friends think I'm not a serious person because I have too much fun. I believe seriousness and fun are quite compatible. I do color my hair ashy blond. But it doesn't mean I'm less capable than Betty and Karen, who use auburn.

Ann, Betty, Karen and I have explored woods and fields on foot, and rivers and streams by canoe, on and off for about ten years. We all love the outdoors and enjoy learning from one another. Our only competition is to see who can retrieve a reference book from a backpack the quickest. Our varied interests in nature provide reason to explore old rivers and local land acquisitions. It also gives us time to yak about what is going on in our lives.

Our excursions are seldom exciting, unless one considers a stream that unexpectedly runs out of water seven miles from a road, exciting. A trip to the sea seemed a natural extension of our day-long adventures.

Maybe empty nests signaled a need to soar. We never really discussed it. Articulating reasons for this particular adventure seemed inappropriate. Freedom from childcare was an obvious factor, but, for me, the postmenopausal years had sharpened my edges. I had cut away guilt and closed down the responsibility department. My husband considers it a favor to join me on a trip. I do the accommodating, organizing and planning, and he accompanies me. Not that he isn't good company. But so are Ann, Betty and Karen. They are also enthusiastic. And they pull their own weight.

I had concluded years earlier that our husbands, in their abstraction, were cut from the same mold. But we never discussed particulars. My husband's response to this trip was not unexpected: "What, camp? At your age? No shower? Bathroom? Hot food? TV? No need to please the kids? I wouldn't do it. *I'd* rather stay home." If he noticed that husbands weren't invited, he never let on.

Ann, Betty, Karen and I divide basic tasks easily and efficiently. We all have different amounts of available time, special interests and particular talents. Betty and I did the on-site scouting for the trip while Karen and Ann made phone calls. We planned to begin our trip in early fall and spend three days on the rivers. Preparation and planning took over a month.

Few people today believe the rivers of New England are still navigable, especially through the densely populated suburbs of Boston. Less than thirty miles separate me from Boston Harbor, but three hundred and fifty years of Indian wars, Puritan rhetoric, a revolution and a very large tea party have made it seem like an impossible journey. Nonetheless, we made plans.

Fortunately, we did not have to paddle into Boston Harbor. The Sudbury River, which winds through our town, flows north. Local Indians traveled from it to the Concord, their *Musketaquid* or "Grassy River," and then to the Merrimack River, theirs and ours, before ending up on the coast sixty miles away. The mouth of the Merrimack River ends up in Newburyport, north of Boston.

Still, the Sudbury, Concord and Merrimack rivers run through densely populated cities and towns, some wealthy, others solidly blue collar. Many residents consider the rivers a resource, others a receptacle for sewage and industrial waste.

My time was spent in town libraries trying to peel away the layers of human history to get down to the rivers. I learned that the river valleys were used seasonally by Massachusetts and New Hampshire Indian tribes who came to fish, hunt and gather wild foods. And that later, after Massachusetts became a colony, rivers attracted settlers like sticky, yellow fly tape. Men whose souls were seduced by the quiet embrace of marsh and thicket along the Sudbury and Concord rivers were contrasted by others who saw power in the foamy waterfalls of the Merrimack.

Much to our surprise, most of the "original highways" are accessible.

But we wanted to be sure we could paddle and portage all the way to the sea. So we scoured the rivers, town by town, noting dam locations, points of portage and pollution. Only two small sections of river, both less than a couple of miles long, are totally impassable because they flow through the heart of two large cities.

Our three-day odyssey began on the grassy banks of the Sudbury River, a short distance from Thoreau's beloved Walden Pond. I didn't take any chances and practically committed to memory Thoreau's book, *A Week on the Concord and Merrimack Rivers*, before leaving, insuring a wilderness experience of my mind, if not my body.

Ann and Betty lash canoes to cars better than most men channel surf. They are also very proficient canoeists. Ann was a canoe instructor for a while after college, and Betty married a would-be sailor who took the family boating until their teenagers left home. Only once did Karen and I, the least experienced, go together in the same canoe. After an hour of zigzagging back and forth across the river, we were split up. Now we know our places, and go directly to the bow.

The Sudbury River is an ambler. It twists and turns over its thirty-six-mile course, dropping only a few feet the entire distance. Its laziness creates unique habitats along the way where web-footed and wise animals of all sorts hang out. Long ago, shad, alewives and eels took naturally to these lazy lagoons. Today, the river edge is still overhung with trees, shrubs and tender-tissue greenery that create a productive nesting place for migrating waterfowl that cruise the Atlantic flyway. My heart is warmed knowing I will not have to visit a museum to view trees, as some Native Americans predict.

Those first few hours were a genuine time warp and I felt like a contented Indian woman anticipating summer on the seashore. A half-mile into our journey we entered Fairhaven Bay, a secluded freshwater habitat with a large, wooded island in the middle. The island is best known for the proliferation of painted turtles who lay eggs along the sandy south shore. After the river leaves the bay, much of the shoreline appears almost pristine, thanks to the U.S. Department of the Interior, which purchased twelve miles of floodplain along the Sudbury and Concord rivers for a wildlife refuge. Alongside a natural rock cropping, the fast-paced waters of the Assabet River meet the meandering Sudbury. The Sudbury, apparently shocked by the encounter, awakens and takes a few steps backward. Then it quickens and continues north as the Concord River.

The Concord River meanders through several affluent communities, Concord most notably, where much time and effort have been spent protecting remnants of the past. Ralph Waldo Emerson was seduced, so he claims, by the waters of this historic river. It is no wonder.

I am shaken out of the seventeenth century a half-mile down-river by the classic wooden arches of Old North Bridge whose reflections are perfect in the quiet water. What could the Indians have thought when the Brits turned against one another? Indians had enough trouble trying to figure out the difference between the French and the English. Imagine how difficult it must have been to learn the difference between a loyal Brit and an angry one.

At the bridge, on April 19, 1775, a group of local minutemen confronted British soldiers who had come to confiscate colonial stores of powder and munitions. Captain Butterick's imposing brick mansion, which now houses Park Service headquarters, looked down on us from its perch high above the river. As we passed under the bridge I was reminded that river waters had not only carried Indian families to the sea, but had also washed wounded soldiers that April day more than two hundred years ago.

We paddled past tourists, some of them slipping down the muddy riverbanks in fancy sandals, and into the towns of Bedford and Carlisle. The sun was hot for September and Ann and I had stripped down to tank tops. Betty and Karen, always careful not to let the sun hit unprotected skin, had unbuttoned the long-sleeved shirts they wore over tee shirts.

Again, the refuge, together with private conservation holdings and large estates, protects river environs. We had scoured the shoreline for a campsite and planned to stay overnight in Billerica which is a reasonable day-long paddle, given the winds that blow upriver and the lack of current to help us along. Unfortunately, most of the town's shoreline is privately held and lined with small, ranch-style homes. So we forgot wilderness camping and focused on front lawns. We spent several days knocking on doors seeking permission to camp. Seldom did we find a resident at home. Then one day we roused a thin, middle-aged lady who came to the door in a soiled, mint-green apron. After we explained our plan, she asked why we would spend several days in a canoe, much less camp out at night. She sounded like our husbands. I remember the look on her face when we said we were paddling to the sea. "You're going where?" she asked. "The ocean? Newburyport? Oh, dears, I think you must be lost. Why don't you talk to the police," and she closed the door.

Betty had walked around to the back of the house and was standing by the river. "Are you looking for a cooking spot?" I asked. Talented in more ways than all of us put together, Betty is a gourmet cook. She smiled. I could see a spit rotating in her head. Crème caramel spilling from a plastic container. And Dutch butter cookies brimming from empty coffee cans. Karen, on the other hand, was looking at the debris along the shore and thinking *cleanliness*. The rivers are mildly to severely polluted and drinking the water was out of the question, but Karen worried about using it to bathe. I suggested she use up her old colognes.

Determined to camp on *this* lawn, I went around front and knocked again. This time I convinced the nice lady that we just needed a campsite for one night. "You want to sleep on my lawn?" she said. "Okay, but call me the night before. I live alone and don't go outdoors much." And she closed the door once again.

In the end, our efforts to sip the stillness of night on the river, or the surround of birds in the morning, were in vain. We made such good time paddling, it was noon, not night, when we arrived at our civilized campsite. We waved to our invisible hostess and pushed on. If she was at home, and saw us, she must have been convinced her first impression was correct. We *were* lost.

We ate an early lunch on Billerica's Jug Island, a small spit of land in the middle of the river, which looked as if it had just hosted a Woodstock concert. There was paper, foil, wire, glass—about every man-made product ever manufactured—strewn along the shore, in the woods and hanging from the trees. Karen stayed as clean as possible by never leaving the canoe. The rest of us poked around like rats at a town dump. As we boarded our canoes to leave, Ann stood up, one foot in the mud, the other on her seat, and declared, "I'm putting in a request for federal superfunds for this site!"

By now I was firmly back in the twentieth century. I had no more illusions of cozy wigwams along this stretch of the river.

Our first portage around a defunct dam in North Billerica came shortly after lunch. In 1711, long before the Revolution, when colonists were still trying to eke out a living from the land, an enterprising young man named Osgood raised a natural dam on the river to run a small gristmill. Eight decades later, the dam was built up even more by a group of entrepreneurs who wanted to raise the water in the millpond. The group had been granted the right to build the first canal system in the United States, using the water in Mr. Osgood's millpond to fill their canals. The Middlesex Canal, as it became known, extended from the Charles River in Boston to the waters of the Merrimack in Lowell. The earth was cut for six miles from the millpond north to the Merrimack River, and another twenty-two miles south, to the Charles River. By the early 1800s, lumber and granite, among other goods, were being shipped from New Hampshire to Boston. And manufactured goods were returning north. The canal, cut into the Merrimack River above Pawtucket Falls, eliminated a longer overland route into Boston.

It took about 150 years for residents upstream to realize that a twenty-mile-long millpond had been created after the dam was raised to fill the Middlesex Canal. Hundreds of acres of grassy meadowland along the Sudbury and Concord rivers disappeared, and land that produced a ton to a ton-and-a-half of good hay per acre turned to soggy, wet marshlands. Residents, not realizing what was happening, slowly lost their livelihood.

Neither the millpond nor the dam are marked, and fishermen warned us that the lack of signs had resulted in several serious accidents. We took our canoes out at the millpond, portaged past a series of newly renovated mill buildings, through a parking lot and down a steep embankment to the river behind the mills.

A half-mile north of the dam, the river broadens to accommodate large areas of marshlands, and for a while we were shrouded in wilderness. This three-mile stretch of river passes under several major highways and high-tension lines but traffic noise is absorbed by the lush marshlands and dense woodlands that protect the river's edge.

We approached Lowell, original home of the Wamesit Indians, at dusk, a whole day ahead of schedule. The distance from our takeout, above the two dams and Class II rapids, is only a mile-and-a-half from the confluence of the Concord and Merrimack Rivers but we could not go all the way. Today the river runs right through the heart of the city and portaging is hazardous to the health.

The Concord River runs perpendicular to the Merrimack and meets it after the latter tumbles forty-four feet over Pawtucket and Hunts Falls. Unlike the sluggish, turbid waters of the Concord River, the waters of the Merrimack River run swiftly. They hurry out of icy lakes in New Hampshire, where they get started, and swell as they flow forty miles through the mountains. The incredible power of the forty-four-foot falls gave a Boston merchant, Frances Cabot Lowell, the idea to create America's first manufacturing center below the falls at the confluence of the two rivers. A series of canals were designed to bring water to factories whose huge looms turned out cotton cloth on a scale never before imagined. During the 1820s, many of the more than thirty-five million immigrants fleeing Europe and other parts of the world crowded into Lowell, eager to work for subsistence wages.

Since much of downtown Lowell was built around the rivers, the city is filled with remainders of its famous, or infamous, but long-departed textile industry. Red-brick mill buildings line the Concord River below the falls and an elaborate network of small canals connect them. Today these buildings are occupied by a variety of computer and high-tech companies.

We took out below an old railroad bridge and I went with Karen to find a telephone booth to call for a ride home. Fortunately, among us, we'd produced a half-dozen teenagers, all with cars gassed up and ready to go.

To our dismay, the food, water and clothing we carefully portaged for our camp out was eaten, drunk and changed in a dusty parking lot alongside the river.

We returned to Lowell early the next day and put into the Merrimack River below the falls. We found a small path alongside the city's septic treatment facility (an ironic twist on nature, where the refuse gets the view). Before Frances Cabot Lowell laid claim to the falls, Indians from all over New England came each spring and fall to fish. I had a clear vision of large, brightly colored salmon flying into the air as they fought their way up over the falls where Penacook Indians stood waiting with their nets. The Merrimack River was the lifeblood of the Penacook Indians whose great sachem, Passaconaway, reigned over the area at the time of English settlement. By 1660, however, Passaconaway was tired of trying to make peace with the English and made his son,

Wonnalancet, chief.

Wonnalancet, a Christian convert, was sure he could bring about the peace his father was unable to accomplish. But while *he* adhered to Christian teachings, his mentors did not. The English were so cruel to the Penacooks that within a few years many of them were dead. His spirit broken, Wonnalancet fled to Canada.

By the end of the nineteenth century, the rivers were severely polluted and fish, like Indians, had disappeared. Recently, however, fish ways were built in the Merrimack and the river is becoming clean again. Shad will soon be reintroduced and encouraged to go home to the Concord. Salmon, always too noble for the Concord, are already back in the Merrimack and doing well.

Beyond Lowell's huge septic facility, steep, man-made, granite embankments shoot up along the river's edge. Like a giant culvert, they hold dammed-up waters that extend ten miles downstream to Lawrence. In late summer the river is as calm as a lake. But I'd walked the banks on a cold March day when wind blew from the north and filled the broad waters with ominous looking whitecaps. We ate lunch that day on the edge of a corn field which borders the river. It was possible, once again, to slip back in time and imagine Wonnalancet's wigwams nestled among the tall cornstalks.

We took our canoes out of the river in Lawrence, the second impossible city portage. Lawrence, like its sister Lowell, upstream, is another mill city that holds a mile or more of the river in its bosom.

In 1845, not long after Lowell became a thriving city, a group of enterprising Boston Brahmins discovered there was additional waterpower available at Bodwell Falls downriver in Lawrence. Prepared to justify yet another assault on the river, they claimed this new mill town was designed "to produce woolens and cottons in a morally sound environment." Such rhetoric earned Lawrence the reputation of being *the* town in which to live and work for the next five years.

We knew there would be no camping out at this point in our journey and had arranged for our teenage chauffeurs to pick us up. Large red signs lined the north bank of the river where we took out. DANGER! DO NOT GO BEYOND THIS POINT. DAM AND POWERHOUSE INTAKE AHEAD. They are not kidding. Great Stone Dam is twenty-six feet high.

The next day we returned to Lawrence for the culmination of my long-awaited dream. We launched our canoes on a small island below Great Stone Dam. North Canal was cut to connect the Merrimack and Picket rivers, and textile mills filled the island area.

We had twenty-seven miles of river left to paddle that day from Lawrence to the sea, but it was an easy one-day trip. Tidal waters back up fifteen miles and greatly reduce paddling time. On the day we chose to end our journey, high tide on the coast occurred at 11:30 A.M. and peaked upriver, in Haverhill, forty minutes later. That gave us enough time to leave Lawrence in the morning, paddle to Hale's Island in Haverhill, eat lunch and take advantage of the outgoing tide.

Shortly after we launched our canoes, we began to look for the mouth of the Shawsheen River. We had walked the banks of the river upstream where it had considerable size and were surprised to see how little water entered the Merrimack.

After our canoes began to scrape bottom, we had to curtail side trips and stay in the middle of the river. There were sandbars all along the next seven miles, so we quit talking and paid closer attention to paddling.

Beyond Lawrence, the onslaught of industrialization softens. Towns haven't become cities and though I couldn't envision Indian encampments, I saw many remnants of old, worn-out fishing villages. The towns of Metheun and North Andover enjoyed a great deal of rivalry in the early 1700s. Andover was known as the Plain of Sodom while Metheun was called Gomorrah.

Beyond Andover, cormorants perched like a string of arcade figures on high power lines crossing the river and a thin, white church steeple reflected in the clear water. "Look at the clarity of this water," I exclaimed. Ann frowned from her canoe. It was obvious the images that overlaid the river's rocky bottom belied water quality.

We enjoyed lunch in Haverhill, the Indian's Pentucket or "Place of the Great Cascade," once a bustling center for smoking and exporting salmon, and picnicked on the grassy banks of Hale's Island. It is easy to understand why so many Indian tribes lived together and shared the resources of the area. All along the way, freshwater streams feed into the river and fertile farmland runs down to the river's edge. Yet most Indians offered little resistance to English settlement. They sometimes accepted a roll of clothing in exchange for all the Indian land a white man could walk in a day on foot. They never thought the land sale would eliminate fishing and hunting rights on the river and its environs. Settlers took less than a century to usurp the Indians along the river and build towns of their own. They kept only a few lyrical Indian names, such as Merrimack and Massachusetts.

After lunch we stopped briefly at Pine Island in the middle of the river. A large Indian settlement once covered the island, and Nancy Parker, a tenacious and industrious old woman, stayed there alone after all members of her tribe were gone. Nancy farmed the land and sold her produce to local fishermen until the end of the nineteenth century. Fishermen described her as "tall and wild looking, but harmless."

As we approached Amesbury and Newburyport, boat traffic increased and we had to contend with wakes from fast-moving motor boats. In compensation, we were delighted by a soaring, young sparrow hawk whirling above us, and a great blue heron ascending slowly and gracefully out of the water each time we approached, staying just ahead of us all the way to Newburyport.

Salisbury, situated in lowlands along the river, was once an important sturgeon-fishing village. The shore is lined with affluent yacht clubs with large motorboats waiting patiently to be powered up and taken out to cut up some salty waves.

As the waters of the Merrimack flare out to meet the sea, a number of small, sandy islands fill the river's mouth. We could not stop to explore, however, or the tide and darkness would turn on us before we reached our destination. We had also been warned that the swells created when the river meets the oncoming sea are hazardous in a canoe.

Our journey was over when we reached Cashman Park, developed for public use by the town of Newburyport. We had accomplished what some people believe cannot be done today. We had paddled, portaged and penetrated some of New England's first roadways and savored a tiny portion of Thoreau's beloved wilderness. For me, it was the wilderness experience of both mind and body promised by eloquent prose.

And, like the Indians before us, we did not leave the coast without eating fresh shellfish. We celebrated the attainment of my quarter-century dream with clams, fish chowder and lobsters at a waterfront restaurant. It was a fitting finale.

NEAR EIGHTY—
AND TALL IN THE SADDLE

Betty Wetzel

*A machine will show folks the man-made things but if people want
to see God's own country thave got to get a horse under them.*
—Charles M. Rusell, Montana cowboy artist

"Now this," announced our outfitter, "is a horse."

The seven of us stood in a circle inside the corral at the Holland Lake trail head as trim, white-moustached Jack Hooker explained the basic mechanics of riding a horse. He was obviously a good hand. His quiet handling of the big appaloosa mare, already saddled and bridled and ready for the ascent into the twenty-four hundred square miles of Montana's Bob Marshall Wilderness, was reassuring.

I needed reassurance. After living for many years next to North America's largest roadless preserve but never venturing into it, I had made up my mind to experience "the Bob" before my fast-approaching eightieth birthday. My husband, four grown children and six teen-age grandchildren all pleaded too busy or too far-flung (or too chicken?) for the ten-day pack trip. So I signed up with the White Tail Ranch of Ovando, Montana, on my own.

Jack Hooker and Bret Clarke, a wrangler, boosted me into the saddle of a big brown gelding called Badger, and adjusted the stirrups. Badger and I would become well acquainted but now it seemed to me that I was much higher off the ground than I remembered being when I grew up on a ranch out of Roundup, Montana.

Jack headed us out without ceremony—twelve riders and seven pack mules. The well-maintained trail along the shore of Holland Lake, past roaring Holland Lake Falls and Upper Holland Lake, was lush with ferns and greenery, but it was all uphill. Occasionally, Jack called a halt to let the horses breathe and us dismount. This proved a questionable relief when I found my legs would barely support me, and I faced the problem of remounting. It seemed hours before we stopped to eat the sandwiches from our saddlebags at the crest of the Swan Mountains and looked back on the Holland Lakes and distant Mission Mountains.

It was a perfect, cloudless July day; the trail was spangled with brilliant wildflowers—whole hillsides of Indian paintbrush, lavender salsify, magenta vetch, golden arrowroot and giant tufts of beargrass—but the afternoon was agony. I gasped at the splendor and the steepness of the trail, and from pain.

The pack string passed us, but I was too preoccupied to notice. It was late afternoon when we left the trail to follow Jack to a secluded meadow where, to our great joy, camp was set up. After a short walk to reactivate our legs, we claimed our duffel bags and spread air mattresses and sleeping bags in our tents. I stripped off my clothes, got into my sweat-suit night gear and washed up in an icy stream nearby. Supper (turkey, mashed potatoes and gravy, cranberry sauce, corn on the cob, tossed salad, olives, fresh peaches on angel food cake with whipped cream and coffee) was served at six o'clock.

We were a motley bunch as we became acquainted around the evening campfire: a couple from Ireland who had read about the Bob in *National Geographic;* a woman from Texas on her ninth Bob Marshall trip; a seasoned couple from North Carolina in their forties; a Seventh-day Adventist preacher from Lewistown, Montana; and I, the senior member. Still washing dishes was Karen, Jack's wife, who ramrodded the outfit as cook, business manager, nurse, friend and counselor.

Two men in their twenties were our wranglers. The eldest, an Arizona State basketball star, bore the unlikely name of Mike Redhair and was in his final year of law school. Bret Clark hailed from Oregon, loved horses and the mountains and hoped someday to own a ranch. Both were tall, lean, congenial and never slept. Riding herd on that bunch of horses and mules, saddling up, packing and unpacking the mules, setting up camp and helping us kept them on the job night and day. At odd times they could be seen taking what they called a "dirt nap" in the shade.

Although it was not yet nine o'clock and still daylight, I left the campfire circle for my tent. I was exhausted. Everything hurt. Jack Hooker had just reported that we had ridden fourteen miles uphill from 4,031 feet at Holland Lake to our Lena Peak camp at 8,364 feet. It was obvious to me that he, knowing there is no painless method of equestrian conditioning, had elected to get it over with.

The morning commotion of horses and mules, the smell of wood smoke and coffee and the feeling of excrutiating pain wakened me. It was humbling for one who fancied herself fit, if aged. It was some comfort, however, to hear groans coming from neighboring tents.

In the morning light everything from the chiseled mountains surrounding us to the miniature flowers just creeping out from receding snow banks was stunningly beautiful. The ground was carpeted with trillium, spring beauty, gentians, Alpine forget-me-nots, mountain heather, and glacier lilies. It was springtime in the Rockies.

After a breakfast of pancakes, bacon and eggs and much strong coffee (the Irish had tea), we rolled up our sleeping bags, packed our duffels and prepared to hoist our sore and chafed bottoms into the saddles. Fleece padding appeared to cushion two of the women.

Yesterday, we had complained that the ride was all uphill. Today, it was all downhill over steep slopes and rocky switchbacks. The vertical ride rubbed fresh saddle sores and tortured different muscles. We rode silently, balancing ourselves as best we could, as our horses picked their way down the impossible trail overlooking a deep canyon.

In and out of north-slope forests of lodgepole pine and tamarack that shaded mosses, ferns and bouquets of foamflower, queen's cup and white bog orchids, we plodded, with now and then a blessedly level meadow brilliant with wild pink hollyhock, fireweed, golden arrow leaf, balsam root, gaillardia, yarrow. Even in our state of torpor, this overabundance of beautiful sights and smells gladdened our hearts. The ugly reality of the burn of the 1988 forest-fire season ended the splendor. Instead of lush forest, the charred ghosts of trees hovered over us mile after mile. But it was interesting to see a new, young forest of lodgepole pine springing up to begin rejuvenation.

A downed tree blocked the trail and we dismounted, crawled under or climbed over and waited up the trail while Jack and Karen led the horses and eventually the pack mules around the high side. While eating our lunch as we waited, we saw a western tanager, Montana's most brilliantly colored bird.

On the trail again, we faced the steepest downhill yet to the canyon floor and the swift, knee-deep water of the South Fork of the Flathead River that had sculpted this gorge. Jack didn't even pause as his horse plunged into the stream, but I was breathless as Badger slipped and struggled for footing in the swift current. We were more than ready to camp in a grove of trees beside the river.

This was the favorite campsite of the fisherpeople. They whipped out their fly rods, donned their waders and scattered up and down the river. This barely fished river is famous for native cutthroat trout.

It had been another fourteen-mile day. Around the campfire that night, Jack told us how to ride a horse. It was about time. Don't just sit there, he said. When the horse takes a step, you take an imaginary step so that your weight in the stirrups coincides with the movement of the horse. Move the weight off your bottom and onto your feet and knees. Downhill, lean back in the saddle and point your toes out, putting your weight on your heels. Try to sit up straight and maintain a rocking motion with the horse's stride. For the rest of the trip, I concentrated on Jack's instructions. We rejoiced that tomorrow was to be a layover day.

The next morning, Jack led a nature hike through meadows and forests above camp showing us how to distinguish lodgepole from ponderosa pine, larch from fir and spruce; how to spot the slash on giant ponderosas where Indians had stripped inner layers for food in the last century; edible plants and berries; pitch blisters on pine and fir that will stanch a bleeding wound or help kindle a fire; where to find squirrel nests or plants for tinder—in short, how to survive in the wilderness. (Jack and Karen know the names of every flower, bush, tree, bird and mammal. Peterson's *Field Guides to Rocky Mountain Wildflowers and Birds* were packed with the kitchen gear and available for reference.)

On the highest point overlooking the valley where the Middle Fork meets the White River, we came across the grave of a packer marked by a tombstone made of five horseshoes.

During the long twilight that evening, the anglers again fanned out and in no time returned with breakfast trout. It was catch-and-release from then until dark. Even I caught a fish.

Rejuvenated by sleep, a rest day and a fine breakfast, I became aware for the first time of what was involved in packing up the camp kitchen: wood-burning tin stove, cabinets, picnic tables, folding stools, dishes, cutlery, pans, meat, produce, bread boxes. All had to be bundled into tarps and loaded onto the mules, together with the tents, duffel bags and other equipment. I had already noticed the simple but delicious food that Karen produced. It was the result of careful planning and packaging of first-class ingredients prepared without fuss by a great cook. During our ten days, the dinner menu varied to include Mexican, Italian, Chinese and American cuisine. We ate steak, ham, chicken, pork chops; salads and vegetables; cheesecake, cobblers and brownies—everything but ice cream. (This was no weight-loss outing.) And coffee! Here's the recipe: Bring a two-gallon pot of spring water to a boil; add one-and-a-half cups of regular grind coffee. When the pot again boils, add a cup of cold water.

Technology such as lightweight tepee tents with zippers and floors has added greatly to the comfort of today's camper. What an improvement over heavy, leaking, mosquito-ridden canvas tents! "The blue room," a portable-toilet tent, is an aesthetic and practical comfort, as well as sanitary protection for the Bob. Tennis shoes with heels are replacing cowboy boots and hiking shoes, serving both needs with comfort, although they do, perhaps, lack somewhat in style. I found the spandex girdle worn by cyclists helped prevent chafing under riding pants.

I hadn't hired out to be tough. My great-grandmother crossed the country in a covered wagon, but she was young and accustomed to hardship. As a twentieth-century octegenarian, I cherished comfort. But I was eager to tackle the next day's ride which would parallel the White River and bring us our first view of the storied Chinese Wall. Using my newly learned horsemanship, the morning went well, almost without pain. Riding was becoming fun!

We lunched on a bluff opposite Needle Falls, which spilled out from a pool behind a stone "eye" and sprayed into a reflecting pool below. Some horses were grazing with a herd of elk on the mountain above the falls. Whose horses? Jack opined that they belonged to an outfit camped on another drainage. It dawned on me that in four days we hadn't met or passed a soul since we entered the Bob.

I was unprepared for the feeling of isolation. I had never encountered it in my several busy lives—growing up in Montana, raising four children and leaving the West in middle age to live and work in Southeast Asia. We had returned to live and work on the East Coast before retiring in Montana.

I've seen the Great Wall in China. Montana's unstructured, asymmetrical, disorderly, savage, freeform wall has it all over the rigid, artificial, forbidding, man-made fence that snakes over the Asian horizon. There's no comparison.

We stayed for a day in a grassy meadow underneath the wall, sharing our camp with deer, marmots and Columbia ground squirrels. From this vantage point and as we rode underneath, over and around the great wall, changing light and imagination seemed to people the weathered stone with giant heads from the Easter Islands, saints from European cathedrals, Buddhas from the Orient. Here and there mountain goats jumped with aplomb along the stone face, grazing on unlikely green clumps. The wall in China didn't have mountain goats.

We rode to the top of a ridge for an eagle view. Ranges of mountain wilderness stretched as far as the eye could see, a distance of about seventy miles—all of them in the Bob. We were reluctant to leave our camp, but struck out for the top of the wall, then veered north, gradually dropping down with no sign of a trail across vast slopes covered with wildflowers. A field of white bear grass bobbed in the wind like balloons. Sweet vetch and elk thistle, favorite horse food, kept our mounts on the alert for snatched treats. My horse, Badger, deserved treats, as did all the White Tail Ranch stock.

Jack Hooker knows horses—and mules. Every animal was sleek, surefooted, well-behaved and strong. (We had been warned to stay away from the mules, which are sometimes spooky.) Not once was there kicking, biting or bucking. Over the long, tough trail not one horse became lame or threw a shoe. When I complimented Jack on his tack and his horses, he said, "We treat 'em well and we work 'em hard."

The other side of the wall seemed like an anticlimax as we dropped down into low country with well-maintained trails, flies and mosquitoes—and backpackers and other outfitters entering the Bob from the east. I felt surfeited by the scenery, the same as I did when I stayed too long and looked at too many paintings in an art museum. My eyeballs were tired. The last day's ride to Benchmark staging area was easy.

My husband, Winston, and some of our family members were waiting at our home on Flathead Lake. They seemed relieved and amazed that I'd survived the 140-mile, ten-day pack trip. They had, it seemed, worried about grizzly bears. Well, we saw bear scat and claw marks, but bears avoid noisy humans and strings of two dozen horses and mules. So what if I'd been felled by a grizzly in the Bob Marshall Wilderness of Montana at the age of eighty? What a punch line for my obituary! What a way to go!

DOVES

Wuanda Walls

Spiritual Affinity. It is wrong to think that love comes from long companionship and persevering courtship. Love is the offspring of spiritual affinity and unless that affinity is created in a moment, it will not be created in years or even generations.
—*Kahil Gibran*

It all seems so logical in retrospect. Nevertheless, I'm still mystified whenever my devoted doves appear, always calm and peaceful.

In 1977, I moved into my paternal grandparents' homestead. Both were deceased but their home stood solid and stark. Green and white, the two-story wood-frame house possessed a coal furnace, pantry cellar, an inviting, sunlit, airy kitchen and a well-used front porch facing the village's quaint post office.

According to family lore, my parents met by way of the porch. When my mother's family moved from rural Maryland to rural Pennsylvania, the mail fetcher's task was given to her. My mother's future mother-in-law, Helen, was a friendly, generous, sweet-humored woman who immediately saw the young maiden as the perfect match for one of her two sons. Often she invited her in for chitchat and her legendary cinnamon rolls. Eventually, the porch became the "in" place, providing a diversion from farm chores for Mother, which suited Helen just fine. She delighted in introducing the newcomer to her neighbors, church members, professors and students from the nearby college and a few flibbertigibbets.

Two months after I moved into the house my father died at age fifty-four from a massive heart attack, just two years after his mother's death. No one was prepared for the challenge of grief, the void and finality. It was a shock that pulled everyone from the mundane. Although as Catholics, we (my mother, sister, brother-in-law and two nieces) had our faith, which was comforting, it was the unceremonious, intimate presence of friends and family, their kind words, deeds and love, that helped to strengthen and console.

For me, living in my father's parents' home, which was located next to his grandparents' property, was providential. Everything I touched and saw took on a new, more historic and spiritual meaning: the changing seasons, the sounds of crickets, buttercups in bloom, my great-grandfather's cradle and Mom Mom's cookbooks and china. Surrounded by cherished keepsakes that evoked heartwarming memories of my ancestors, I felt connected to something primordial, mythical, wise and loving.

One day while reflecting and sorting through things in the attic, I discovered my father's Boy Scout manual and a colorful, handmade Saint Valentine's card made for his mother. Touched, I called my mother, and we both rejoiced. Over the years she had kept all of his cards, and asked me to save my prize if I didn't want it. Admittedly, I felt a tinge of selfishness, but realized the joy was my discovery. Without hesitation I wrapped it in vintage newspaper and sent it with love.

My parents had a special love affair crowned with harmony and romance. There was no room for competition. A quiet, devoted family man, Dad was endowed with an understanding heart and humanitarian spirit. He adored his wife and daughters. Their happiness was his happiness. A breed apart, many called him a saint, shaped by the morals and genteel nature of his ancestors.

One of my fondest memories of my parents is when they had their new convertible which was forever in motion, heading nowhere special or for uncharted territory. They liked to drive along the super highway as carefree as birds, basking in the glory of it all, the beauty of life. They led a charmed life, wholesome, and uncomplicated. Their closeness intrigued and delighted many while others may have kept an envious eye camouflaged.

Spring was near, budding pussy willows, crocuses and forsythia teased anxious hearts. During this period I made it a matter of intent to appear cheerful, free from anger, sadness and resentment. These feelings, related to my grief, had a tendency to creep up when I questioned my father's death. My conversations with God were spirited, at times amusing and always forthright. I tried to keep my mind working at a breathless pace, focusing on my studies, research and writing. Nevertheless, I did allow myself to feel pain. In fact, frequently I invited it by looking at family photographs, those of us ice skating on the village pond, and the treasured one of my father and me taken the day I was christened.

Much later, when my mind was filled with images both felt and observed, due to a series of ill-timed events I was compelled to meditate out-of-doors on one of those humid, enervating summer days. The perfumed air blending honeysuckle, roses and bee balm vivified my soul as I walked near the pond. Then, without warning, a flock of birds landed directly at my feet. Startled, I stayed motionless, struck by their delicate beauty, boldness and serenity. My pulse quickened coupled with an intensely peaceful sensation which overtook me; thus, the birds transmitted their energy to me. The air resounded with their musical whistling as they flew away.

During the next years I lived in Europe and the Caribbean. My life changed a little but for the most part I was studying languages, writing and traveling. I didn't see the birds. However, I often thought about them while living in Spain because almost every household kept some type of bird. Besides, the fact that Spain was such a Catholic country heightened my curiosity about how I was raised. I was prompted to begin studying the history of the Catholic church.

After spending days in the archives in Seville, I came away disillusioned. My discovery revealed horrors encompassing corruption, sexism, racism, violence, the Inquisition and more. Notwithstanding, the lives of several saints captivated me along with the symbolism of birds, mainly doves, and certain rituals and pilgrimages. Eventually after a time I was able to put the horrors into their proper perspectives. To my delight, from time to time, I saw white doves, those painted by Picasso, and contemplated their divinity.

Back in the states, several years later, trying to find a place for myself,

I decided to visit a close friend in Texas before moving to Colorado. My life consisted of coming back from one place, only to seek a new one. This decision was not easy and my friend, being the sensitive, loving person she is, invited me to spend time with her family before claiming my new home. On day two, I refused to stay immured in an air-conditioned haven. Instead I opted to inhale the suffocating, warm air as I walked to find shade. Upon returning, my thoughts were sober, bordering on melancholy. Was the Southwest the place for me now? Then I heard them: their unmistakable cooing. At once, my eyes scanned the dry field catching a glimpse of their etched, white tail feathers. Somewhat befuddled, I couldn't help thinking their appearance was a good presage related to my new home. Quite unexpectedly, smiling images of my father gratified my soul. I remained in the field for some time hoping they would reappear.

When I told my friend about the incident she said she believed I was connected to the birds in some deeper dimension. I agreed, knowing that over the years following my dad's death I had begun to understand how everything in nature is connected. In addition, I embraced meditation, Native American spirituality, and communicated with my ancestors on a daily basis. These things, plus the acceptance of certain metaphysical tenets, undoubtedly made me more receptive to supernatural phenomenon. I relinquished both my attachment and disenchantment with the Catholic Church and found strength and guidance in nature.

That evening, as I sat in the middle of the bed, I remembered stories about birds associated with peace and good omens. In the Holy Scriptures there are four instances when the Holy Spirit appeared, once as a dove at Jesus' baptism. As the stories kept coming, I remembered one about an eagle and eagle feathers used by Native Americans in their prayer markers, tobacco pouches tied with string taken into sweat lodges. The eagle is revered because he flies high, close to the sky realm of the Great Spirit. Then I had a flashback of a conversation I overheard my parents having about death. Half-jokingly, my father told my mother that if he died first, he wanted to visit her in the form of a bird. This really amused me because our religion did not believe in reincarnation.

The beauty of Colorado enthralled me. Walking, biking and hiking became my favorite activities. My consciousness relating to health, the environment and endangered species expanded. My penchant for certain material things diminished. The breathtaking beauty of the majestic Rockies satisfied needs on many levels. My vision waxed clearer. I evolved into a minimalist.

More settled one year later, I moved into another house in the same Denver neighborhood. When I met my neighbor, Mary, I knew we were kindred spirits. Her back yard reminded me of my grandfather's garden. Irises, roses, violets, lilacs, peonies, mint and the state flower, the columbine (the Latin word is *columba,* "dove") enchanted my senses. We connected instantly with no thought to race (I being an eighth-generation African-American and she of French-German ancestry) or age (she being my grandmother's age). Having a nimble mind, enamored with universal pleasures encompassing history, music, nature and the arts, Mary became my confidante.

On a lovely, clear spring day while lying in my hammock, I spotted two birds perched on Mary's slanted roof. I moved cautiously as I approached her back door, hoping to find her in the kitchen humming to the music coming from the radio. When she noticed me, she smiled kindly and said, "Isn't this a glorious day!" I whispered, asking her to come and identify the birds. Her blue eyes lit up when our voices disturbed them and they flew away. She quickly exclaimed, "Oh, they are mourning doves. They visit me every spring."

When I heard the word *mourning* I repeated it and commented that I never heard of morning doves. Mary off-handedly spelled out the name. I was taken aback, as the word *mourning* conjured up images of gloom. Momentarily, I sensed some significant break-through; however, it was nebulous. I was unsettled. I felt movement toward some incredible revelation that would connect me with the spiritual world and I opened myself to receive.

For some reason, I didn't share my mystical experience with Mary but went instead to the library to research the bird. The first book I picked up proved useless, but the second one amazed me. Here were the mourning doves depicted in a lovely color illustration, their countenance as delicate and beguiling as in reality. I discovered that the birds mate for life, and if one mate dies the other mourns forever. Both are protective, doting parents. The beautiful mournful cooing gives the bird its name, and it is a protected songbird in some states. Suddenly, I understood their connection. My father possessed those same traits. At that moment, his spirit seemed to embrace me tenderly. My heart rejoiced.

A few weeks later while walking, I decided to explore an unfamiliar neighborhood. Cottonwood, aspen and poplar trees graced the wide street. Immersed in the glory of the season, I was in my own world until one small dove landed directly in front of me. This time I greeted the bird and blessed it with a prayer. As I entered the food market I heard a customer ask the clerk for the date. She replied, "May the first." Literally, my heart skipped a beat as I breathed deeply, realizing it was my father's birthday.

The sky was calm and clear, and the air lulled me like a philter as I made my way home, secure in a newfound knowledge, wearing comfort, peace and serenity.

ADVENTURES OF THE
WOMAN HOMESTEADER

Elinore Pruitt Stewart

May 15, 1928*

My Dear Friend (Mrs. Florence Allen),

Although I vowed that never, *never* again would I deliberately run into discomfort and danger when I came home the other day, I find I cannot trust myself or believe my most earnest avowals. And I was in such a resentful frame of mind, angry and disappointed over the failure of my outing.

My outings are so rare and I feel that I *earn* every one I get. So to have been defeated and turned back, to be so sunburned, scratched and bruised and to be called a damn fool filled me with ire but there was no one on whom I could vent my spleen so I attacked the job I hate worst, cleaning the stove. I had just emptied the soot box. An agravating little breeze had thrown it back over me so that I looked like a chimney sweep when Mrs. Pond rode up and hailed me.

"Hello! You look like the devil sued for murder. Is that your idea of beauty?" Uninvited, she slipped easily from her horse and came on into the yard. She seemed not to notice my lack of friendliness, went about among the flowers, picking one here and there. "I like poppies, especially these Shirley poppies. They are so bright, silky and cheerful—"

"Come in." I envited. Some how she looked so wistful and little and

---

* Please note that the original spelling and syntax of this piece has been retained.

old that my heart melted and my anger vanished. Soon the soot and ashes were cleaned away and the stove was as clean as I could get it. We were chatting gaily and she had called me a damn fool tenderfoot two or three times. I told her frankly that I felt cheated.

"Of course you were but hell, woman, I didn't do it. You would never been allowed to go up to the chimneys alone if you went at all. One of them moonshiners would have gone along just to steer you away from their cache. I had an idea they had a still there, you know the Agents burned Ave Hank's big still and outfit over there two years ago. I thought maybe they had rebuilt it but I didn't think of a cache 'way up under the rim like that."

"It cost me the only outing I am likely to have this year and when one stays at home month in and month out even a day in the woods counts tremendiously."

"Don't worry over what it cost. The moonshiners can do that, it cost them. But let's take a little time away. Let's go up to Hoop's lake and see if there is not some wild raspberries. There used to be lots of huckle berries up there too. Then on over to Beaver Creek there were worlds of choke cherries. Let's go up and stay all night. Are you afraid to camp out?" I wanted to go terribly. We couldn't start that day, too many neglected tasks to do but she went to work and right good help she is. It ended in our getting an early start next morning.

If there is any thing to open the heart to the whole wide world it is a long ride in the hills these golden September days. Golden aspens in little hidden places in the hills fluttering in delight in the friendly sun, blue haze, distance; views of little brown homes. I loved it all. We were both silent but the numerous pails we had tied on our saddles jangled and clanged like a tin pedler's cart. Mrs. Pond led the way but when we came to where we should have turned off into the bald range she kept right on past the fork of the road.

I called to her, thinking she had not noticed. "There's another trail on up past Hank's. I want to pass the Hanks place so they and every one else will know we are not out on any secret mission. That is why I wanted so many pails. They make enough noise and glint so in the sun that we can be seen for miles and every one will know that we don't care if we are seen." A few minutes brought us around a shoulder of a cedar hill and almost up to the Hank's door. The plain, travelled road runs between their house and the meadow. The two men we had seen the other day were out hammering a tire on a wagon wheel. They were sullen and furtive-looking but Mrs. Pond was very pleasant. She told them where we were going and why, told funny fibs about me, called me a damn fool tenderfoot repeatedly, her fibs illustrating my greenness.

"But I've lived here a good part of nineteen years, can I be called a tenderfoot?" I asked.

"Look at the face of her, peeling with sunburn, she doesn't know enough to powder when she goes out in the sun and wind. She caught that trying to get up to the chimneys the other day. Is the road open up that way? Could we get up there if we should want to as we come back?"

"The road is open pretty well, a few wash outs but we've been hauling posts out. But you can't get to the chimneys. There's been a slide," Wicks answered.

After a little we rode on, this time we turned off into the high hills leaving all the ranches and homes far below us in the valley. It was glorious, I was happy, happy. That day will be a beautiful golden page to put into the drab book of Winter. We scouted around hills, up little draws, some times up narrow canyons, through pines, out again on to rocky flats. A few choke cherries, a *very* few raspberries, a handful of service berries rolled about in our pails. Always up, up away from all the cares and worries. Suddenly I was aware of Mrs. Pond's voice, talking, but not to me. "Yes, I'm coming, God, right up to where I can almost touch the hem of your garment. I know you are near and I love you, Father. No matter what I am in the valley, I am your child and you are my dear Father when I come to the high spots—"

I drew rein and dropped back for I felt it was a holy communion. She rode on, not missing me. I saw her gesture. Slowly I followed and when I came up with her she had alighted in a little shimmering grove and was briskly unsaddling her horse. "Get off your horse and attend to it, so it can rest while we eat a bite. This is a good place to noon."

A little spring gurgled up from the earth, the water cold and sparkling. Grass and weeds grew among the aspen and our horses cropped eagerly. Mrs. Pond had put up the food for the trip while I did the many chores that must be done before I can leave home. She handed me a generous sandwich and this is what it contained; one thin slice of whole wheat bread covered with cheese, on the cheese a pinch of raisins, on that a thin slice of buttered white bread. The reason I am telling you is because on all my outings it has been a real problem to take enough food. One eats ravenously on these trips. But this one sandwich made a delicious and satifying meal. The few berries we had gathered furnished dessert.

Our grove was on a high, sunny slope. We could look across the gorge at the real mountains rising in solemn grandeur one after another, the snow peaks gleaming over the wooded hills. Faintly across the gorge came the sound of the wind in the pines but only the dappling shadows of the quaking leaves showed there was any wind on our sunny slope. After our lunch we lay resting on the warm earth. I was wondering whether the hard ride would affect the breaks I had last year.

Suddenly Mrs. Pond said, "If every one lived on a hill there would be no sin. No one could live this high up, this near God and not love him and all the world too much to even think of doing Wrong. I firmly believe that all wrong doing is just ignorance, any way. Of course any one doing wrong knows he is but he thinks it is going to lead to better things and then he will do right. But wrong doing is like a chain, one link leads to another. If tempted persons could only get away to the mountains, 'way up to where it is quiet he could *feel* God."

I lay watching a hawk away up in the blue, the sun glinting his wings to silver. There seemed nothing to say to her observation so I made no answer. After a reflective moment she went on.

"I *know* that sin and wrong doing is only ignorance. Many people doing their very best to do right do irreparable wrongs. My father did. You might never guess it but I was most carefully brought up. My father was a minister and he was so narrow that if he had been any thing else but a man he would have been a shoe string. He worked with out a salary on a circuit that he mapped out himself. Every Friday he left home on his old brown mare with his saddle bags filled with his bible and what ever else he had to take. He would preach that night at Sarotelle. Next day he would reach Grafton in time for service, Saturday night he preached at Bonville, Sunday at Rockford, Sunday night at Burnside. All these were just communities, not towns. Monday he got home and Wednesday night was always prayer meeting night in our meeting house. We were renters. We lived in a little house of Squire Haddam's and tried to farm. We had a cow and our other horse beside old Julie that father rode. You can see how much time father had to help make a crop. We were poorer than any church mouse, we had only the plainest, coarsest food and not always enough of that. There were three of us children, Bart, the only boy, then Lottie. I am the youngest.

"My mother was a saint. She couldn't be any thing else. Both my parents belonged to the old school that believes a man is the head of the house. Mother was so meek and humble and father was so determined to live a godly life, he firmly believed in a burning hell and he tried to save his own family and every body else. Well, we grew up that way. Grace was a good deal longer than the meals. Clothes were a hit-and-miss-come-by-chance. Every summer there would be a big revival meeting where my father fondly believed he garnered souls for God, where Mother, under instruction would always start the shouting and shout until she was exhausted and lots of others in a frenzy. Father would call for mourners—Well, he was a good man but I can remember when I began to think that he was working more for his own glory than for God's. Lottie and myself were expected to be models for all other girls and father was determined to make a preacher of Bart. There had always been a preacher in the Taylor family, so Bart would *have* to be a preacher.

"Up the creek from us there was a small settlement that my father had long given over to hell. I guess they were a rowdy lot; they were woodsmen and tho' they came to the revivals they never got religion. We used to hear of dances they had. One night while father was gone I happened to be awake and heard Bart creeping to his bed in the side room. Next morning while we were in the cotton patch he told me that he had run away and gone to a dance. Right then I became possessed of some thing of my own. A secret. It was a very real some thing to me and I kept it jealously.

"One of our neighbors was Mary Maude Dixon. She was a widow and older than Bart but she took a notion to him. She was what we used to call "well fixed"; she could shout the loudest and longest of any one in our neighborhood. Well, the next thing we knew, I found Bart in the cotton seed house very sick. I ran to Mother and—well Bart was drunk. Father came before we could get things straight. I don't know what was said or done but I do know that that eighteen year old boy was made to marry Mary Maude Dixon to save his soul. I never will forget the look in his eyes the day father married them. He said 'Father, you yourself, have sent me to hell.'

"Lottie was sixteen then, pretty as a flower, quiet and shy. Both Lottie and I helped out at Mrs. Haddam's. The Haddams were the richest folks in the county. Mrs. Haddam was always sick and always had a baby. So Lottie and I helped her and were paid one dollar and a half a week.

"Three of the children were wrong, couldn't speak, just idiotic. Mrs. Haddam died, consumption they said. Mrs. Haddam and father had been friends for years and after Mrs. Haddam died the Squire was at our house a lot. Lottie got to acting queer. One day she disappeared. One day Mother got a letter from her, she had run away with Willis Stokes and they were married at the court house and had gone to Denver. It nearly killed father, I know it hurt him but mother didn't seem to be upset at all. When I was nineteen father told me that Mr. Haddam has asked for me and that he had told him he could have me, that I must set the wedding day soon and then get some new things to be married in. Lord! I couldn't stand old Haddam, he had more beard than Moses, and all the young ones, some of them older than I.

"Well, I couldn't quarrel with Father, he wasn't the kind you could argue with or reason with, his word was law and he had passed it. That night I eloped with Mr. Pond. We made it over the mountain to Aunt Lola Pierce's and were married in her house. She lent us the money and we came West to hunt up Lottie but we never found her. Mr. Pond came of a drinking family. We both thought he would be freer from temptation out West, but—Well, after awhile my boy was born—My darling boy. He was just every thing any mother could wish for. For sixteen happy years he made the world heaven for me. At first I thought his father would cut out the booze for Tate's sake. My boy's name is Taylor, but when he was tiny he tried to say Taylor and called himself Tate so we always called him that.

"Mr. Pond would keep perfectly sober for months then go on such a drunk he was months getting over it. He was fine with sheep and I always went with him to cook for him until Tate was born. When Tate was big enough to go to school I insisted on a home. I washed, I cooked, I did every thing in the wide world I could to make an honest living for my boy. I did every thing I could to keep him from knowing his father's weakness. Often I have thought I might have got a divorce but that was my weakness. I couldn't cast off my husband. Tate was so quick and bright to learn, so eager to go on. He soon finished the grades and we planned, he and I, for him to go away to school. Mr. Pond was away with sheep. We hadn't seen him for months. I knew what that meant but Tate had not learned. But we figured out a way to get the money. We put in a big crop of potatoes then he went away to herd sheep while I stayed home and tended the potatoes. He didn't come back when he should have."

She turned over on her face and was silent for a while. Across the gorge the wind crooned and mourned in the pines.

"When next I saw my boy he was drunk. Sodden drunk. For two years it was a whiskey hell. Often father and son drunk together, too drunk to get out of each other's way. Every dollar they could get went for booze. Tate got a shadscale thorn in his foot while they were out with sheep along near the end of the two years. He limped around on the sore foot herding until blood poison set in. They got word to Hackitt, the man they were herding for and he came out. He brought whiskey.

"My boy was dead drunk when I got to him. I got him to the hospital but it was too late. He awoke just before he died and asked me to get him a bottle of whiskey. The doctor had told me he couldn't live but I couldn't bear for him to die drunk. I—refused—him. He dozed off but woke again, he stared right at me. He said 'Mother, death is not what we think it is. We do not *die*, we just quit this body. And hell is just wanting some thing so terribly we can't stand it and not being able to satisfy the want. But I will not have that to bear. I've conquered whiskey.' He closed his eyes, slept. I couldn't believe he was going but he never spoke again. You have heard that Mr. Pond died of delirum tremens, he did, six months after Tate left me. Tate died of blood poisoning but *I* know whiskey killed him. And—I'll fight whiskey til I die thoe' I have to do it on the sly."

We reached the lake just at sundown—it is a lovely spot but there were no berries. We made camp, broiled some bacon, had supper, and larioted our horses out to crop the little meadow. Extra blankets under our saddles supplied us with bedding. We cut pine boughs for our bed and did all the camp work in silence. There was much to think of and nothing to say.

It was too chilly to sit up, Mrs. Pond would not have a real fire, just a smudge, so we crept under the blankets. I was tired, stiff and sore but I couldn't sleep. Around and around my mind kept milling with the story I had listened to. So much wasted endeavor, such futility, mysery. Our camp was right in the pines and they kept crooning. It was easy to imagine that they were discussing the eternal Why—

We were up very early, coffee, bacon and toast, each of us held long sticks with a slice of bread on the end over the fire. But we didn't dawdle for we had decided to go further.

"In my sheep herding days I knew this country like we do our homes. Over on Sage creek there is a long ridge, a kind of a bluff, where the cherries were never known to fall. We will not need to go back to the road. We can just cut through the timber until we come to the open and we will pass some real fossil beds as well as the Indian wall. The wall is a rock face to a hill. The Indians once had a battle there, the Utes and the Sioux, I think. Any way, they chiseled pictures on the rock wall that tell the story of the battle."

I couldn't resist all that so we set out. We had turned North-West and were jogging along in the forest. Nothing much to see except as we came to occasional openings which allowed us views of distant peaks and dreamy beauty spread every where. Then a turn would plunge us again into the forest. We saw the ranger's telephone box fastened to a pine. Mrs. Pond got off to examine it. "Locked and no key in sight. What if I knew of a fire. I'd have to ride for miles to get to the station to report. It is a wonder they wouldn't leave a key here."

We came out of the timber, across a rocky mesa, down into the flats where the mesa's side made the rock wall. The pictures are there but the wall is soft sandstone so that blowing sand has almost worn them off. I could have spent a great deal more time studying them but Mrs. Pond is a fidgety creature and hurried me on, on across the flats to a low range of blue, badland hills, the fossil beds. So much of enterest to be seen, old diggings and quarries to be looked into but no time to do it in.

"Come on!"

"No, not yet. Let me examine this."

"Come on. We have to ride up if we are going to get any choke cherries."

"I would rather have one fossil than all the cherries—"

"Well, I wouldn't. You can't eat a fossil and our grubstake won't hold out for a week."

Exasperated, I followed her up the narrow blue trail, made by sheep in the ash-like soil. The sun was scorchingly hot and I was thankful when we emerged out upon the bench where the breeze was so pleasant. A flock of sheep was being lazily tended by a herder, he was some distance from us but as soon as he saw us he came riding toward us. We rode slowly, Mrs. Pond eyeing the approaching herder, his sheep, the range. Not at all like the woman who told me the story the day before. The herder came on up, greeted us very pleasantly and began talking about how dry the summer had been. We agreed and Mrs. Pond told him that we were out for cherries, raspberries or huckleberries.

"Good Lord, did you think you would find any over here in the badlands?"

"We didn't know we were coming to the badlands. We thought we had better get out of the timber and out into the open where we could see before we got lost."

"You came to the wrong place for any thing like that. I've not seen a one all summer, it's been so dry nothing could grow and the sheep kill out every thing, you know."

By now we were headed almost east and some way, the herder kept edging us along. There was no road, no trail, just bare, hot ground, heat glimmers in the air and the smell of sheep insulting our noses. Mrs. Pond rode along talking gaily, asking questions about sheep, did they pay well? Was it hard work? What did they do with the sheep at night? Just any thing that came to her mind and she had been out with sheep for years! Presently we found ourselves around a badland knob and right on the highway!

"Well, I guess I'll be leaving you folks, I got to get back to my sheep." Mrs. Pond waved to him as he turned the knob again.

"Bye-bye Mr. Sheepherder what aint," she said to herself; he couldn't have heard her. We rode slowly along the road, once more among the badland hills. "You see that white streak of road that goes over that rise away ahead of us? Well, that is the last place he can see us with out following us. He will be on some of these hills watching to see if we cross that. When he sees us go over that white rise he will think we are hitting for home. But I have been around in these hills myself and I know my way about. But I want to be *sure* I'm right before we make any change. You take my bridle and lead my horse right on. I want to sit back ward in the saddle so I can watch the hill tops." With out dismounting she turned face to tail and we rode slowly along the hot road. Pretty soon she chuckled.

"Right! He is watching but all his doubts and suspicions will be settled when we pass the white place."

Slowly we rode on, she still sitting backward. The very minute we passed over the high spot she jerked our horses around toward the west, out of the road, up a dry wash. We kept in the washes but kept as close to the hills as we could. It was past noon when we got back to the fossil diggings. We crept into the scant shade of a ledge and ate some sandwichs. Mrs. Pond took off all our pails and cached them with our food under the ledge. Then we mounted and rode west, still keeping close under the hills. After a while we came to where the badland range of hills narrowed to a point and a broad, dry wash ran north. We rode around the end of the point, came to where a ledge of rock, kind of a rim rock began. Buck brush and a few cherry bushes grew along, we found a shady spot for our horses and tied them closely where they couldn't get them selves into view.

We carefully worked our way through the brush to the north side of the ledge and began going east. The bushes grew taller as we went along but the going was hard and slow. We had to be so careful, not a bush must shake unduly, not a stone roll down. We didn't know what we were looking for or how soon we would find it. Cherries had to be our alibi and our pails were miles away.

Cautiously, slowly, silently, at last we gained a vantage point and looked down on a strange scene. We were high up under the ledge but there was sufficient brush to conceal us. Down below us the dry course of Sage Creek twisted its self into the letter S. In the curve of the S next to us we counted twelve log houses and a huge, low barn-like structure. We could see what looked like silos, not so tall as others I had seen but I can think of nothing else to compare them to.

As we looked a truck backed out of the barn, it was loaded with casks; presently another came and was driven into the barn. We could hear the thumps of the loads being placed, some filled wool sacks were thrown on and a tarpaulin was tied over each truck then both trucks drove away, right up the Creek bed. No road, not a sign of a trail or any thing to show there was a place. We had the only place from which the place could be seen with out walking right into it. I don't know how we made our way back, I was so excited that I couldn't talk. There was no mistaking what the place was, the smell betrayed it. It was not the smell of a sheep ranch. We mounted and just as carefully as before we made our way back to our cache. Still keeping in the draws instead of across the mesa we rode for the forest. Mrs. Pond forgot that I was with her, her face shone, she kept talking.

"Just let the daylight last, God, just let me get back into the woods, God, and you and me will raise hell with the moonshiners."

It is not easy to ride in timber, usually we have to pick our way. This time we didn't. We rode madly, recklessly. I never once thought of the ribs that have not ceased to be tender or of the chest that a jolt causes pain. More scratches were added to the collection already made. "We *must* get to that telephone box while we can see to find it. Oh we must! Hold the sun, God, just as you did for Joshua."

"Why not hunt up the road, go on home tonight and telephone—"

"Fool! All the phones are party lines and you know it. Every word would be relayed to them. The ranger's line connects straight to Evanston and is no party line—." We reached the telephone box. Madly she hammered and pried til' she got it open. She tried hard to control herself but her voice trembled as she called central and gave a number.

"Oh, Dr. Wilson, will you *please* come. The Tetlow baby is very sick. We've done all we can for it. We have given it sage tea. We used badland clay for a poultice but it does no good. I think it is the creek water they are using, it is not clean, it may be typhoid the child has. I think we should take it South but perhaps we had better go further West. But please come and if you can get it bring help, we're all worn out."

At first I was astonished. The Tetlow baby had been sick but was out of danger. We scooped out a little pool in a tiny little rivulet and caught water enough to give our horses a drink and to wash the sweat from their backs. We hung our saddle blankets up to dry and by that time it was too dark to cut boughs so we just rolled up in our blankets and lay down, no fire, no supper. We mustn't even talk where there was a chance for some one to creep near enough to hear, not about our find must we *ever* talk. I was so tired, so uncomfortable that I didn't expect to sleep but I was awakened before it was light by Mrs. Pond. "Get up. We've got to get home as fast as we can. We must get to a telephone where we can talk to as many as we can so as to let every one know where we are today all day. More than that the horses had a devil of a hard day yesterday and not a damn bite to eat."

Going toward home the horses traveled better. We kept away from the road so as not to be seen. By going through fields we managed to reach home without meeting any one. Mrs. Pond left amediately and I heard today that she is a silly old thing, that day before yesterday she telephoned about every body in the neighborhood. Today she came back.

"Lord, they've been raising hell with the moonshiners. Biggest raid ever over on Sage Creek. Seems the prohibition men were out after sage chickens and ran on to a whole town of moonshiners. They ran their still night and day. Had a big spring piped right into their plant. It was three or four miles off the road yet they had a thoroughfare right up to their very door. They used the creek bed for a road. Sage Creek never has much water and this time of the year it is dry. It makes a fine road and mighty little sign to show that it is a highway, not a sign of a road to show that any one ever went that way, just a few mangy sheep grazing about with a watchman-herder to steer non-wanteds away, a few families here and there with party phones picking up every item of gossip that may chance over the line. It seems that the government man had no idea of finding such a *big* thing. They were not prepared to fight such odds, they almost made a fizzle of their raid but a plant like that is too big to get away entirely. They caught the four ring leaders. They apprehended thousands of gallons of booze and destroyed thousands of dollars worth of equipment.

"And to think of *families* living in a moonshine dump; every thing as modern as town, big delco plant furnished light, a great engine pumped water so that every house had water, a sewer system, every thing!?"

"I would like to have seen the raid," I said.

"Like hell you would. Why it was like a battle, machine guns even. But it was a complete clean up, everything wrecked. They even had an airplane. It was a great day."

Both the Stewart and I think the airplane must have been a mail plane off its course. There would have had to be a landing field and there was no clear space any where near the place. This P.S. is being written May 15. Just home off a wild horse hunt. Sore, *sore,* stiff, blistered and reblistered. Love, lots of love to you.

E.P.S.

WHAT MAKES GRACE RUN?

——————————————— *Heather Trexler Remoff*

I suppose the more accurate question is, What *made* Grace run? I mean, after all, she is dead, has been dead for ten years now. But accuracy is hard to come by. This is an emotional issue for me, not one that's easily sorted out with facts. The fact is, I never knew Grace. So why do I feel so close to her?

Grace Andrews was killed by a hit-and-run driver shortly before Christmas of 1985. She was sixty-eight. He was drunk. She was out with her dog, going for her nightly loop around the lake that is the heart of this mountaintop community we call home. One of her daughters tells me that she tried to persuade her not to run that evening. "Let me go get the paper for you, Mom." Part of the daily ritual in Eagles Mere, Pennsylvania (population 123), is to walk or, in Grace's case, run over to Enza Laurenson's to pick up a copy of the local paper. Grace wouldn't hear of letting her daughter take over this errand. "Oh no, I *need* to run."

It would be nice if I could tell you that that statement was the start of the peculiar intimacy I share with a dead woman, but I've only recently had this mother/daughter exchange played back for me. So it wasn't the start of my identification with her but merely affirmation of something I already knew. I understand what it's like to *need* to run. This is something Grace and I have discussed, mostly when I'm out running when I shouldn't be, when I have cracked ribs, or a swollen knee or have just had a chemotherapy treatment. I started running in the late seventies, about the same time Grace did. I didn't live in Eagles Mere then, but was a New Jersey graduate student going through an unhappy divorce. I was almost forty. Grace was sixty when she started to run. Her marriage was a long one, and I've heard rumors about it. But any union that produces fourteen children has to have had its moments of accord. However, the accord was pretty much over when Grace started running. Dene, a victim of Parkinson's disease, was moved to the nursing home where he would, within a few years, die. And Grace began to run.

What makes Grace run? She had no history of athleticism, except, in her words, "years of chasing after fourteen kids." When pushed as to her reasons, she gave the answer that is word for word the same explanation I've provided curious friends. "It's just something I always wanted to do."

There were other things Grace always wanted to do. Going to college was one of them. And so, in 1982, when she was sixty-five, she enrolled at the College of Misericordia in Dallas, Pennsylvania, a good hour's commute over hilly rural roads that are often covered with snow and ice. She liked English, psychology, and Russian history.

Are there elements in Grace's past that would have predicted this future? My sources are all biased ones, but even those reveal more than the informant would intend. Eagles Mere is a funny town. It has a history as a summer resort catering to the wealthy. Grace was one of those who catered. At least the wealthy she served assumed it was catering she was doing. Tourism and lumbering are the two major industries in Sullivan County. There's only one traffic light in the entire county. We drive almost an hour to get to a grocery store whose produce counter displays more than iceberg lettuce, cucumbers and cellophane-wrapped pseudotomatoes. We don't have a viable commercial base, so a majority of those with deep roots in Sullivan County work in the service trades. Grace babysat the summer children. She grew flowers that her brood of fourteen peddled to the big old Victorian hotels. She cleaned houses. She baked for those in the summer cottages. It should be noted that these "cottages," boasting upwards of fourteen rooms, are cottages in name alone. Built for occupancy only during the months of July and August, they lack central heat but are elegant in every other respect.

Grace wasn't the only one in her family who worked hard. Dene drove the ice truck, the milk wagon, and even when suffering from Parkinson's, put in long hours on the road crew. But in the legion of stories that Grace Andrews has inspired, his role is a peripheral one. "He had a bit of an affection for the bottle," one woman told me. "But such a charming man. He always had that gentlemanly air about him. He was kind of the town character." "Character" is a word the summer people use often when talking about those with local pedigrees.

What makes Grace run? Spirit has something to do with it. In 1965 the Andrewses' house burned, leaving the family temporarily homeless. One of the summer people, knowing of my love of running, asked me if I had known Grace. I confessed that I had not. "Oh, she was a character. You knew her house burned down, didn't you?" I nodded. "Well, do you know the Dillons?" I had to admit that although I knew *of* them (everyone knew *of* them), I didn't know them personally. "Well, you're new here." My informant glossed over my obvious lack of social standing. "You know where their house is. The family has been coming up here for generations. Now old Mrs. Dillon was especially fond of Grace. Grace worked for her, you know, helped out with running the house. Well, after the fire, Mrs. Dillon went down to see Grace." Anticipating the punch line to her own story, my newfound historian began to laugh. "That Grace was such a character. Anyway, Mrs. Dillon said to her, 'Oh, Grace dear, be sure and let me know if there is anything I can do.' And would you believe it? Grace handed her a laundry basket full of dirty clothes. Here was Mrs. Dillon, who'd never washed out so much as a pair of silk stockings, suddenly being asked to do the laundry for fourteen children!"

Many of Grace's sons and daughters and grandchildren are also runners. The year following her death, they held a race in Eagles Mere in her memory and honor: Grace's Run. It has been held every year since then and has become a race associated with the triumph of spirit. Because Grace started running late in life, it is a race that puts special emphasis on the athletic ability of women over fifty. Although there are prizes in all gender and age groups, the large Grace Andrews Memorial Trophy is awarded to the first woman over the age of fifty to cross the finish line. I had just turned fifty when my second husband and I moved to Eagles Mere. That year I amazed myself by winning the Grace Andrews

Trophy. Her progeny rejoiced with me. I felt they were all really happy to see someone from Grace's hometown capture the honor. It was around that time that I began talking to Grace.

What makes Grace run? That year I told myself it was her competitive spirit. After all, Grace, like me, had not been content simply to run, but started entering races shortly after she'd developed the conditioning to run more than just a mile or two. It was the same with me. The first race I entered was a 10K. Within six months, I'd completed a marathon.

That was seventeen years ago now. My mother was still alive, alive but not really well. She was in her seventies and seriously afflicted with emphysema. Mother had always been a shy person who kept her deepest feelings to herself. I thought of her as sedentary, conservative, not given to display. Her one act of rebellion had been to take up smoking when my sisters and I were all still in elementary school. From almost that time on, my memories of her are played against the background accompaniment of a hacking cough. She had her first nervous breakdown when I was in college. Misdiagnosed for thirty years as schizophrenic, the category of drugs the learned doctors administered aggravated her physical condition and did precious little for her mental one. She was in and out of hospitals. It was only in her eightieth year, the last year of her life, that she was correctly diagnosed as delusionally depressed. Lithium gave me my mother back. I try really hard not to be angry at the loss of all those years.

What makes Grace run? Maybe it's the same thing that made my mother run. Now, there's a surprise, this quiet, sedentary woman a runner? I didn't know this about her. I told you she didn't reveal too much about herself. She thought it was wrong to brag, to draw attention to herself in any way. But that year, the year I ran my first marathon, she pulled me aside and shyly admitted, "I used to love to run."

"You did?" I asked in amazement. "When was that?"

"When I was a little girl. It was before my mother died so I couldn't have been more than seven. Sometimes she would send me on an errand, and I never walked. I always ran. I didn't run because I was in a hurry. I ran just because I was so happy. I had a nickname then. All the neighbors called me Legs Almighty."

I ran my second marathon in Philadelphia, the city where I'd grown up and where my parents still lived. By then I'd shared Mother's story with my father. Daddy drove her down to Boathouse Row to watch me cross the finish line. She laughed, looked a little embarrassed, but was mostly pleased when I ran past her wearing the tee shirt my father had had specially made just for the event. Large letters proudly emblazoned across my chest identified me as Legs Almighty.

What makes Grace run? I began to answer the question with more certainty around the time I moved beyond talking *to* Grace. We were talking *with* each other now. I can't really pinpoint the moment when Grace began talking back to me. It was probably sometime after I had run a few more times in her race. There were years there when I just couldn't nail that trophy down. Someone was always faster. It was then that Grace and I decided that running wasn't about winning but about being in the game. And what a game it was.

Anyone lucky enough to run in Eagles Mere soon comes to understand the profound beauty sketched by the natural world. A runner's high takes on a whole new meaning when the transcendence occurs beside a mountain lake surrounded by deep woods. In addition to Grace, I have an *actual* running partner. Carol is six years younger than I am and shares with me a deep appreciation for all the wildness here. We, like Grace, both run with our dogs. Two laps around the lake, five mornings a week for almost eight years now and each run has been different from all the others. We've never seen the same sunrise twice. Every silvered shade of peach is lifted from a slightly different palette than the one of the day before. I really mean it when I call out, "Oh, look! I've never seen that deep a red in the morning sky." Sometimes deer will cross in front of us, drawing the dogs quickly to attention, but they are both good boys and won't give chase. In the spring, tiny spotted fawns teeter on their spindly, little, bent-kneed legs. Once we had to stop and wait while a huge black bear finished calmly scratching behind his ear and finally cleared the road so we could continue on.

We thrill to piliated woodpeckers and great blue herons flapping slowly over our heads, their long legs stretched out behind them. Every season brings a migration of a different sort. We run in rain. We run in snow. We run with cleats strapped over our running shoes on those mornings when ice storms transform our world into a glittering, crystal wonderland. We run in fog so thick that only the memory of the road embedded in our feet guides us confidently on our way. We watch night turn into day. We see the stars and moon fade. We watch them move with the seasons, changing their positions in the sky. We glory in blue-sky mornings. We see wind send branches crashing down. We run in cold so fierce our breath crystallizes and coats our hair with frost. We watch the lake freeze. We hear it thaw, tiny little shards of ice rubbing against each other and filling the air with tinkling melodies. We run when we are tired. We run when we are sick. But we always run. What makes Grace run? Beauty has a lot to do with it.

The year I was doing battle with an advanced stage of ovarian cancer, I ran because I was still alive. Grace understood that. She was a frequent companion that year. I talked to her even when I wasn't running. In hindsight, I see that I didn't listen much. I talked over her, pushing too hard to achieve, to win this one. Seized with a panicked determination to vanquish death, I forgot that Grace's conversations with me were themselves proof that life/death isn't win/lose, black/white. Life and death aren't opposite ends of a continuum but parts of the same whole, a beautiful spinning orb where each is immutably fused with the other.

I didn't think I'd be able to enter Grace's Run that year. The hospital had me scheduled for a seriously mean chemotherapy treatment the week before the race. I knew from experience that my blood counts would be so low as to rule out any hope of racing. But, for a change, a low white count worked in my favor. It was too low for me to receive the promised chemo, and I lined up at the start with visions of being once again the first-place woman over fifty. My husband, Gene, worried about my trying to race, insisted on running with me. I agreed but was secretly certain I would leave him and all the other old gray heads before the first mile was over. My prediction was partly right. By the time we passed the mile mark, I couldn't see another older woman anywhere. In fact, I couldn't see another competitor of any description, not because they were all behind me, but because they were all far ahead of me!

It wasn't until we hit the wooded, far side of the lake that I finally quit fighting the inevitability of my dismal showing in the event and relaxed and found the grace, so to speak, to just enjoy the experience. Grace's Run is scheduled in October of each year. The weather is almost always perfect. Grace's grandchildren give her and God credit for the fair skies, and who am I, with my reputation for imaginary conversations with dead women, to argue with that? On this particular day, I finally listened to what it was that Grace had been trying to tell me. "Beauty," she whispered, yet again, in my ear. And, of course, she was right. We ran through falling swirls of golden beech leaves. The sugar maple burned red and orange against the counterpoint of midnight-green banks of hemlock. Dancing water, mirrored light, the surface of the lake was too brilliant for the unshielded eye. My lungs were washed with air so clean I felt that I could drink it. The rest of the race was as glorious as any I have ever run.

Gene and I finished hand in hand, a deliberate tie for last, far behind the rest of the pack. I chilled easily in that cancer year, and so I hurried past the crowds that cheered us on and dashed home to take a shower. As I was pulling on dry clothes, I heard Gene banging on the bathroom door. "Hurry up," he told me. "You won the Grace Andrews Memorial Trophy." Unlikely though it seemed, I had been the *only* woman over fifty in that year's race. As I stood there accepting my award, I was certain I heard Grace giggle. "You imp," I thought to myself and to her. "How in the world did you ever manage to persuade all those other older women to stay home this year?"

The illness is behind me now. I think the doctors were the only ones who were surprised by my recovery. My runs no longer feel like calls to battle. I bring a different spirit to the activity. Therefore, I guess I should not have been caught off guard by what happened in this year's race. It was another glorious fall day, and I was moving lightly and effortlessly around the course. I was very much in the pack, passing women in my age group, even occasionally pulling ahead of a man or an insufficiently conditioned teenager. We had just a little over a mile to go. I'd pushed hard going up the hill to the Crestmont Drive and was ready for the lovely free-fall down the other side. This is my favorite stretch of road, a gentle welcome downhill where gravity does all the work. I felt that I was flying.

What makes Grace run? I have the answer now. For suddenly, while caught in the sweetness of that downhill, I feel a gentle tugging on my left hand. I turn and don't recognize Grace at first for I have never seen her as a child. Her hair is auburn, cut in a tomboy bob with bangs to frame that laughing face. Her long legs are bare, flashing out beneath a simple muslin shift with each quick stride. This happy, running child can be none other than Grace Smeltzer, little Grace, not yet Andrews, more than a half-century away from formal entry in her first race. Realizing that Grace and I are galloping along shoulder to shoulder, I check and discover that I have moved back in time fifty years. I'm wearing brown laced oxfords, the kind I always hated, but I must admit they stay on my feet in a way that the Mary Janes favored by my friends would not. Grace and I are dashing along, having a giggling schoolgirl time!

But there is more to come. *Three* of us tumble down this hill, for on my other side, keeping pace, running right abreast with Grace and me is Legs Almighty. "Legs!" Adorable, grinning Legs, with her hair held back in a large satin bow, a bow so lovingly tied that only a mother could have put it there. Isn't it a wonder? How can the mind do this, just collapse the decades between us? We can't be more than seven, not one of us, not one of these three little girls running, laughing, calling back and forth like birds, caught up in joy, brimming with the sweet magic of this moment in our lives. What makes Grace run? The answer has been there all along, so plain I couldn't see it. What makes Grace run? It is joy, nothing more. But what *could be* more than this swelling, lifting joy?

ANASAZI SUMMER

Deborah O'Keefe

The first ladder had seventeen rungs made of round branches. The ladders were bolted to the rock, so at least they didn't wobble much. In other ways they resembled the original ones made by the Anasazi Indians. It was hot, ninety-six degrees Fahrenheit. A gray-haired woman slowly climbed the ladder toward the Ceremonial Cave. She was in her late fifties, short, considerably overweight. The ladders were placed close to the cliff and leaned out only slightly, so the ascent was steep and the climber could not place her feet securely on the rungs. Signs at the bottom read, THIS TRIP IS NOT RECOMMENDED FOR THOSE WITH HEART OR RESPIRATORY DIFFICULTIES OR A FEAR OF HEIGHTS. She didn't know if she had a fear of heights; she had never found out before. A little boy looked down at her impatiently from the ledge above. Clutching the rough poles, she lurched up and over the top. The first ledge was narrow, a short dirt path across rock; to the right, the cliff plunged into the stream below.

In the photograph a baby toddles down a straight path between tall flower beds. I am two years old at home in Connecticut in 1941, and I am looking pleased. Bad things may be happening to other people in other places but here life goes smoothly. In this town near the city, nature is tamed but admired. Lines of fine trees shade the houses, grass grows in the little cemetery where I walk with my grandmother, birds sing politely. I become a bookish child, cheerful enough but timid; outdoors is where I go with somebody bigger. I am comfortable following.

1950. At summer camp in Maine the world is new and wild but we are well-protected. I love camp. When we go on hikes a counselor walks in front, another at the rear. We stay in line and never get lost. We are rewarded with hot dogs and marshmallows. On camp outs, birds screech in the night. Sometimes a mean-looking porcupine ambles by. Pungent with Flit, I am warm in my sleeping bag and happy, even though Sally teases me because it is not like other people's; it is a peculiar type with feathers that fly around and make us sneeze.

I am not an athletic girl—it took me a year to learn to ride a bike because I am uncoordinated and fear falling. Rainy days at camp are nicest; we do crafts and read by the lodge fire instead of playing tennis and softball. I do enjoy the team competition, though, because of the group solidarity and the tidy, predictable system of points earned for each activity, and because the Whites always beat the Blues. Sometimes on a fair evening the whole camp goes out in canoes to watch the sunset. Sitting on the lake in rows, we sing a camp song to the tune of "You Can't Be True, Dear": "We leave the shoreline, to realms of dreams we go . . . " But we don't leave the shoreline much. Only the yearly canoe trip up Meadowbrook Stream holds a bit of menace: disgusting leeches cling to our young legs. I spend nine summers at camp, doing the same wonderful things each year. I become a junior counselor but I am still a follower, safe. Decisions are still made by somebody else. At night I lie cocooned in my cot reading Agatha Christie while loons call on the lake.

The second ladder was the longest, twenty-six rungs. She tried not to be distracted by a family of slim teenagers waiting on the ledge below. Her small backpack was clumsy and made her feel unbalanced. A mixture of sun block and sweat covered her hands and face and made her glasses slip down her nose. This time it seemed safer to grip a rung above instead of the side poles, while a lower rung dug into her feet and a middle rung bruised her clenching thighs. She puffed, decided she was not dizzy, not swaying, pulled up to the next rung. She remembered reading,

THE ALTITUDE (ABOUT 7,000 FEET) THROWS AN ADDI-
TIONAL BURDEN UPON THE HEART AND LUNGS; YOU
MUST BE IN GOOD PHYSICAL CONDITION, and smiled. Her
lips were dry and a damp lock of hair itched on her forehead. Muscles
all over her body told her what they thought of her physical condition.
Poking her head over the next ledge, she was not comforted by the
sight: a few stones too near the edge formed a path to the next ladder,
with no handholds reachable. She grabbed the ladder poles where they
stuck up above the ledge, dragged herself up the final rungs and landed
uncertain feet on the rock ledge. It helped to lean against the hot cliff.

1980. The little trail is popular with visitors to Vermont. Labels tell the
names of trees and bushes. Poems by Robert Frost appear at suitable
spots, mounted on weather-proof plaques, for this is the Robert Frost
Trail—nature and culture in one twenty-minute expedition. We stop to
read, "Come In" at the start, "Birches," next to the birches. My husband leads the way, then my three sons, who punch and trip each other
and whisper, "Turdface!" I come last, herding them along. Larry and
Mark slide down a small incline to the stream, while Danny stops to
examine a newt. When we get back to the rustic bridge nobody is whining and I feel we have accomplished something. These days my role is
tending to the people around me; guiding.

We spend summers in the Vermont woods, in a house in a clearing
at the end of a long, straight driveway. I am aware that we are surrounded by miles of wilderness, but I don't have much to do with it. I
take the boys for short hikes on well-maintained trails we have walked
before, Silver Lake and Texas Falls. We admire wildflowers and stones
glistening beneath the waterfalls; it is a sweet time. Mostly I keep an eye
on how they are getting along, making sure each one takes an equal
turn carrying the heavy lunch pack. After our hikes we go to the lake.
They like the pool table and video games in the shed but I force them
outside and into the water. Soft, low mountains surround the lake. I
watch so the boys don't get chilled or stung or drowned. The scene is
beautiful, familiar, not particularly mysterious.

Back home outside New York we work in the back yard. My husband instructs me on how to plant perennials properly. We put phlox

and bee balm and lavender malva, serum and hosta in shadier gardens. We get a lovely jumble of color, all framed and enclosed by the rectangular property line. Next to the house, annuals line the terrace. I water them in dry weather, sometimes with Miracle-Gro. Fine maples tower over the old farmhouse in a double row; they were planted by Farmer Hall before the turn of the century. When their leaves fall the five of us go out with rakes and clean up. I am responsible for people and things. It's like camp, where we all knew who we were and where we were going, only now I am the guide and the one who has to tell the others how to get there.

The third ladder had nineteen rungs. It was shorter than the second but scarier because it ran straight up the main face of the cliff, not sideways to it. Resting on the ledge, she reached for her backpack to get a swig of water, then realized she had taken a drink and left the bottle in the car. The thought of the sticky granola bar in the backpack made her thirstier. The path along the cliff to the ladder looked more and more ominous as she stared at it until, disgusted, she lunged up its uneven stones and grabbed the poles of the ladder. As she started up, she tried not to see what she saw out of the corner of her eye, way down: the fine sweep of the canyon floor. Eyes looking straight ahead at the mottled rock inches away, knees clutching, she thought instead about the thin Keds she was wearing and the long, floppy, blue shorts that were comfortable but klutzy.

1995. I walk out the paved breakwater, past seafood restaurants, rows of moored boats. I count the twenty-six flagpoles, with their bright banners flapping. From the end of the breakwater I can understand the whole scene—harbor, boulevard, palm trees, red-roofed valley and sheltering mountains. Santa Barbara is a well-managed paradise; humankind makes itself comfortable here.

I am lucky, too: now, with my children all on their own, I have this moment in this place, to take stock. It is a new luxury to do things alone sometimes, making choices. It is a new freedom not to be doing what other people expect. I am no longer responsible for anyone but myself, although I am responsible with my husband, as a partner. He is doing research at the university for a couple of months this winter while I write on my portable computer. More often I wander in and around the city, noticing how things relate to other things. For years I have been an English teacher, telling college students how to write their thoughts out in orderly fashion. Now I have left teaching and am organizing my own mind; it isn't as easy as I told them but I like it. I am mastering the grid of graceful city streets, which ones go which way; I am following the shore's edge up and down and learning the names of the mountains. These days, I am mapping.

As I try to see the shape of what I have done with fifty-five fortunate years and what I will do with the coming years, I work on a parallel enterprise: what is the shape and the meaning of this place I am in. I take a Continuing Ed course of nature walks: we visit a baroque garden estate in Montecito, a painted cave of the Chumash Indians, a tide pool full of sea anemones and tiny shrimp and rocks covered with small, slurping barnacles. We walk in the ruins of a financier's hunting lodge at the edge of a cliff in the Santa Ynez mountains; on the trails by a river we identify trees and insects.

I devour the infinite detail of this world (though I forget most of the names), but I also take comfort in the patterns. The valley stretches only a few miles from coast to mountains, with one large highway running between. From La Cumbre Peak I am high enough to embrace city and suburbs and farms, and ocean meeting land in a thick, tan line of beach. But I am also close enough to recognize the weathered-wood wharf and the university lagoon and the individual highway exits. It is satisfying to discover how all these lines connect.

I always liked figuring out maps, even though I have not spent much time outdoors. Last summer, exploring on the roads of central Vermont, I realized that my wandering had a goal: I was trying to cover the whole rectangular county, passing over all the back roads that connected to bigger roads and to each other. I saw not all the roads, but a lot—a lot of spotted cows and silos and rivers and guys next to trailers and evergreens and crossroad gas stations and worn, white houses. Even from one brief passage down these lanes I could get a sense of the web of space, the organization that is really an organism.

So in Santa Barbara in the winter in my rented car I map my way up the coast, east through the mountains, south to the flower nurseries of Carpinteria where the Chumash Indians built canoes. I even follow the whales migrating up the shore, in a windy tour boat that keeps a respectful distance behind the flipping tails. For driving I study road maps of the country; for walking I study tourist maps of the Franciscan Missions, their adobe buildings and gardens. I even stand and peer at the map welcoming you to the zoo—if you know just where everything is placed, sights like the capybaras, indolent giant hamsters, will not seem so weird. The world makes sense when things are where the maps tell you they should be.

We are staying near the quiet beach in Carpinteria. At low tide I walk way up the sand, barefoot in February, to find stones that are like no other stones and shells of colors with no names. The sea is vast and, as it's winter, the sky is dim. But I have tamed the scene enough to be at home in it. I have learned what's on the other side of the barrier of rocks. And I know what to expect of the water, as I read the newspaper tide tables daily in my condo.

The fourth ladder had only six rungs. Above it loomed the great curve of the Ceremonial Cave. She watched a bearded man swing down the ladder using only one hand, self-consciously casual. DO NOT HANDLE ANY BATS OR THEIR GUANO, the trail-guide booklet had warned; she wondered who would wish to handle bat guano. Her heart still pounded but she stepped onto the first rung and moved steadily upward. Anasazi lived here six hundred years ago, in the canyon valley village and the cliffside caves; nobody knows exactly why they disappeared and where they went. Birds swooped over the canyon floor, lower than where she climbed. The rough wood of the ladders had scraped her hands; the backpack straps had dug small welts. Looking up, she saw the sheltering ceiling high above the cave. Stiff, shaking, she reached the top. A woman sitting on a rock said, "Would you like some grapes?" She took three and smiled.

After the grape ceremony, she sat on a stone shelf watching the cliffs on the other side of the valley. Her skin was both hot and cooled by the shaded air, wet from sweat and dry from heat. The grape woman's children laughed and romped but stayed near the inner semicircular wall, for the floor of the open, wide cave sloped slightly downward to its unprotected edge. Thin trees lay far below, and the gleaming river. A rounded dirt kiva, not large, rose from the center of the cave floor. There she saw one more small ladder, two in fact, up and down: there was no end to ladders. This was the cave's own cave. The grape family had departed now. She walked around the inner wall, then ascended the few rungs to the kiva's top and descended through the opening into the heart of whatever the ancient ones did here. The low, round ceiling was smooth. The kiva felt like a tomb where things remained forever and a cocoon where things would burst forth. She stood there awhile.

There are no people in this story, just me. No faces, no dialogue, even though I have always been acutely attuned to other people's wishes and expectations. And it's not much of an adventure; nothing terrible happened. Many women, not so soft, wouldn't have thought twice about the climb, and I guess I knew I would reach the top unharmed. It's more the story of what I've come to in the outdoors after the years of following, guiding and mapping—which seems, at last, to be venturing; exploring without a strict sense of limits and goals.

The summer after the Santa Barbara winter we are in Albuquerque for a month, where my husband is studying at the university. We are staying in a guest cottage inside the courtyard of a handsome adobe house, inside a beautiful locked compound of such houses. I have always liked working inside, in a cool enclosure, but now the hot, stinging air draws me away from my computer. I circle around this strange universe, walk past bright gardens in the compound and see a gawky roadrunner bird running the roads, then out the gate and over the acequia irrigation ditch to the Rio Grande trail. Once again I am trying to learn the shape of a new place, but not just rough linear mapping; there is something else.

This desert city is mostly stark and raw. The ground is bare dirt except where things are watered. Space is infinite and the grid of streets is surrealistic—endless blocks of malls and fast-food places, gaudy signs for spots like "Bubba's Hot Deli Dining" and "Rick's Booze 'n' Cruise." It's an easy town to learn spatially: Interstate 25 crosses Interstate 40 at the city's center, forming four quadrants: 25 is paralleled by the Rio

Grande River and 40 is paralleled by historic, honky-tonk Route 66. This insistent geometry is tolerable, I realize, because it's not the whole picture: the city grid is a small, harmless joke in the expanse of desert, mountain range and riverside bosque. Under that much sky it is mean to quibble about a Pizza Hut or two.

For me now, mastering the map is not enough. Fifty-six years is probably all I need of following predictable lines. There is no end point to a circle: its satisfactions are different. I do not throw away my maps. They give me hints and invitations and help when I know what I want. But as I venture, I sometimes ignore them. As I leave Bandelier Park and the Ceremonial Cave, I do not go back along the Santa Fe route home but turn onto two-lane 4 west, into the Jemez Mountains. As Route 4 heads west it twists up past aspen groves and tall pine forests. In the silent mountains I pass a series of lanes leading into the woods; sleek signs with elegant lettering announce, "TECH 47," "TECH 32" and so on. I suspect these are divisions of laboratories in nearby Los Alamos. Los Alamos is not a place I want to visit. I lose count of the hairpin curves and drive through gorges of the Jemez Mountains in a happy stupor, not knowing or wondering what is ahead.

And then I do find what's ahead: a magnificent, big, green bowl like a child's painting of heaven. At a pull-off spot I search in my guidebook published by Moon Press, and find it: "Valle Grande is a gigantic caldera formed when a series of volcanoes collapsed and the mountains were sucked into the earth. One of the largest craters on earth, the valley contains 176 square miles of grassy meadowland." I get out and walk above the valley. It spreads out a little below the level of the road. No animals or people are in sight, just wide grass. I am in the road, in the great green valley, in the mountains, in the desert. It is a reward, the kind of reward you cannot understand and do not deserve. Walking, I eat a handful of M&M's.

So I return home. Winding Route 4 ends on straight Route 44. The desert here is encrusted with strange formations of bright red sandstone. I whoosh down 44 with a wail of country music on the radio and do not mind when a jug of water breaks on the front seat in a McDonald's parking lot.

Other days I look for other pieces of this puzzle of a state, sometimes trying for the shortest line between two points, other times trying for the longest, sometimes not knowing what the point will be. Sometimes I follow road signs, other times I just admire them—the inscrutable pictures of a cow standing still; the philosophical remark, GUSTAV WINDS MAY EXIST; the fearsome silhouette of rocks falling on a car. I am bemused at a sign that sounds like T. S. Eliot, which appears several times on a barren mountain road southeast of Albuquerque: WATCH FOR WATER. It has not rained for weeks; there is no stream or arroyo anywhere.

I am not on a journey, or anything so fancy as a quest. I am looking at patterns, I guess, without wanting to analyze them. At the ruins of Anasazi great houses in Chaco Canyon, I can only gaze; their intricate circles and squares and doorways are unfathomable. And crossing the Continental Divide, that strange, abstract line which is announced by a small highway sign, I park and look at a few trees in a field; I can see no rivers at all, flowing in any direction, but I like knowing the Continental Divide is here.

Certainly the direct path, the known pattern, is often the best choice. The instructions at Ouarai Ruins, for instance, are not something I would quarrel with: RESPECT THE PRIVACY OF THE RATTLE-SNAKES IN THIS AREA. STAY ON THE TRAIL. But the image I like best is the state symbol: the sun design from Zia Indian pottery. It appears on license plates and tourist brochures and tee shirts but is nonetheless indestructible—the Zia sun still seems full of primitive meaning. It is simple and complex, lines radiating out from a central circle. Four lines (two longer flanked by two shorter) point out from each of the four sides of the circle—but then, does a circle have sides? The Zia sun needs both lines and circle. It's interesting the geometrical language we use: over the years my behavior has been both square and straight, though I like to think that my empathy has no limits, like a circle.

My venturing leads one day to El Malpais, the Badlands west of Albuquerque, a territory that is sacred ground to the Acoma and Zuni Indians. I stop for a trail map in the uranium town of Grants, which has a tiny grid of straight streets with names like Patton and MacArthur. Soon, however, I feel I am on the moon: volcanic lava rock covers the thousand-acre valley of the Badlands. A design of cracks breaks the textured black rock; carved sandstone cliffs loom above the lava valley. El Malpais is a dark brother of the green Valle Grande, also beautiful and complete and completely unknowable. In the baking sun, wearing a goofy white hat, I creep around the top of the sandstone bluffs. As I stare at the paralyzed lava flow below me, a large lizard stares at me, its eyes disgusted but harmless. Lightning flashes in the distance, its jagged shapes echoing shapes in the lava.

Knowing the necessary rain may start, I drive on to La Ventana, the natural arch that rises 125 feet to guard the Malpais. The trail from the parking area runs flat for a while through scrubby desert stuff, not lava here, then climbs past rocks in what look like easy enough stages. When I am partway up, the rain comes, sudden and drenching. In a minute my shirt and shorts are sticking to my body, my goofy hat is worthless. I proceed, since I can't get any wetter, uneasy only over the lightning that has started again. Desert rock formations are not the place of choice in a lightning storm. But it's too late to go back; I grasp slimy, wet rocks and pull up to a higher level. Drizzle continues as I reach the top of the path, perch on the giant boulder right under the arch and eat an apple. I am very wet but I got here and I didn't follow anyone or guide anyone. When some bedraggled people emerge up the path I look down at them and say something quite unlike me: "I own this rock, but you're welcome to come up, too, if you like." They nod and look worried about my sanity, then wander off while I continue to sit on my boulder.

From the arch at La Ventana, the window, I can see miles of golden sandstone castles and black valley. There could be another stage for me to discover after venturing: maybe it's seeing. I haven't really gotten to seeing yet, but at least I'm beginning to look. When I descend to the flat, sandy earth, I go off the trail to look at small cactuses with bright yellow flowers. I wander a little, wet sneakers squilching in the sand, and get turned around so I don't know exactly where I am. But I think I will be able to find my way, ahead and around and back.

BITTEN BY THE JUNGLE

Judith Niemi

We're plowing upstream on the Amazon River in a decrepit boat through brown water thick with sticks, logs and little green rosettes of *chugas,* or lettuce. The river's not friendly, especially on visits to the outhouse perched on the stern: you climb over duffels and scramble monkeylike around the churning motor, to perch where waves splash your feet and bottom and excrement drops directly into the river. This is difficult for trained low-impact campers, but we have no alternative to suggest. One woman wears a tee shirt reading, "Toto, I don't think we're in Kansas anymore."

The boat rocks ominously as we cross currents. It's top-heavy, more so since a half-dozen of our guides are sitting up on the flat roof, and several tourists have joined them. I can't say anything to the Peruvians, but as the tour leader who recruited them for this trip, I feel responsible for all the *gringas,* and nag them about equatorial sunburn on winter-pale skin. I'm just trying to keep the roof population down. I chat up the sunbathers: how did you happen to sign up for this? A live-wire woman from backwoods Minnesota says her husband read two short paragraphs in the newspaper.

"A women's trip in the Amazon! There ya go, Sade!" he had said, kidding, of course.

"The Amazon," she said. "I'm going."

Sadie's impulsive. She got married the same way: went north for a

179

fishing vacation, met the guy, called Mom in Chicago and said she wouldn't be back.

But what about all the rest of us? We're a group of twenty-four to seventy-year-olds, mostly a sensible, middle-aged lot of professional women, not given to soldier-of-fortune fantasies. Some travel a lot. Others, however, just got a brand-new passport, to go to a place the U.S. State Department still does not encourage as a tourist destination. Even my written description warns, "Facts: it will be hot and steamy. Insects will bite. You will be far from medical attention." What *are* we all doing in the jungle?

No one mentions anything such as "seeing the rain forest before it's gone." I've read phrases like that in tourism brochures, have felt chilled at how unabashedly crass a consumer society can be. *Eco-tourism* is too self-conscious and trendy a term. We seem to be drawn by intense curiosity alone, the pull of "the other." We're new to this place, but not quite naive. My own images of the Amazon probably come mostly from reading Peter Matthiessen's *At Play in the Fields of the Lord:* jeweled butterflies floating in Eden, but also disgusting, corrupt functionaries, smoldering violence. One woman rented videos, not only *At Play,* but also *Fitzcarraldo,* and *Aguirre, the Wrath of God*—and she still came. Intrepid, we say. Some of us worry about snakes, especially anacondas. I've been reading nature guidebooks, and my own special horror is of seeing the spiders that are as big as your hand and eat baby birds. And I came across this unforgettable fact: in the Amazon Basin the biomass of ants alone is greater than the biomass of all large Amazon mammals. Gives one pause.

For the record, terrorists aren't on our list of worries. State Department warnings against travel in Peru have severely inhibited tourism in the Amazon, but, in fact, the *Sendero Luminoso* always has had better places to prowl than these jungle villages. It's the six-legged and eight-legged terrorists we're thinking about.

A Three-Toed Sloth

The sheer volume of the main Amazon overwhelms the imagination, wipes out thought. A wide gray sky covers vague, distant shores that will go underwater in two or three months. Water and silt have moved as many as two thousand miles to reach here; there are another couple thousand miles before this pushy river reaches the sea. It's a relief, the second day, to turn into a tiny tributary, the Yarapa. In the clearer, dark water, dolphins are rolling and blowing. The close, almost impenetrable shores have a curtain of heart-shaped leaves hiding the darkness within.

This will be home for two weeks, and right at the river mouth we have one of those nice little moments in women's travel: insubordination, moral action, bonding. The guides spot a sloth and nudge our boat into the overhanging cecropia tree. It's a young sloth, waving its head in that spacey, drunken way of its kind. Cameras click. Paul, the *gringo* owner of our tour company, races out onto the deck, into the tree. He wants to catch the sloth for photos.

"Leave it alone, Paul."

"No, really, it won't hurt it. "

"Leave it *alone*. It's just a baby."

"But—"

"Paul," says Sadie, sternly, "We're *mothers*."

Crestfallen, like a small boy, Paul climbs back aboard. We've started to claim this place. The little sloth climbs away, dreamily.

In camp we adapt quickly to jungle time, to being cooked for and guarded carefully. Usually one to paddle my own canoe, I discover the joy of boat travel with absolutely nothing to do but be passive, receptive to the jungle. The surfaces are fascinating; what's beneath, hard to know. We spend hours photographing pink water lilies the size of soccer balls, *victoria regia*. When flipped up, their six-foot lily pads reveal wicked spikes beneath. You can float an infant on them, says our guide, Rosario. She shows us healing trees, a fish trap set to catch the rare *paiche*. Only when pressed does Rosario identify the warty *arbol brujo,* a bad medicine tree.

Caimans

Night falls, sudden and complete. The hot, sticky air cools. The breeze carries sweet, erotic odors from trees with names such as *capinuri* or *machimango*. Floating downstream silently in the dark, the air a perfect temperature, or no-temperature—could this be what it feels like in the womb?

We float into a little lagoon good for finding frogs, tiny blue and green and translucent beings with red eyes and big finger pads. Or, in the dark of the moon, looking for caimans, alligator relatives. Mostly white caimans, just a foot or two long; the guides delight in lying over the bow, flashlights in their teeth, and swift as herons, grabbing the caimans, thrashing, toothy little beasts. This night, Moises finds none. He has to content himself with snatching a sleeping red-capped cardinal off a branch; laughing, hoping he's pleased us, he releases the flustered bird.

On the other boat, however, from far across the water, Jose Luis's powerful flashlight picks up the red glow of an eye, then another—wide apart. *"Muy grande! Muy grande!"* he hisses. Black caimans, maybe the biggest yet seen in Lake Uvos. They slide closer. Under the beam of light a bumpy profile emerges, a head twelve, fifteen inches wide, suggestion of a tail twelve feet behind. Nobody breathes. The ancient beast lies motionless, primordial. Alejandro is young, an extra jungle hand hired just for this trip. Hoping to demonstrate his potential as a tour guide, he whispers to Sadie, "Your night camera. Get a picture!" He shoves her forward over the bow, holding her shirt. By the time the flash goes off, the caiman has had bloody well enough and lunges at the bow. A crash of water, the boat rocks, a flashbulb goes off, someone falls into Jan's lap. Jan isn't sure who falls overboard with the croc, her friend Sadie or Alejo, but both turn up safe and soaking wet on the floor of the boat. It should have been a great accidental photo, all white spray and caiman jaws. But all Sadie's flash catches is a blur of what might be boat, against black night. Not so easily captured, mythic caimans.

Shamans and *Tunchis*

As we settle in, life at our base camp seems less fraught with excitement. We float down the river at dawn watching toucans and paradise tanagers. There's a bunch of bananas ripening in the corner of our sleeping platform; every now and then a soft banana plops to the floor. If we don't get it right away, the ants do. I watch how our guides and the local people move around, try to pick up from them the little habits of jungle life. Don't touch brilliantly colored bugs, often poisonous. Don't sit on fallen logs, which are probably teeming with ants. Some bite so violently that there's a dance, the *tangarana,* named for them.

We venture out away from base camp, in small groups. The "Outwardbounders" explore another, wilder river for days. Women paddle dugout canoes, fish for piranhas, hike through the steamy jungle, swing from vines.

I'm one of four (in the care of two guides and a cook) who spend a few days in a nearby village where the Ashuara people still speak their native language as well as Spanish. We hope the shaman will agree to show us some of the plants he uses. As we follow Ramon through the jungle to gather *aja sacha* for a ceremony, MaryAnn trips, over nothing we can see, slashing her shin open. Although she hikes with the energy of a much younger woman, her skin is delicate, brittle and splits in a series of ugly gashes. Sterile is out of the question here. Doing the best we can, we spray her leg with our bottled drinking water that we brought on the boat from Iquitos and carried on the muddy path through the jungle. Cautious peeks through the dressings show no signs of ghastly tropical infections, but playing it safe, we ask the shaman to check it out during his ceremony.

"He says tell her not to worry, " Rosario translates. "He says, 'Tell her I think that was intended for me.'" We're not sure that makes us feel better.

Back at base camp we all reunite and exchange stories from our adventures. We're not surprised that Sadie and Jan have the wildest tales. They'd been on a "survival hike." Excitedly, they tell us about the rising water flooding their path, about quicksand. About the metallic taste in your mouth, the way your hair stands on end, when you wade with electric eels. And snakes, deadly fer de lances; Alejo kept the fangs of the two he killed. And there's something else they aren't talking about openly. Two of us pull them aside.

"We hear you saw something outside your tent. You're not crazy—we'll believe you."

"Jan saw it first, but I wouldn't look. The next night I saw it. White, larger-than-human—"

"—and it didn't quite touch the ground. Right?"

"How did you know?"

"We've been reading jungle folktales, Milly's book of her grandfather's stories. People down here see them often. It's called a *tunchi,* a form ghosts take, unhappy ones, but not malevolent."

"Oh. Well, OK then."

Bitten by the Jungle

On one of our last nights we lie, each shrouded in the privacy of our mosquito nets, listening to the clicks, croaks, pipings, hoots of the jungle night. Suddenly, close by, a terrible shriek cuts the air. Those of us with any reason to feel on duty—two nurses, the women in the nets next to the shriek and me—scramble out. Everyone else stays sensibly in their nets, asking, "What? What?" It's Sadie. Something, we assume an insect, made its way under her tightly tucked net and bit her. Right on the eye. No sign of the biter. In a while, she can see again; it's clear she'll be OK.

At about this time I figure out that Sadie will certainly be coming back, and soon. Caimans, fer de lances, electric eels and tunchis are not deterrents. They may be attractions. A nurse herself, she sees the desperate medical needs of the villagers. A free spirit, she's found a place wild enough for her.

Within weeks, she and Jan are filing 501-C3 papers for a nonprofit medical foundation; within months she is back with a small study team. Now and then I get lively telephone reports.

About travel on the public water taxi: "Supposed to be three hundred people, we had six hundred, plus water buffalos and chickens and pigs. When the men peed overboard, the wind blew it back at Abby, but at least that got rid of the cockroaches on her. You've gotta come with us."

After working, one team went to Machu Picchu, as tourists: "Wouldn't you know, there was a landslide. I had to hire a Russian Sikorsky helicopter to get everyone out on time. You've got to travel with me sometime," she said.

"How the hell did you find a helicopter?"

"Walking around town, talking to everyone, to see if a solution would turn up. Then," she said cheerily, "there was the time Kathy and I went up in a Cessna, but the pilot spoke no English and the fuel gauge didn't work. You should have been there." Right.

Siete Raices—Seven Roots

Those of us with less need for adrenaline rushes also return. Sometimes I've felt struck by a strange homesickness for the jungle.

Back home, I try to sum up the first visit: visions of heaven—late sun on the wings of blue and gold macaws; visions of hell—the floating city of Belen, when the river that serves for bathing, sewage and drinking water rises far into the streets; and definite intimations of mortality. Here I'm thinking not particularly of poisonous snakes or injuries, but of the everyday, routine voraciousness of the jungle. Growth, decay, flooding. Nothing lasts. There's no rock here, only slippery clay, decaying vegetation. A dugout canoe leaks right away, rots out in ten years. You clear a water trail, a garden, and the jungle immediately starts to reclaim it. Life flourishes, overwhelms, but mortality is the main event.

I wouldn't want to live there; couldn't. But it's instructive, and oddly energizing, to visit.

So a few months later I'm back, escorting another group. None of these women, either, can say exactly why they came to the Amazon. The reasons for travel, even jungle travel, must be either too self-evident to discuss or beyond articulating. Two of the women, in their seventies and eighties, whom I come upon one day matter-of-factly discussing burial plans, are about the most durable of any of us. "You really gave me the third degree on the phone," eighty-six-year-old Claire accuses me. "Well, sure, I wanted to be certain you knew what we'd be getting into, that you weren't signing up for some fantasy trip." But when I learned she'd recently been hiking in Central American rain forests and in the Himalayas, my cross-examination stopped. She and the rest of the group unanimously choose to go on a camping trip far upriver from the relative comforts of base camp.

As the little open boat chugs upstream, the jungle changes, subtly but distinctly. Rosario points out new sights. "Monkey brush. Killer-bee nests." So far Eden seems to be marginally ahead, since the number of blue morpho butterflies we've passed outnumbers the killer-bee nests. The total number of bees doesn't bear thinking about. The final tiny stream we work up is notable for the impressive amount of ant-nest biomass we knock into the water while slashing our way through the green tunnel.

The actual slashing, of course, is done by a guide, Roy. He's merely a teenager, irrepressible and sometimes irresponsible, who demonstrates the use of ant eggs as a poultice on his face to prevent zits. But he's dead serious for once as he does a man's job with his machete, balancing barefooted on the prow of our boat, ignoring the ants biting him. There's plenty of action for the rest of us, too, smashing the ants that fall into the boat. Up in the bow, Claire and I are on the front lines. Claire is quite unflappable and agile, slamming her sturdy hand down on the gunwales. One tiny ant who makes it past our defenses bites my leg, and although I use an extractor to draw out its venom, the pain is impressive. I wonder how many bit Roy.

The campsite is memorable for the number of spiders, mostly poisonous, that scuttle under the brown leaves or drop out of the decaying thatch of an old shelter. They seem to choose the boots and duffels of the most arachnophobic among us; you have to try not to take things like this too personally. Just beyond the clearing, the jungle floor is covered with red blossoms fallen from lush trees. Monkeys whoop. This ragged, little field seems an affront that the jungle is eager to erase.

In the evening our little band collects in front of the least decrepit hut for dinner. We perch on stumps and duffels, lounging in our mosquito jackets and bush hats. Looking right at home in this setting is Fern, seventy-five years old, an avid traveler and conservationist. In Iquitos Fern and I sat at an outdoor table at sunset, looking out over the wide river, drinking *pisco* sours—a vile drink, but befitting the decadent *Fitzcarraldo* scene. We were talking about overpopulation, the difficulties of bringing birth control to jungle women, who are eager for it. Would condoms last in this climate? How would the men ever be persuaded to use them? We fantasize replacing the local toast, *"Salud, amor, y dinero"* with something such as, "To responsible fucking!" Fern was lamenting the passivity of women, including the surprising timidity of her own daughter. "I keep hoping," she said, "that menopause will beat it out of her."

Now, far upriver, we're being offered a grubby bottle of *siete raices,* a potent sugar-cane rum that's pure essence of jungle. Patty, a *gringa* who works for our tour company and is a true soldier-of-fortune type, says this brew does promise health, love and money, besides being, of course, an aphrodisiac. It's sticky, with an acrid, woody flavor. Fern surveys the tangled jungle and in her ladylike voice offers a toast that captures the spirit of the place: "To chaos."

"To pristine chaos," Patty amends it.

"To pristine chaos—cheers!"

Career Changes

Another year later, I'm back again, and it happens to be when Sadie and her medical team are working just upriver. One afternoon we go to Libertad to meet them. Walking the path back, I hear one more story of her jungle luck. The villagers rarely expect snakes here, but on Sadie's last trip, on this very path, a fer de lance came darting out of the bushes and wrapped itself around someone's leg. No one was surprised. And listen, they insist, it didn't bite, so all's well.

Our tour is almost over, and I think about how happy I am to have brought together these people and this place. But I itch, and my Minnesota metabolism is exhausted by heat; secretly, I'm harboring thoughts of home, hoping there will be snow when I get back—antiseptic, soothing snow. In the future, I think, I'll let other leaders come here—I belong to the North. Still, when I think I may never see this place again, tears are near the surface and I try to absorb every color, sound, odor. I want to imprint this place on a part of my spirit that I hadn't known before.

Women are showering, padding off to the dining room for a warm bottle of *cerveza* or Inca Cola or the syrupy red cola, Bimbo. Shirlee looks languid, too, swaying her hammock with the tiniest motion of her toes, but I look at her intense eyes and smile, and suspect the Amazon is laying a claim on her.

"Maybe I'm ready for another career change," she says. Her checkered past includes theater, country living, social change; lately she's had a professional, support-the-family career, but now her son is almost grown. She talks about coming back alone. Asks about Sadie's work.

Wonders how she can help with what the *riverenos* need.

"Let's go visit Kerrie Lynn!" she says suddenly.

Kerrie Lynn. Now there's another one. A *gringa* who came here as a casual tourist, on a trip like ours, and rewrote her life. A pharmacist, she now runs a small first-aid station. A pleasant, pregnant, middle-aged woman, she welcomes us and as soon as Shirlee says, "I work for a pharmaceutical company. What supplies do you need?" the two of them are off at top speed, rattling off names of drugs, corporations, CEOs. Two professionals, movers and shakers, happily schmoozing. But their dance, their rising enthusiasm, has other meanings in this setting.

A woman with two tiny children comes for aspirin. Kerrie Lynn rummages around in the dim supply room. "Nah, don't come back here—there's one of these big guys on the loose somewhere on the shelves."

She points toward her wall, where she's hung a glass case housing a dark, dead tarantula—its hairy legs could span one-and-one-half octaves. Unnerving decor. The lower part of her bamboo-slat walls are stained dark, from the high water last May. Maybe she can get the floor raised by next year. Still, she says, when the jungle is flooded, the poisonous snakes come aboard any dry place.

"What do people *do* here in high water?" I asked Rosario once.

"Go around like caged tigers," she said, with a wicked grin.

But Kerrie Lynn is cheerfully talking about going to the States to have her baby and being back by May. She invites Shirlee to stay there.

"You could come upriver by the river taxi, but get a guide to bring you over from Libertad. You'll have to come by boat then."

And Shirlee, I now see, is very likely to return in May, not in spite of the high water, but maybe because of it. As we boat home in the dark, she's spinning lists, thinking of sources for school supplies, Spanish primers, drugs. One more, I think. Another wild *gringa* who's found something vital in the jungle.

NATURE BUDDIES

Barbara Beckwith

When my grandson was born, I gave his parents a gift. I would baby-sit for Daniel each Sunday while they took yoga classes. I was sure that grandparenting would come naturally to me.

I was wrong. Daniel wanted only milk or motion. I didn't have milk-filled breasts to offer, so I used my arms to jiggle him as we speed-walked around the apartment. The moment I stopped, he'd cry. After a month of Sundays, I started weight-lifting classes to strengthen my baby-sitting arm.

But I still didn't get it right. "Daniel's diaper needs changing!" my son declared on returning from his first yoga class. "But I kept check-ing! It was dry," I said in my defense. "These are nineties diapers, Mom," he explained. "They're maxi-absorbent. The top layer wicks liquid away. You have to check how heavy his diaper feels."

I had failed my first grandparenting test. I panicked. I could lose my baby-sitting privileges. Humbled, I asked my son and daughter-in-law: how do you change him, carry him, amuse him, put him to sleep, wake him up? I no longer felt like an all-wise grandma. I was a bumbling Mommy-Daddy substitute. The special bond that Daniel and I were meant to have, just us two, was fraying.

I myself never had a grandparent. At least, not the lap-sitting kind. One grandparent lived far away and two others died before I was born. The grandparent I did see frequently was more interested in entertaining his grandchildren than in getting to know them. He'd line us up and scramble our names to make us laugh. He didn't know or seem to care that I climbed trees better than anyone, was a champion at mumblety-peg, and wrote poetry and stories.

I was determined to be the warm and wonderful grandparent that I'd never had myself.

Daniel was born in winter. For months, we were stuck indoors. I occasionally tried stroller and carry-pack outings, but the stroller wheel skidded on the ice and the Snuggli-pack straps stumped me. They'd loosen after a block or two, and I'd be left carrying my grandson's chilled body in my arms.

Finally, spring came. Daniel was now four months old. He could see yards ahead instead of only inches away. One Sunday in April, his father said that I could take Daniel to the city pond nearby. He warned me, however, not to get Daniel sunburned. He draped a blanket over the stroller and pinned it tight: "to keep the sun out," he said. To keep the *world* out, I grumbled to myself.

Off we went, they to their yogic Salutes to the Sun and Daniel and I to the shady pondside path. On arrival, I removed the blanket. Now Daniel could see the natural world. He turned his head to watch the trees above him. Their shapes entertained him as I pushed the stroller around the pond.

When we came to a clearing under a canopy of maples, I lifted him out of the stroller. I whisked off his socks, and set his feet—maybe for the first time—on Mother Earth. His toes explored the grass, a tree stump, a granite boulder. He wiggled and bounced on the bumpy grains of mica, quartz and feldspar—ooh, nice feel!

I knew, right then, what we'd do together, Daniel and I. We'd be nature buddies.

I'd show him what I loved as a child: salamanders, Indian pipe, pine trees, red shale, gooey marsh and trees to climb. Daniel may be a city kid, but still, we'd "do nature" together. We would explore his neighborhood's natural spots, one by one. We'd feel inchworms, catch ladybugs, collect pine cones, skip pebbles, make maple "noseys," blow dandelion seeds and kiss soft moss.

Later, I told his parents about our nature adventure. They were not pleased. "His feet are dirty!" my son remarked, as he grabbed a Handiwipe. "I see a cut on his foot."

I remembered my own country-toughened feet as a child. I showed off their calluses—proof of a summer of barefoot play. But I did not argue with my son. Instead, I promised that I'd be more careful next time.

The next week, my son and daughter-in-law brought Daniel to my house. Off they went to twist their limbs into unnatural positions, as I resumed my quest for a natural place in Daniel's life.

Daniel and I went out to look at trees that he'd seen from afar on our pond walk. I held Daniel in my now-muscular arms and stood on our porch where tree branches dangled across the railing. He grabbed a leaf and held tight. I flapped the branch up and down to show him how it moves. He got the idea and jostled his limb. His leaf soon ripped; he grabbed another. He burst out with a belly laugh. I did, too. We stripped the branch of leaves, but we didn't care.

His parents liked my story of Daniel's leafy fun, but they were alarmed as well. "He could have fallen off the porch!" my son said sternly, and then: "What about the squirrels? They crawl on those branches and they could leave droppings." He reached once more for his Handi-wipes.

As a child, my son was golden-haired and sweet, but not the outdoor type. We brought him on camping trips. There, he swatted the mosquitoes and refused to eat the campfire-blackened hot dogs. He was a city boy. He wanted his stickball and Legos, his comics and TV. It wasn't until he married a woman raised in the Sierras that he came to love woods and wilderness, for himself, if not for Daniel.

One recent Sunday, Daniel and I explored his parents' back yard. We left the plastic toys inside; I took out a twist of paper bag as a plaything. I threw aside the blanket his parents usually kept between him and the earth. I sneaked off his socks and let him feel the grass. He pulled and babbled. I got down on my belly to see what he saw. I liked the view. We rolled on the ground, grabbing whatever we could reach.

I heard the bumblebee's drone before I saw its huge and fuzzy body. It hovered over us like a helicopter and then dove straight toward my grandson. I threw the blanket over Daniel's bare legs. He yelped with surprise. I clasped his body to me. *Can a bee sting through blankets? What if he's allergic? Where's the nearest hospital?* I had no idea.

The intruder circled us twice, as if gauging our sweetness. Then it zoomed off to the next yard. Minutes passed. I slowly lifted the blanket.

Daniel blinked, his fists still clutching tufts of grass.

The beast was gone, but the yard was transformed in my eyes. Underneath the grass we had played on, bugs crawled. Black ants, red ants, beetles, sowbugs, centipedes—and a spider-like insect I couldn't even identify. *What if it burrowed in Daniel's clothes and bit him in the middle of the night?*

I saw that spears of grass were sticking to Daniel's hands and I worried: *what if he puts his fist in his mouth? He could choke on a single spear! And the paper bag twist—could the Bruegger's Bagels label on it be printed with an ink that's bad for babies?* I snatched away the bag and shoved it into my pocket.

Daniel had now rolled onto his back. He was cooing at the trees overhead. I rushed to turn him back onto his stomach—what if he looked at the sun and went *blind?*

When my son and daughter-in-law returned, they were glad that Daniel had been playing outside. "But he didn't eat dirt, did he?" my daughter-in-law asked. "Because it's got toxic lead in it." She's a soil scientist; she knows these things. "No," I said, but I felt chilled. I had never considered the dangers of back yard dirt.

Driving home, I remembered from my own childhood: the snakes in the lake, the splinters and sprains and poison ivy, the sea surf knocking me down, my howls when I fell off my bike into mud: "I'm blind!"—but I wasn't.

More soothing memories rose up: my mother examining daddy longlegs and worms and beetles with me so I wouldn't fear them. My father standing at the window to marvel with me at the flashes of lightning as my mother retreated to her room so I wouldn't catch her fear.

I knew then that my son would discover—as all parents do—that his son is tough. And I knew that my grandson would climb rocks, skate on ice, pick up snakes, take a dive and show off his callused feet.

Last week, I took Daniel to a park where a miniature Old Faithful shoots water up from a stone circle. At his first sight of the spurting water, he cried. That's OK. Next time he may reach out and feel the gushing water. Later, he may jump and splash in it. One day, he will play in it till he's soaked. He may fall and scrape a knee. Or swallow water and have to cough it up. Then—after a hug from Grandma—he'll go back for more.

JANUARY JOURNAL

Marcia Bonta

January 1, 1991

Seventeen degrees at dawn and crystal clear. The gloom of December has been cast off, at least momentarily. I can only hope that the new weather pattern of light and peace will symbolize the new year which everyone is fearing with its looming threat of war in the Middle East. Now that we have celebrated the birth of the man who symbolized light and peace with our usual mix of idealism and materialism, we have resumed business as usual in the real world.

I sat, at sunset, tucked among the Norway spruce trees while dark-eyed juncos zipped in so closely over my head that I felt the wind from their wings. They made their clicking, scolding sounds when they saw me. But eventually they settled in for the night in nearby spruces, one or two to a tree.

Suddenly a loud screaming rent the pre-dusk stillness somewhere below me in the vicinity of the Far Field Road. At first I stayed where I was, since usually my investigations of odd noises are fruitless. But the sounds continued unabated, and I finally stood up and walked to an area overlooking the road. Still I could see nothing, but the screaming went on. I sat down and scoped the area below with my binoculars. Almost at once I spotted a large bird, looking mostly dark in the dim light except for a white line above its eye, leaping around on the ground

193

and screaming like an angry troll. As I started toward it, the bird took off fast and low to the ground and was gone in an instant. Fixing my sights on the place it had been, I climbed down to find one small, downy, gray feather. Had the bird been pummeling small prey, such as a junco, or was the feather one of its own? Although I searched the area, I found no other clues to the bird's identity or hints regarding the behavior I had observed.

I hurried home to check my field guides. The most likely bet, I decided after studying the pictures, was an immature northern goshawk, but the experts claim that northern goshawks are silent except during the mating season. Next I listened to my bird-call record and easily identified the screaming as that of a northern goshawk. No other bird of prey sounded even remotely like it. To cinch the matter, I called our local bird expert, who told me he had seen a couple of northern goshawks in the valley below our property a couple of days earlier. Later, I talked to a graduate student who is studying northern goshawks and has been a licensed falconer for many years. I had witnessed, he said, what biologists call "play behavior" in young northern goshawks.

What a wonderful beginning for the new year!

January 2, 1991

Twenty degrees and cloudless at dawn, warming up to forty-eight degrees in the sun by mid-afternoon with clouds rolling up from the south. I sat in the woods overlooking the Far Field thicket and listened to the earth sigh and mutter with every vagrant breeze. In the distance, pileated woodpeckers called. Other birds cheeped occasionally, but mostly the woods were wrapped in winter silence. Walking back up the Far Field Trail, I heard a quiet tapping and looked up to see a female hairy woodpecker working over a red oak tree branch. She was the only creature I saw during my two-hour walk.

I wondered, as I moved along, why I feel compelled to be outside every day, and I finally decided that my job is to bear witness to the beauty of the earth. I am neither a scientist nor an environmental writer. To me, the outdoors means just that—being outdoors—not to hunt, fish, hike, canoe, bike or bird, but to be, even in the winter—especially in the winter—when nature is stripped to its bare essentials and few people are abroad.

Sometimes I'm tempted to move somewhere else, to another country even, and to learn a whole new culture, a whole new concept of nature. But I cannot bring myself to say good-bye to these old hills forever, despite the fact that they have been degraded by humanity's misuse. So I remain, a stubborn naturalist of place, content to look for the unusual in what many see as a commonplace and unexciting area that lacks the glamour of the north woods, the seacoast, the Rocky Mountains or the desert. But there is always more to discover here, as I learned yesterday.

Again I sat in the spruces after sunset, but instead of a northern goshawk I heard a pair of great horned owls calling back and forth while occasional dark-eyed juncos flicked into the grove to roost for the night.

January 5, 1991

Forty-five degrees at dawn, raining and foggy. But there was a swift clearing late in the morning. Despite fierce winds and warmth reminiscent of March, the light is still January, casting its long shadows in the woods, gleaming rosy on the fields and mountaintops, seen in brief snatches as the clouds race across the sky. I could almost feel the earth spinning beneath my feet.

I seemed to be alone with the wind and the light and the fantastic, cloud-studded sky, when I walked down First Field and paused to soak in the spectacle. Then a flock of dark-eyed juncos flashed across the field. As I stopped to watch the birds, I suddenly realized that I was being watched when the gray-and-white silhouette of a deer materialized at the edge of the woods. We stood looking at each other for several minutes until the deer stamped its right front hoof in alarm, flicked its tail and ran off, followed by two others I had not seen until they moved. Amazing how well the gray winter coats of the white-tailed deer meld with the tree trunks and snow.

January 8, 1991

Twenty degrees at dawn and fair, with a fresh layer of snow on the ground. I love such January days. When else is the sky as blue, the air as clear, the light as bright?

I was out early in the morning to listen to the silence and to identify each bird as it called. A crew of woodpeckers—downies and hairies—worked the tree trunks accompanied by the yanking calls of white-breasted nuthatches. Black-capped chickadees and tufted titmice gleaned insects from shrubs and tree branches. Crows cawed across the sky; evening grosbeaks quarreled over the shabby remains of fall webworm nests still hanging from the tops of black cherry trees. Then a pair of common ravens croaked along Sapsucker Ridge, one in front of the other, their wedge-shaped tails a distinctive badge that separates them from their smaller crow brethren.

Deer trails wove through the woods and over the fields, and I glimpsed several deer watching me from a distant hillside. I moved over the fields and spied the rounded, brown body of a meadow vole as it emerged from its tunnel and then popped back in again as soon as it saw me.

The fields are a good place to search for insect life. Goldenrod ball galls swelled on dried goldenrod stems, and I found the hardened foam of a praying mantis egg case firmly attached to a dried weed. Suspended from a sapling spruce at the top of First Field was a round, beige, papery ball that looked like a small oak-apple gall.

I broke it open and discovered spider silk gently cradling hundreds of minuscule crab spiders. Even though it was cold, I could see them wriggling under my hand lens, and I apologized for dooming the whole lot because of my insatiable curiosity.

I continued on to the thicket. Hieroglyphic-like marks made by a dangling grapevine brushing over the snow were a sharp contrast to the precise, fresh tracks of ruffed grouse. Two grouse erupted in front of me with an explosive noise, and I wondered how they could have been so close in that snowy landscape without my spotting them. The thicket also sheltered a couple of white-throated sparrows, a female northern cardinal and a scattering of juncos.

I walked for miles, following no trails, weaving in and out between the trees, slogging up and down hillsides, ducking under grapevines, pushing through thickets of briers, savoring the incomparable beauty of a perfect winter day.

January 11, 1991

Twenty degrees with fine snowflakes sifting down at dawn. The snow picked up momentum and fell heavily off and on all day. The feeder was mobbed with house finches. One female and two male northern cardinals and eight tree sparrows joined the party, while a solitary female purple finch pushed herself between the house finches on the feeder at midmorning.

Winter does not fit into our society's plans. Even I grumbled when a day I had planned for library research and shopping was scuttled by the weather. Tomorrow, the statewide Audubon Conference is supposed to be held in Harrisburg. Even environmental and nature-related organizations blithely plan conferences with no contingency plans at the worst time of year for traveling. Will the conference be held, and, if so, will some of us struggle there because we own four-wheel-drive vehicles made to defy nature? At least the local schools are smart. They have canceled school for the day. Too bad our whole work-and-conference-ridden society doesn't follow suit. Then we could all relax and admit that where nature is concerned we should adjust instead of resist.

Later in the day the conference was canceled, but not because of the weather alone. Our state's most environmentally-minded congressman, who was to be our speaker, couldn't come because of the impending vote in Congress regarding the Iraqi situation. Will there or won't there be war with Iraq on the fifteenth?

Despite depressing world news, I took a walk in the snowy sleet of the afternoon. Woodpeckers, both hairy and pileated, were abroad, along with white-breasted nuthatches and tufted titmice. Best of all were the golden-crowned kinglets with their high-pitched calls that, like the voices of happy children, spread instant good cheer as they foraged close to the ground.

Maybe that's why I need to get out every day—to connect myself with the sane world of nature and forget the often insane world of humanity.

January 16, 1991

Thirty-six degrees. I awoke to hear it raining this morning, and all day I have been encased in fog up to my doorstep. A song sparrow flew into the feeder. So did a single American goldfinch in his winter garb. Both are new arrivals to the feeder for the year. In mid-afternoon I watched a male downy woodpecker examining the dead, bent-over stalks of pokeweed below our back porch, but he was not tempted by the suet on the feeder.

Near dusk I took a walk in the fog and had about fifty feet of visibility. Nothing stirred except the juncos in the spruce grove at the top of First Field. I sat there, wrapped in muffled silence, the usual sounds from the valley muted by the fog. Raindrops hung in solitary splendor from the tips of the spruce needles. Juncos chirped at me from their sheltered perches deep within the spruce boughs. They seem to come into their night roosts one by one and from different directions, not in a concentrated flock as some researchers have reported. The same is true of the juncos who use the juniper bush beside the house.

A good day to start a war—gloomy with rain and fog—and so the Gulf War began early this evening with bombing raids on Baghdad. Yet here on our mountain it is so peaceful and beautiful, even on a rainy, foggy day. I am grateful to be living in such a place during these troubled, tumultuous times. Yet when, in the history of civilized humanity, have the times *not* been troubled and tumultuous? To take solace from nature instead of humanity is the true balm of Gilead for the human spirit, distraught as some of us are with the warrior mentality of so many human beings. Where is the peace of God "that passeth all understanding?" Why does the Prince of Peace's message fall mostly on deaf ears, even among Christians? I believe it is because religion, for most people, is helpful only in times of trouble. Otherwise, it is highly impractical, and its basic tenets are easy to ignore if you look at humanity with clear-eyed vision. In fact, religion has served as a rallying war cry more than once and is now doing so again.

January 18, 1991

Twenty-six degrees at dawn with snow flurries, but later a wind swept in and cleared the skies. The squeaks, groans and peeping noises of trees substitute for bird calls in winter, although I heard, for the first time this year, the spring-like *fee-bee* calls of black-capped chickadees.

Fresh ruffed grouse tracks wound along Laurel Ridge Trail, but mine were the only human tracks on the trails. Here on my mountaintop I can enjoy a stunningly beautiful, peaceful winter day while lying against the Far Field Road bank. I can contemplate the blue sky and scudding clouds, soak in the sunshine and breathe deeply the bracing winter air. But halfway around the world missiles have been launched at Israel by Iraq, and most of the rest of civilization watches the action live from Tel Aviv on cable television. What a sorry world we have where the winter entertainment is watching people at war. In the words of poet Richard Shelton, "Wars occur because men want them and peace occurs when they are tired." I hope they are soon tired.

January 21, 1991

Thirty degrees at dawn with a light, wet snow falling—a wedding-cake snow that brought in large numbers of birds to the feeder this morning. The tree sparrows doubled to ten and fed among the sixty-five house finches mobbing the porch and feeder. Those feisty sparrows frequently threatened the finches and any other birds in defense of their turf. The tufted titmice, black-capped chickadees and white-breasted nuthatches seemed more intimidated, so they waited until the finches were spooked off and then snatched their own food. Twenty dark-eyed juncos, too, held their places among the finches and were not intimidated. The northern cardinals were their usual royal but ultracautious selves. Taken one by one, the other birds will challenge a house finch and usually win. But the overwhelming finch numbers defeated the others. When fifteen to twenty house finches crowded the feeder, pushing, shoving and yelling like a gang of bullies, no other species dared intrude except an occasional extrabold tree sparrow or white-breasted nuthatch that slides in from the side. But when a red-bellied woodpecker sailed in, they all scattered as chaff before the wind.

Shortly after noon the snow stopped, and the sun shone in fits and starts as I walked along the snow-covered trails. A puffball of snow sat on every mountain laurel leaf. Tree limbs and shrub twigs, with their two-inch-high snow layers, created a lacework of white against a deep blue sky. The snow glistened with light, and I spent unforgettable hours of beauty wandering through snow showers spilled off the tree branches by the wind. Once I sat quietly on the Far Field Road watching three deer peacefully feeding on the bank not far away. Chickadees *fee-beed* despite the cold. It must be the increased light, and not the warmth, that triggers them to sing their spring song in the midst of a snowy day.

January 25, 1991

After a two-day trip to Pittsburgh I returned to the mountain. To most people this place would be relegated to the realm of unreality, but to me this is where my real life is. All other is illusion.

Thirteen degrees at dawn, clearing and beautiful. I found the top off our trash can this morning and a few plastic strips from the orange juice containers on the back step. Then, while following fox tracks from the old garden area up to the top of First Field, periodically losing them where the snow had melted, I spotted a jelly jar lid with puncture marks in it and its edge slightly bashed in as if an animal had carried it in its teeth. In all likelihood it was a fox.

I continued to follow multiple fox tracks over to our neighbor's property, up his logging road to the top of Sapsucker Ridge and then back along the ridge top on our land heading for the Far Field. In some places veritable animal highways wound through the woods, and I wondered if the highway-building mentality originated from our mammalian connections. Most animals, like people, follow the crowd. But occasionally tracks deviated from the norm as if the creature *were* marching to a different drummer. Some took the way most traveled by; others followed their own instincts. Who says that animals are different from people? To follow animal tracks in the snow is to wonder just how different animals are from us. Some took the path of least resistance; others seemed to delight in the exotic. Still others chose the more challenging trail. But all eventually went over the rock-strewn mountainside where I could not follow without fear of falling. So, in the end, I was defeated by the physical superiority of the creatures I was following, left to ponder what I had seen as I drowsed against my favorite Far Field log in the winter sunlight.

Walking back along the Far Field Road and down First Field, I saw so many fox tracks that I envisioned the long, white, winter nights filled with dancing foxes paying court in the moonlight.

January 27, 1991

Seventeen degrees at dawn with a fresh inch-and-a-half of snow, clearing into a sparkling day with Dresden-blue skies. Nine deer fed on the Sapsucker Ridge power-line right-of-way. Others crossed the Far Field Road and grazed above and below it. The silence was broken by the brisk scolding of a Carolina wren and the cawing of a gang of crows. At the entrance to the Far Field I discovered a maze of fox tracks with a sprinkle of urine on a raised hillock. Near the thicket I found a scattering of ruffed grouse feathers surrounded by small fox tracks.

Today is Super Bowl Sunday so no one is abroad, but since yesterday was positively the last legal hunting day (the end of the extended ruffed grouse season), and fur prices are low, what is there to bring people out into the woods? They will make no profit except for their souls. Consequently, the only human prints on the mountain are mine.

As I sat at the base of a tree, golden-crowned kinglets came swinging in overhead to call and feed in the tree branches above me—wonderful birds with whom to share a peaceful Sunday morning. They acted as if I were not there and foraged within ten feet of where I was sitting without showing any alarm. Golden-crowned kinglets are the best and most satisfying of winter birds—easy to see and identify, not dependent upon or even interested in bird feeders, and able to make a good living off the meager offerings of winter. This winter, unlike other years, I have been finding them in same-species flocks. Previously I would often discover a couple feeding with tufted titmice, black-capped chickadees, downy woodpeckers or brown creepers. They, like Carolina wrens, have been increasing over the last several winters, welcome additions to the fauna of January.

January 28, 1991

Thirty-one degrees at dawn with a light frosting of new, wet snow. But the sky cleared quickly, tufted titmice *peter-petered* from every direction, and there was a steady *drip-drip* from melting snow.

I was sitting at the base of Sapsucker Ridge by nine o'clock in the morning, soaking in the sunlight, basking in the beauty, listening to the birds—tufted titmice, black-capped chickadees, American crows, Carolina wrens, white-breasted nuthatches, northern cardinals and downy, hairy and red-bellied woodpeckers. Jet trails disappeared almost as quickly as they were etched across the deep blue sky to the northwest, but they remained in the southeast a little longer where there were still light clouds. The barn roof steamed as if on fire from the evaporating snow. Individual droplets dangling from tree branches twinkled like stars and captured prisms of light to dazzle my eyes. Mostly they were translucent, but a few flashed yellow, orange and red.

I walked over to our neighbor's land, now owned by a lumberman, and passed her old garden—lost dreams, lost hopes, a sagging fence, a broken-down shed, an abandoned car. I remembered the happy days when her brother was alive, when a friend cultivated her garden and helped with her bee hives, when she had at last found some peace of mind after a troubled life. But now she is gone, her brother is dead and her friend has left his wife to live with another woman hundreds of miles away. There are no more human footprints. The back acres have been reclaimed by the foxes, and the birds sing with joyous abandon. In the end, all flesh is grass. Nature's peace settles like a mantle over the reclaimed land. Rivers of deer tracks flow through the snow, and the squirrels proclaim their rights to the trees.

January 29, 1991

Twenty-four degrees at dawn with Sapsucker Ridge lit scarlet from the rising sun. Jet trails remained like long white fingers in the southeast while the rest of the sky was blue. The machines at the limestone quarry in the valley were so loud that their noise penetrated the walls of the house this morning, and later, when I sat above the Far Field Road, I could still hear them. Other valley sounds also funneled up distinctly, shattering the illusion of winter's peace.

Several days ago the war took on an even more horrifying aspect as Iraq began flooding the Persian Gulf with Kuwaiti oil, creating the largest oil slick in history. Experts on cleaning up oil spills were rushed to the Gulf, and a bombing raid was launched to destroy the pumps emitting the oil. But what madness! They are destroying an entire ecosystem from which all the Gulf area residents prosper. Birds and fish are dead or dying, and the slick is moving inexorably toward Saudi Arabia, where desalination plants process saltwater into drinking water. And there lies the explanation for what seemed at first like unreasoning madness. Destroy a civilization's water source and you destroy a civilization, especially a desert people's. But such a deed demonstrates how sick humanity is—always putting the petty ambitions of people above the nurturing of the natural world. The planet seems too small to support so many rapacious humans bent on victory at all costs. Of course, we did the same thing in the Vietnam War with defoliants, and we tried to talk Peru into using them to wipe out the drug trade. Why must nature pay for humanity's deeds? Or, more to the point, when will we discover that everything *is* connected to everything else and that when we fiddle with nature we imperil our own survival?

An incident from William Warner's *Beautiful Swimmers* says it all regarding humanity's relationship with nature. A Maryland biologist tried to explain new conservation measures to the Tangier Sound Watermen's Union on Smith Island and asked for discussion. According to Warner, one islander finally rose to his feet and responded, "Mr. Manning, there is something you don't understand. These here communities on the shore, our little towns here on the island and over to mainland, was all founded on the right of free plunder. If you follow the water, that's how it was and that's how it's got to be." The right of free plunder has beggared us and will continue to do so.

I sat quietly in the corner of First Field listening to the tapping of an unseen woodpecker. After a time I found it: a female pileated quietly tapping and then lifting her head as if she were listening for the sound of carpenter ants in the bark. She repeated that several times before flying off. Next, a pair of foraging golden-crowned kinglets flew into the area, followed by a white-breasted nuthatch, several black-capped chickadees and a female downy woodpecker. The downy landed in a tree next to me and made more noise than the pileated. All ignored my presence as they went about their business, so I had the rare pleasure of feeling as if I were an integral part of the scene and not an unwanted interloper.

Continuing my exploration of Sapsucker Ridge, I discovered a new fox hole at the base of an old stump near the Sapsucker Ridge powerline right-of-way. I also disturbed two deer basking in the sunshine of the Sapsucker Ridge thicket. One bounded quickly up the hill, while the other leaped slowly along. The bottom half of its right front leg was missing, probably shot off during hunting season. Several years ago we watched a doe that had lost most of her left hind leg not only learn to run nearly as fast as the other deer, but give birth to twins and raise them to maturity.

On the veranda, in the warm sun of mid-afternoon the thermometer registered fifty degrees. Through the walls of the house I heard a raven croaking and went out to watch as it flew from its perch in the woods.

January 30, 1991

Forty-eight degrees by midmorning and absolutely clear. I sunbathed against the Far Field Road bank in utter peace. Winter silence on top of a worn-down, ancient, Pennsylvania mountaintop, with only the cries of occasional birds to keep me company, can be as purifying an experience as forty days in the desert. Life is stripped to its barest essentials to survive the winter, and the sun pours from the sky unimpeded by tree leaves. I can see far in any direction, so I tend to spot the shyer creatures, such as porcupines, foxes, even a bobcat once, in the winter. But my companions today were more commonplace: a pileated woodpecker flying silently past, a golden-crowned kinglet calling and fluttering in front of me, a tree sparrow flying up from the brush to shake its feathers at me, four deer filing up Sapsucker Ridge.

Later, I sat at the crest of First Field, surveying the landscape and thinking, I hold all the joys of life in two hands—a loving, encouraging husband who has nurtured my growth and unselfishly lived here for my pleasure, three sons who were my close companions in their childhood and youth and who still share most of their lives with me, a home that is warm and simply furnished with minimal fancy furniture and maximum books, a handful of friends who share my concerns and interests and a stable lifestyle dependent more on spiritual than material things.

January 31, 1991

Thirty-three degrees at dawn. An absolutely radiant day, not a cloud in the sky, and I was out at eight in the morning to walk down Laurel Ridge toward the Tyrone Gap. As I reached the end of the ridge, I had a graphic view of the limestone quarry. Layer after layer of gouged-out hillside with all the noisy, earth-eating machines sitting at rest in the bottom of the desolation. Without that sight and the sound of vehicles from the valley, the view of blue-misted hills and rolling farm fields would have been timeless. But people seem to adjust to the gradual degradation of their environment, anything to further the technological success of our civilization. What? Question the folly of removing whole mountainsides as quickly as possible to fix up and build more roads? You can't hold back progress.

Winter is the time to see visions. I seem to hear prophetic voices, railing at humanity's failings, prophesying the end of the world. Light pours from the sky, bathing my thoughts with the heat of conviction. They are voices crying in the wilderness, preparing the way for doom that no one believes and no one heeds. The earth withers away as I watch, and I am stunned by the rapidity with which it destructs once it begins to unravel from too much use and too little love.

IN SEARCH OF THE
BLUE-FOOTED BOOBY

———————————————— *Marguerite Guzman Bouvard*

I discovered nature when I was nine years old and my family moved from New York City to a Midwestern suburb. After school I would lie on my bed for hours dreamily watching the clouds or take long walks with an elderly neighbor who pointed out the Indian trail trees in our town. When I became an adolescent I had three favorite books that I read over and over: *Secret Tibet,* by Fosco Mariani, *Half Mile Down,* by William Beebee, and *Kon Tiki,* by Thor Heyerdahl. While hungrily turning the pages, I was climbing the Himalayas chanting *Om Mani Padme Hum* as I rounded the peaks; I was in the bathyscaphe, Trieste, peering at electric fish; I was on a raft listening to the water hissing between the slats. Our house in Wilmette was not far from Lake Michigan and at night I could hear the waves heaving and tossing through my window, a sound that became so much a part of me I felt torn when I was away from it. I had begun my double life: the secret self who takes flight in nature and solitude, and the social self who goes about the practicalities of life in this world.

> *First there was the sky*
> *with its continents and in the center,*
> *a green country from which I sent messages.*
> *Nights I was always on deck. When I woke up,*
> *there was still the crash of waves in my ears.*

Although I studied political science in college and eventually became a professor in that discipline, nature always occupied a large space in my imagination and my being. I found that we live in different selves, each following its own path throughout our lifetime: the visible one, and the invisible unfolding of the dreamer. They also have their own calendars, and while rearing a family and pursuing my career as a professor, the dreamer went underground. It was only when my children reached adolescence that I returned to my earlier interest and began to write poetry as well as to keep a journal. That journal contained an impassioned and meticulous observation of nature, which for me was an inextricable part of self-discovery.

While my children were growing up, we vacationed in the Alps where my French husband had summered as a child, and we hiked and picnicked among cloud-covered slopes. Those scenes took root in my poetry and my journals. But the Alps have been settled since time immemorial and there are traces of former inhabitants and passersby in the most isolated mountain passes.

In 1978, I experienced the wilderness for the first time on Ossabaw Island off the Georgia coast when I was in residence at an artists' retreat. Living on that island evoked so many emotions: fear, exultation and, ultimately, a deep peace. I learned to avoid copperheads, wild boars with their young, and to step through the dense foliage with alertness and respect. This did not come easily; once, I encountered a sow with her brood across the path and found myself running backwards in terror. Most days after working on my poetry, I would walk through the woods with as much trepidation as wonder. I heard so many sounds I couldn't identify, such as a very loud splashing in a pond which I imagined could have been an alligator entering the water. Since my walks were solitary, no one could see me retreat behind a tree when I encountered strange rustlings in the brush, nor could anyone know how my heart was pounding while I sat on the edge of the water, drawn by the beauty around me while wrestling with my unease at the unknown.

But I also discovered the regenerative powers of being in the wilderness; I became part of a vibrant web of life and the problems of the outside assumed their proper proportion, moving away from the focus of my concerns. My boundaries fell away as I soared with a tern I watched near an estuarial river most afternoons or nestled in the middle of a dead tree on the edge of a solitary beach. Writing in my journal, I traced my journey away from the burdens I had brought with me and into my deepest self. I had come to regard nature as healer as well as a source of wonder and delight.

> When she first arrived she kept a journal
> Then she began releasing
> her breath until it mingled
> with the damp breath of palms.
> Then her hands wriggled free
> finding their own way
> and her pauses lengthened like ripples
> on a windswept lake.

At the other end of the island was a residence for scientists and graduate students engaged in various projects. One of them was a tall, athletic, young woman who visited us one evening with slides of her stay in Ecuador as a member of the Peace Corps. She spoke of clearing fields and learning Quechua as if they were the most natural things in the world. I was, and am, thin, with mostly dormant muscles, and could hardly imagine myself in her shoes. Those experiences were not for me, I concluded, until a slide appeared on the screen of her trip to the Galápagos Islands: a nest of blue-footed boobies. My heart lurched with longing for these rare birds. They are endemic to the islands, more absurd than beautiful and insistently unique. I was younger then, forty, but I stored that memory the way one harbors the face of an early love. I never dreamed I would have either the opportunity or the determination to actually visit those islands. They swam below my consciousness as I rushed from teaching classes in political science to caring for my children, from volunteering to housekeeping, all the routines that are so necessary yet make inroads on the soul. Buried beneath those roles was the poet and the woman who loved zoology, watching nature programs on television with a passion.

As I moved through middle-age, my fiftieth year loomed before me as an important turning point. I imagined myself climbing Mont Blanc in France, knowing full well I was not physically in shape for such a venture. My son teased me, suggesting that he drop me at the summit by helicopter. It was not so much Mont Blanc with its blue-green glaciers that attracted me as the need to experience a sense of freedom and to explore the wilderness in my own heart.

One afternoon in the late fall of 1988, exactly ten years after my experience on Ossabaw, a close friend and I were sitting at my dining-room table critiquing each other's poetry when she announced dreamily that she had a sabbatical coming up and would really like to visit the Galápagos Islands. "I'll go with you," I replied immediately, with abandon. We discussed the possibility as if we were talking about the most mundane matter. At the time, it seemed so far-fetched, but after a number of discussions our plans were in full swing. My friend Martha was a professor of literature at the University of Massachusetts and I was teaching at a nearby college; we would go in January between semesters. Setting off on such an adventure was the realization of my younger self who had lived in the world of her books.

I was fifty, and would turn fifty-one in January, and experiencing the first year of what would eventually become a debilitating illness, interstitial cystitis. Although I didn't know it at the time, this would be the last wild adventure I would be able to manage. I worried endlessly about the arrangements, whether the small boat we were planning to take would have the facilities for someone who needed to get up frequently at night. In fact, I decided to cancel the trip at one point unless we found a craft with the minimum facilities. My friend was a top-notch planner and thanks to her we found a package that included a flight with Air Ecuatoriana, a few days in Quito before and after a week on a vessel accommodating a small group of passengers. My daughter put together a kit for me which included all kinds of implements, such as a Swiss knife that became an octopus of cutlery at the press of a button, and my husband bought me a pair of field glasses so I could observe wildlife.

The night before we left, I was in terrible pain and slept very little. My husband convinced me that it was the chance of a lifetime and that I should go anyway. Exhausted but terribly excited, I set off on a wintry January afternoon for the beginning of an adventure which would also include the journey to Quito. Martha and I sat over coffee at Logan Airport in Boston as we waited for our departure to New York, amazed that we were actually en route. We arrived at Kennedy Airport in the early stages of a snowstorm and waited for our flight to Quito. Ecuatoriana Airlines kept sending messages over the loudspeaker about the unfortunate delays in our departure, while the snowfall became more and more serious. By midnight, the announcements ceased and we joined a cluster of worried passengers standing around the Air Ecuatoriana counter. Martha fell asleep leaning against a wall when at three in the morning, the airline finally announced its decision to put us up in a motel for what remained of the night. Our flight left at noon the following day, not for Quito, but for the steamy port of Guayaquil where we spent a night in an equally steamy hotel.

When we finally made it to Quito, we watched with dismay as the emptied luggage carousel circled without our bags. It was summer in Ecuador, eighty degrees in the city, and as the days passed, our luggage failed to arrive at the hotel. I was dressed for winter in a heavy coat and padded boots which thudded against the sidewalk as we trudged through the city.

We spent our days trying to trace our baggage and combing the stores with little to show for our efforts. Strangely enough, there were places that sold such modern items as contact lenses, but the clothing stores had little in stock and practically nothing in our size. One saleswoman in a shoe store suggested I stuff a pair of too-large sandals with paper so they would fit, and in desperation, I followed her advice. Besides the huge sandals, I found a long tee shirt which could double as a nightgown, and a pair of oversized shorts. More serious was the fact that Martha's suntan lotion, a luxury unavailable in Quito, remained in her bag in New York City. My olive skin was much more resistant to the sun than hers, and what I had to share was insufficient to protect her.

After a few days in Quito, we left for James Island. As our small plane landed on the island, Martha was overjoyed and exuberant, but I was tired from lack of sleep and alarmed when I saw how small our craft was. The fact that we had few possessions proved to be a blessing because our tiny cube of a room had no space for luggage. There was a single hook on the wall and the small portholes doubled as drying racks for our underwear. The size of the boat would turn out to be an advantage as we trawled among the islands unobtrusively.

We were welcomed on board by a silent, middle-aged captain, Rolf Wittmer, a handyman, and a cook who put out a wonderful spread for us, including wine made from oranges, and a voluble young Ecuadorian woman who would serve as our guide. We were a congenial group of nine who read Darwin at night in the galley where we ate and relaxed, sleeping below deck. The passengers included a German couple on their honeymoon, a young couple from Washington with whom I stayed in touch and a woman from California who became a lifelong friend. Heidi lived out my fantasies of climbing mountains; an inveterate trekker, she had just scaled Cotapaxi before joining us. An American woman married to an Ecuadorian brought her two lively sons and invited us to her home in Quito. It was an auspicious beginning.

I remember the wonderful feeling of rocking on the water as I fell asleep the first night and of being wakened at 3 A.M. by a loud barking. In my half-sleep I thought of dogs and Manhattan, but I was hearing the joyous baying of seals in the ocean.

The Galápagos is an archipelago of thirteen large and six smaller islands as well as forty exposed rocks and islets that lie on the equator. The cool Humboldt Current flowing up from the Antarctic Ocean brings seals and penguins to the islands and prevents coral formations. The islands are made of black shield volcanos which rise symmetrically, giving way to wonderfully patterned lava plains; they are populated by primitive reptiles and by a wealth of birds. A few of them have some feral animals such as goats, pigs, cats or dogs, the only traces of former settlers who tried to eke out a living in agriculture. Our group slowly made its way among the smaller islands, landing at James Bay and proceeding to Bartoleme, Seymour, Baltra, Santa Fe, Espanola and Floreana. We also stopped in Puerto Ayora on Santa Cruz where the Charles Darwin Research Station was located and where we were able to see the Galápagos turtles which give the islands their name. Then we sailed to Rabida and back to James Island.

The first morning we came ashore on the Isle Bartolome at six o'clock to avoid the noon sun. Even at that hour, the island seemed to be carved from light that shimmered on the waves and on the stretch of beach below the black volcanic cones. When I saw a group of seal families bunched around the sand, I was so overcome, I lost my footing and landed on my behind with field glasses I had been clutching careening against the rocks. As I hauled myself up with much embarrassment and ruefully examined my dented field glasses, our guide warned us against touching the baby seals because the mother recognized her young by their smell and would reject them if our odor remained on the pups. We also saw what looked like truck tracks along the sand, which were the paths of sea turtles as they moved from the ocean to dig nests and lay their eggs before returning to the water.

If the wildlife was abundant—seals, frigate birds, flamingos, lizards, marine iguanas, sea turtles—the islands were bleak with little vegetation, cinder cones rising up in their nakedness beneath a brutal sun. The scattered clumps of *tiquilia* plants on the sands of Bartolome remained pale gray, their leaves covered with tiny hairs to help prevent the evaporation of moisture, and to serve as protection against that pitiless light. Other islands were glistening flows of *pahohoe* lava, their swirling patterns like frozen waves. It seemed as if we had moved back in geological time. There was a beauty and integrity in the stark landscape where our voices and our very presence seemed out of place. We were dwarfed by the sky which turned cloudy in the afternoons, the huge expanse of ocean and the islands stubbornly asserting themselves against the elements. Although the Galápagos have long been regarded as a biological and geological mecca, this was also a space that required much of those who shared it, making claims on the soul as well as the imagination.

> *She knew that on the mainland days go by*
> *as trees blur past a speeding car,*
> *but she could barely remember all that.*
> *She was putting by for the winter,*
> *storing moments carefully.*

What the islands required was the practice of concentration, seeing with the whole self; the Sally lightfoot crabs scuttling over lava fields, the different varieties of finches flitting through the branches, the distinctive black markings of the masked boobies, the largest boobies. In the seeming bleakness of the landscape were lessons of adaptation and evolution and the infinite diversity of being. I remembered my biology professor in college lecturing us on the practice of observation, telling us that we had to return to the same specimen beneath the microscope day after day until we really saw.

It seemed as if I was slipping into meditation as we gradually made our circuit, visiting a different island each morning and late afternoon. Tired from our long days, we generally went to bed soon after supper and a quiet period of reading from the small library on board. As we progressed, I became used to walking among colonies of seals, to the silence punctuated by the waves, the combination of vastness and intimacy of the wilderness. What struck me most was the indifference and innocence of the animal populations. The seals would doze lazily in the sun, uninterested and undisturbed by our presence as we walked by. The bird colonies of masked boobies and swallow-tailed gulls had established ownership of the coves and cliffs, and we were of no more importance than the passing winds. I found that oddly comforting, as if we had returned to our proper places in the rich tapestry of life, no longer the center, but a small thread in a pulsating animal and mineral world that would outlive our transience. Awed by the spectacles, our group moved quietly along the trails, melting into the landscape. I remember gliding through a salt lagoon in the dinghy and watching the sea turtles rise to the surface, singly or in pairs, tumbling and mating. Thunderheads hovered above us as we bobbed in a sphere of water. The days and hours were seamless; I felt as if I had been released into a peace and freedom in which my inner and outer worlds coincided.

> *The land tamed her just as a fox*
> *once tamed a prince*
> *and taught him how to watch for the first*
> *eddy in the wheat heads,*
> *how to wait for him at the same time*
> *inching closer every day.*

My concepts of nature altered during our voyage as I learned that lizards frequently have heart attacks from the sun, and watched the marauding frigate birds with their eight-foot wing span and magnificent red pouches. While majestic in flight, they are, nonetheless, predators of smaller birds. Our guide informed us that male seals are given to murder, shattering my view of humans as the only species that kills wantonly. Martha and I were swimming blissfully among a group of seals when our guide ordered us to hurry out of the ocean because of the danger from the large male churning the waters near us. If we were present at the process of both geological and biological creation, we were also witness to its ruthlessness. As well as scenes of rare beauty, the islands and their inhabitants offered a naked view of the essentially raw and violent battle of life.

Although our group was always alone as we moved along the bays, and we felt as if we were the first to step on the pristine shores, the outside world had cast its shadow of destruction. We learned that on some islands, the sea turtles were dying out because so many rats from the cruise ships had migrated to the islands, invading their nests and devouring their eggs. There was no remedy which would not destroy an already-fragile ecology. Occasionally, we skirted large and noisy ships whose passengers would certainly land among the wildlife with no concern for its well-being. Once we took the dinghy to the famous Devil's Hole for snorkeling. After days of solitude and silence, I was stunned to see mobs of people splashing in the water, jolting me back to the world I thought I had left behind. Despite the fact that the Galápagos National Park incorporates nearly ninety-seven percent of the area, that no one may travel there without a licensed guide and visitor sites are limited with the trails marked in order to preserve it as a wilderness, I worried about the havoc too-large groups of visitors would wreak on the wildlife. I remember we were just leaving one of the islands when a large group of tourists poured out over the sands and began to disperse, ignoring the paths. I began to wonder whether I was contributing to the destruction of this Eden by my own presence.

If our guide was enthusiastic and informative as she escorted us across lava flows and up sandy hills, our captain was dour and silent. He intrigued me; when we landed on the island of Floreana where he was brought up and where his elderly mother lived, I grew even more puzzled. I had an overwhelming feeling of eeriness and unease as I confronted a gravesite with a stone monument that seemed anomalous in a world where matter was transformed in an endless cycle of destruction and birth. It turned out to be the graves of our captain's father and older brother. Close by was a hotel with a few empty rooms and a small shop with postcards, tee shirts and sundries run by Mrs. Wittmer. Further inland was a wooden post-office box where once passing ships would gather messages and where we could drop off mail visitors would pick up as a courtesy. Martha and I dropped off self-addressed cards which we later received with New York postmarks. Aside from that jerrybuilt box, the island seemed empty, with a single and short path. Mrs. Wittmer depended on passing ships for her livelihood. Silently she served us a typical German meal on a lace tablecloth by the light of kerosene lamps.

Our guide gave us fragments of the events that brought Rolf Wittmer's parents to South America, and later I read about the strange and violent saga of three families pitted against the wilderness and each other. The Wittmers migrated from Germany in the early thirties in order to build a new life as homesteaders. Heinz and Margaret Wittmer had read William Beebee's book, *Galápagos: World's End,* and were attracted by this seeming paradise as Heinz had suffered in the trenches during World War I only to face the economic insecurity of the post-war period. The Wittmers' son, Harry, suffered from health problems, but they were unable to afford proper care and hoped that life on Floreana would provide him with a chance to recover. They set off in 1932 when Margaret was six months pregnant with Rolf.

Living on the island was a philosopher and medical doctor, Freidrich Ritter, and his ailing mistress, Dore Strauch. They had set off from Berlin in 1929 in search of a rather grandiose utopian vision, ill-equipped for the rigors of living in an isolated wilderness. This provoked serious tensions between them and exacerbated the already-frail mental condition of Dr. Ritter. They were later joined by a woman who called herself Baroness Eloisa von Wagner Bosquet and who held one of her two lovers, Lorenz, in virtual slavery. He managed to escape by posting a notice for passing ships on the wooden post-office box, but was found dead along with the captain of a Norwegian vessel that took him away from the island. Friedrich Ritter died of a mysterious poisoning in 1934, thus ending his bitter feud with the Baroness's household and his own tortured search for a mystical paradise.

As soon as they arrived, the hard-working Wittmers constructed a wooden house and later a stone dwelling, adapting themselves to the island by using the materials at hand and planting a garden. They frequently supplied their reckless neighbors with food and water, even harboring the desperate Lorenz during the last days before his flight from the island. The endurance of that family through periods of drought and the inroads of their neighbors was reflected in the faces of Rolf and Margaret Wittmer. While Dore Strauch, the Baroness and her lover fled the island after a few difficult years, the Wittmers created a life for themselves and became one with their adopted home.

For me, Floreana had two identities: its unsavory past hung in the atmosphere, but it also had a beauty that remained untainted by the events of the 1930s. As the evening sun hung low, we watched flamingos moving quietly and regally along the edges of a small pond, their colors reflecting the pale orange swaths against the horizon. The noise and tumult of human events represented no more than an instant in time and space. In this scene of utter serenity, I felt as if I had reached the heart of the world and the unfolding of an enduring reality.

I celebrated my birthday by climbing a cinder cone on Hood Island with Martha and a few of the other travelers. It was not Mont Blanc and it was only a short hike to the top, but I felt as if I had reached some sort of pinnacle in my imagination; like Fosco Mariani, I had left behind work, country and routine and entered another world. In a photo of Martha and me, our arms companionably entwined, we are wearing our broad-brimmed hats and long-sleeved shirts borrowed from the men on our tour, our binoculars slung around our necks, looking very much like nineteenth-century travelers in the desert.

Before completing our circuit back to James Bay and the flight to Quito, we spent a wondrous morning walking through a nesting ground of blue-footed boobies whose turquoise-colored feet were startling in the colorless landscape. The chicks were newly hatched; dozens of white, fluffy balls were standing erect, each flanked by a parent and vibrating with great intensity to mitigate the intense heat, a scene of the utmost privacy and beauty. It was as if my secret self had moved to the center and my public life had vanished into its insignificance. This was the moment which would nourish the dreamer for years to come.

And while the woman learned to read
the flight of birds
the islands moved closer.
They learned her gait,
the contours of her body.
Then slowly they entered her, singing
through her blood.

OVERLAND TO KAIETEUR FALLS

Elizabeth Evans

Most people only can dream of seeing one of nature's most glorious waterfalls. Now I was going to see Kaieteur Falls for the second time! I had seen Victoria Falls during my Peace Corps days in Africa and had visited Niagara Falls while passing through New York State with my Swiss friend, but after seeing Kaieteur Falls during a Springfield College/YMCA summer exchange project in British Guiana, I never expected to return the following year to see again this secluded, hard-to-reach waterfall in the middle of a dense tropical forest. But I was back with a second group of Springfield College students who were going to hold coaching clinics and recreation-leadership seminars throughout the country. After a flight from New York City with an overnight stay on the island of Curacao, the group was welcomed in Georgetown at a formal gathering where the appropriate speeches were made. Each member of the group was assigned to a private home to stay the night.

Guyana is on the northeastern curve of South America. Squeezed between Venezuela and Suriname on two sides, with Brazil to the south, this former Dutch possession became a British territory in the early 1800s. In 1966, it gained independence, dropped the *British* and changed the *i* in Guiana to *y*. When someone in conversation slipped out of habit and called the country "B.G.," embarrassment was quickly covered by implying that the initials stood for Before Guyana. I had the good fortune to bring students to the country the summer before and the summer afterward. Although the land size is about that of the state of Idaho, nearly ninety percent of the people live in a forty-mile-wide coastal band that the Dutch made habitable by draining the swampy land and building sea walls. Inland, the topography ranges from jungle and rain forest to upland grassy savannas. The word *guyana* is thought to be an Amerindian word implying "land of many waters." Long rivers drain from the interior to the sea. As they descend there are dozens of waterfalls. Great Falls on the Kamarang River drops sixteen hundred feet. However, the world's most famous waterfalls are rated not only by height, but also by the volume of water flow, the crest width and a number of other considerations. In Guyana, people generally want to see Kaieteur Falls. We did, too!

Formalities aside and with a good night's sleep, we met at the boat launch in the early morning to start a trip designed to combine sightseeing and project-planning before starting to work. The first stage of the trip took several hours in the relative comfort of a large passenger boat on the Demarara River. The college students, mostly undergraduates from middle-class suburbia, had never been out of the United States. They sat with eyes glued to the passing scenery, fascinated by the sights of the countryside. Never before had they encountered houses elevated for air circulation (necessary because much of the coastal land is below sea level), let alone houses without window glass and only huge shutters to keep out the sun and rain. At a distance the structures resembled grayish-white marshmallows on toothpicks. Somewhat closer, they looked like frosted gingerbread houses on stilts.

From the deck of the boat, watching cars pass on a single-width strip of gray tarmac road with red dirt edges and a drainage canal on either side became a game to see who could guess correctly which car would give way first. A second game evolved, trying to guess which way a vehicle would go to dodge the bicycles, chickens, pigs, goats, donkeys, people and other assorted creatures who wanted the center-of-the-road right-of-way, too. Several of the students thought that if they watched closely enough, they might see one of the gentle manatees that inhabit the canals. Since the canals are really sluice ditches contaminated by sewage, garbage, dead animals, laundry by-products and anything else someone wants to get rid of or wash out to sea, it was impossible to see anything other than dirty water. How these unusual and gentle creatures survive in such a filthy environment surely must be another of nature's great miracles.

Observing other passengers was a multicultural experience for the students. Guyana is sometimes called the "Land of Six Peoples." More than half of the Guyanese people are descendants of the East Indian indentured servants brought into the country to work in the hot, humid sugar cane, rice or tobacco fields. About thirty percent of the population has African slave roots, and much of the remainder of the populace contains some sort of racial mixture. This mixture includes those of Chinese, European and indigenous Amerindian descent. While the official language is English, one hears a mixture of accents and dialects. Several students asked me how I was able to understand when people spoke to us. Usually, they found it difficult to tell if they were speaking English or Hindi. I explained that most of the people in Malawi, where I served in the Peace Corps, were Africans and/or East Indians speaking English as a Second Language. So I was accustomed to hearing accents and intonations similar to those we were hearing in Guyana. I also had the advantage of having been in the country the previous summer, and I knew that in the local patois the verb *to be* is usually omitted and *th*, as in *Th*ursday, is pronounced *tur* as in *tur*key.

At the end of the boat ride, we piled our gear and our bodies into the bed of a big lorry. Then we spent the better part of a day being jounced around the flatbed of that rather decrepit old vehicle while traveling west toward the wide, placid Essequibo River. Breathing the exhaust fumes and road dust was bad enough, but the constant bouncing around was even worse for me. I thought about those motel beds where for a quarter the bed vibrates and decided someone should do a research study to determine at what level does being jiggled around change from being pleasurable to annoying or even debilitating. Everyone was glad to reach the end of that stage of the trip, but it took a while to get our land legs again and to adjust to being on a nonmoving surface.

After an overnight stay at a guest house, fifteen college students, faculty leaders and several Amerindian guides loaded dugout canoes for the trip up the Essequibo to the Potaro River in newly independent Guyana. While the canoes were no doubt similar to those used by Amerindians in the interior for hundreds of years, a major concession to technology was that each canoe had a small outboard motor to assist the paddlers. Of the foreigners, only I knew what to expect: drinking river water the color of diluted root beer; the humidity of the air; the exhaustion of portaging equipment and supplies around those places the canoes could not manage to navigate; the pork-knockers dredging for gold on barges in the middle of the river; the climb through the lush forest to the top of the falls; the sounds and smells of the interior. After they got used to being in the canoes, the first thing I suggested to the passengers was to fill all personal water bottles with river water, then to add water purification tablets so the chemicals would have time to work, and drinking water would be available when needed. Some were a bit hesitant about the prospects of drinking brown water, but they got over their fear when it was pointed out that minerals, not dirt, made the color. Actually, the water was so clear that it was possible to see tree roots along the river's edge, stones on the bottom and fish. After this reassurance, they began to focus on the beauty of the river and the surrounding scenery. For the first part of the voyage, the surface of the water was smooth and peaceful, disturbed only by the paddles of our passing canoes and the occasional dipping of a passenger's foot or hand.

We left the calm Essequibo and started up the smaller, faster-flowing Potaro, past Tumatumari, where the British Guiana Consolidated Gold-fields Company had built staff and worker headquarters. Some ways upstream, it became impossible for the canoes to pass. The first portage was difficult. Loads were heavy. Footing was slippery. The air was hot and sticky. After we got back on the river, the water became more turbulent. As we passed the first of a number of barges anchored in the middle of the river, I explained the process of goldmining and how a barge sucked up the river bottom and spewed out the unwanted waste. How much gold actually was retrieved from this process, I never found out. Next, it became a game to see who could find a gold nugget lodged on the river bottom. As the sun rose in the sky, and the heat grew more intense, more of us trailed hands and feet in the cool water. This probably made it more difficult for the guides to steer, but they never told us to stop.

The second portage was longer than the first. It was no easier, but prior experience made us more efficient. Upstream, as we neared our destination, and the canoes approached the bottom of the falls, the river ran faster and the crescendo of falling water ahead of us made it necessary to speak loudly to each other. Upon our arrival, we were welcomed by the keeper of the guesthouse and his wife. The building was little more than a sparse wooden structure partitioned into several rooms. One large room was a communal eating-sitting room. Men and women were assigned by sex to one of the two large sleeping rooms. Cooking and outhouse facilities were located behind the main building. Painted yellow on the outside with natural wood inside, all walls, including those on the outside, were open at the top for air circulation. Floors were uncovered, and bare light bulbs dangled from the ceiling in each room.

Each member of the expedition unpacked and went to work hanging a handwoven Amerindian hammock for sleeping. These handwoven pieces of art had stripes and long, fringed sides that can hang down as decoration or be flipped over to become a sort of blanket for the occupant. While we went about our chores, the Guyanese cook who accompanied us readied the evening meal. A short, stocky woman of mixed racial features, she was perhaps in her late fifties or early sixties. Surely the eldest in our party, she had the only bed in the house—a small cot in the corner of the room where the women were to sleep.

Hungry and tired from the heat, the reflection of the sun in our eyes and portaging, we were glad to sit down to eat supper. The food—plain rice with a sort of vegetable stew on top, a glass of lemon squash or a cup of English tea and a banana for dessert—was as welcome as the chance to sit and rest. This simple but satisfying meal tasted great and was quickly devoured by all. However, the coffee addicts among the group were not a happy lot. When supper was over, we sat around the table and talked about the hike to the top of the falls which was planned for the next morning. Before heading to the sleeping quarters, everyone talked about the river trip and wondered about the adventure we would undertake the next day. Students were impressed by the fact the distance the river water dropped out of the Pakaraima Mountains was greater than that of Niagara and Victoria Falls combined. The cook especially was eager to see one of the wonders of her country, because very few of her compatriots ever had the chance to go to Kaieteur Falls. Those who did go rarely went on the difficult overland route. If they could afford to, they flew in to the top of the falls on a pontoon plane. Mostly it was tourists, Bauxite or diamond mining officials, sugar cane plantation owners or business men associated with rum distilleries who had enough money to travel that way.

Though this day's component of the trip went much as I expected, what I did not expect was to happen during the night. Lights were put out, and everyone except the cook climbed into a hammock to sleep. The cradle-rocking effect of the hammock combined with the energy depletion of the exhausting trip made it easy to fall asleep. At about two o'clock in the morning, I was awakened by a noise. I found my flashlight and turned it on. Scanning the room with its beam, I noticed the cook sitting up in bed with her hands holding her foot. I scrambled out of my hammock and went over to her. Blood was soaking into the sheet. I didn't know if the wound really didn't hurt, if she was in shock or if she was being stoic, but she was not crying or complaining. I asked what had happened, and she whispered that something had bitten her. On her heel was a bright pink wound about the size of a nickel. In the center were two parallel, dark lines.

Trying not to awaken the others, I hurried to get the first-aid kit. It was lacking in modern-day supplies. I found a small bowl and mixed iodine with water. With a ball of cotton, I swabbed the wound, bandaged with gauze. By this time, several people were awake and wandered over in the dark to see what was going on. As I administered first aid by flashlight, the cook explained in a low voice that her foot was sticking out from under the sheet, and a vampire bat had bitten her heel. The anticoagulant it injected had made the wound bleed. I ran to the small structure behind the guesthouse where the keeper and his wife lived. Knocking loudly, I woke them up. It took a few minutes for them to put on some clothing before they opened the door. I explained the situation. Not to worry, the man assured me, it happened all the time to the miners' noses! He told me to have everyone go back to sleep, but to leave a light on so the bats would stay away. Then he closed the door and went back to bed.

By the time I got back to the main building, all of the lights were on, and everyone else was up. There was much commotion and loud talk about how to avoid the cook's predicament. Several of the students were putting on socks and hats and pulling the beautifully woven, long edges of the hammocks over themselves to make bat-proof cocoons. Why they didn't suffocate I'll never know. In any case, I made sure that the sheets were tucked in firmly around the bottom and sides of the cook's cot as she lay down to go back to sleep.

In the Peace Corps, besides teaching English, history, hygiene and art, I was in charge of the kitchen. In addition, the headmistress designated me the school "nurse" because I was the only staff member who had studied anatomy, first-aid and prevention and care of athletic injuries in my college courses designed to prepare me as a physical education teacher. In Africa, I learned about hookworm infestations, schistosomiasis, smallpox, tuberculosis, wax build-up in ears, malaria and a host of other conditions. I experienced my first donation of blood for a transfusion to help save the life of the mother of one of my students. An Israeli doctor even taught me how to give injections. The Peace Corps physician wrote down how I should mix and use the powders and liquids found in the school medicine cupboard. But here in Guyana, I was not prepared for a bat bite. Not knowing there was an incubation period, I climbed back into my hammock, wondering how long it took to get rabies and what would I do with the cook if she were sick in the morning. With no answers, I finally fell asleep.

The next morning, the cook was up making breakfast and insisting she would make it to the top even if she had to crawl in order to see the falls. Since I was in charge of the group, I decided that she might as well try. If she made it to the top and couldn't make it back down, a plane was scheduled to fly in above the falls on the following day. Getting her out that way would be easier than taking her back on the overland route. It never occurred to me that there might be no room in the plane or that it might cost a lot of money which I didn't have with me or that the schedule could have changed.

With our cameras around our necks and our hiking boots on, we gathered in anticipation of the trek up the steep path through the damp, dark green foliage. Our cook was there, too. I looked at her feet. Because of the bandaged heel, she was wearing flip-flops. They were totally inappropriate for any type of hike, but especially one where the steep terrain was muddy on the surface with lots of slippery rocks. She insisted she would be fine and that she could make the climb if someone would walk beside her. I picked the biggest men in the group and assigned one to each side of her. Off they went, elbows in elbows, three across on the narrow trail. The air was warm and muggy but cooled as we climbed along the shaded path. The trail we hiked wound around through the rain forest growth. The noise of the falls changed its timbre, depending on our distance from the river and the thickness of the intervening trees. In a couple of hours, everyone made it to the top without mishap.

From the top of the falls, the rush of the amber-colored water created frothy, golden foam and a roar as it fell 741 feet to the river below. Reflections of the sun in the brown-and-white water droplets brought to mind topaz and diamonds—odd, I thought, on a river mined for gold. As the water rushed over the semicircular shelf of rock into a steep-sided gorge, its force made the ground vibrate under my feet. This noisy creation of natural beauty led individuals in the group to turn inward and become very quiet. Some just sat and stared. Others wandered upstream a short distance in order to be alone. As I stood looking downstream, I saw no evidence of human habitation, only a sea of treetops all the way to the horizon.

In the early afternoon, the group gathered for the descent to the guesthouse. Because the light had changed, leaving the open area at the top of the falls and entering the dense rain forest growth was a new experience from that of the ascent. Directly overhead now, the sun's rays filtered through the foliage to make irregularly shaped polka dots of light on the trail. Except for the heat and humidity, everything seemed so different from the bush of Africa, where trees were sparsely scattered over the plains, leaving little shade. And the colors were totally different. Here existed every imaginable shade of green with dark, fertile-looking browns. There, colors of ochre, raw umbre, and burnt sienna predominated the landscape.

The walk back down the trail was somewhat easier than the climb up. Yet we had to be careful of foot placement, and the eccentric contraction of quadriceps muscles made thighs ache. While conversing with a student, suddenly my foot slipped on a wet rock. Now I was the one in a predicament. Before I knew what had happened, my camera was swinging from my neck, lodged in the crook of my right elbow, as my right hand held on for dear life somewhere behind my head. Hanging there by one hand, I was looking down into a deep ravine with a sloping wall of low undergrowth and large rocks. I reassured the student that I was OK and caught my breath—more embarrassed than hurt. As she rushed to my aid, I was able to place one foot on a solid piece of ground, get turned around, and climb back up. Just as I started to brush myself off, the cook and her two bodyguards sped on by. With her flip-flops flapping and her muddy, bandaged heel looking less than sterile, she made it back to the guesthouse with no repercussions.

After washing up and eating dinner, many of the students made journal entries, and all of us prepared our belongings for an early departure the next day. In the morning, we had a light breakfast, packed the canoes and began the trip back to Georgetown. In reverse, the portages were much easier. Not only were the loads lighter, but the newly experienced group worked more effectively. Traveling with the river current, the canoe trip ended too soon for some and not soon enough for those who wanted a hot shower and a soft bed.

Having off-loaded the canoes, eaten and slept, it was time to reload once again. Leaning against our gear and bouncing around in the flatbed of the lorry, it was impossible to hold a conversation. Most of us reflected privately on our wondrous adventure, because the next day we would have to get busy preparing for, and carrying out, our sports and recreation projects—the main reason we were here.

In comparison to our previous three days, the trip back to "civilization" and the seacoast was uneventful. The cook was immensely pleased with herself. I, on the other hand, was much relieved that she appeared to have no ill effects from her ordeal. All in all, I was proud to boast that I had been to Kaieteur Falls by the rigorous overland route two years in succession.

ON ASSIGNMENT IN THE SAHARA

Eirene Furness

I began making my living as a journalist in 1965 when I moved to Algeria where I worked as a stringer for *Newsweek,* the *Financial Times,* the *Daily Express, United Press International* and some others. I was fifty-four. The next fifteen years I spent reporting from North Africa were crowded with events, intensely busy and exciting. I saw a newborn nation stray into what seemed an unfortunate political path. I covered a successful coup d'état and several abortive attempts, saw hijacked airplanes, a desert war—not yet over, interviewed international terrorists, attended an unforgettable, unique Pan-African Cultural Festival. I learned about *yellowcake* and the mysteries surrounding the exact volume of a barrel of crude petroleum oil; I saw Red Adair boldly extinguish a blazing oil-well fire at Hassi Messaoud; I encountered Ghadafi at his desert frontier and Eldridge Cleaver in Algiers, among many other newsmakers. Except for the eight days I was incarcerated in a desert prison, the operative word was *Rush.*

Today, thirty years later, those times continue to be a vibrant part of my being. The following episodes, spun off from the daily deadlines, are relevant to my experiences in the golden Sahara, the somber Red Desert, and to my contacts with the brave, generous peoples who touched me personally and stole part of my heart.

. . .

Somewhere in the five hundred miles of empty desert that separate Tamanresset from Djanet, our Land Rover bogged down in the sand. Revving up on the four-wheel drive only dug the vehicle in deeper. There was nothing in sight but sand and stones, our water supply was very low and the sun, high in the sky. I had a sense of déjà vu, but from films, not real life! After desperate struggles, we managed to lift the front wheels onto a strip of rusty metal the driver had liberated from an abandoned air base, and we thankfully got rolling again. Since I remembered those old movies, I was not surprised when we ran into mechanical trouble a few hours later. Black nomadic tents dotted the horizon, and we limped over to the nearest one to await the supply truck. I stayed in the Land Rover with our guide, not cheerful, irresponsible Sayeed this time, but older, more serious Bou Salem.

A young Arab, lean and dark with fierce moustaches, came from the tent to greet me and escort me to his wife, seated in the women's section of the tent with a sturdy little boy of about three. She was very young, with beautiful black hair concealed under a scarf. We spoke no common language. She fetched some water for me, clasped my hand and touched my cheek. The woman was gentle, subservient, pregnant. These were desert Arabs, not Touareg. Outside, I could see a camel and a few goats, and a huge expanse of desert. Water had to be brought from a well nearly a mile away, traditionally, from biblical times, the women's task.

It was ineffably calm and peaceful looking out from the dark tent— its floor covered with thick, glowing carpets—at the blinding light of the desert, the nearest sign of human presence a black dot on the horizon. The little boy, dressed only in a short tunic, toddled off to the men's side, where his father and my guide were smoking and chatting. The child was healthy and beautiful but I refrained from expressing any admiration. The djinni may be listening, I thought, become jealous and snatch the child away. I hugged the mother, who kissed my shoulder. Children are precious and prized in the desert; their lives are so precarious they never know anything but love from both parents.

Darkness loomed as the sun dipped below the horizon and a late swallow flew into the tent, as if returning home. I do not remember what we ate but surely it was the best they could provide. I slept through the chilly night on those royal carpets, to be woken before dawn by Yasmina with tea.

We loaded the Land Rover, which had been repaired by the supply truck already en route. Yasmina went to fetch water in two bright yellow jerry cans. My host clasped my hand and then touched his to his lips and heart. We had entered their lives as briefly as the swallow, to be received with touching hospitality. Communication was limited but this lack was overcome by our common humanity, a sharing of the basics: family, love, shelter, provisions—and a glimpse of the extras: peace, dreams, beauty—enough to weave a tie of affection and respect.

The tent faded to another black dot as we struggled on to Tamanresset. Tamanresset is a thriving oasis a short distance above the Tropic of Cancer. It is, and was, an important market and staging post between black sub-Saharan African and Mediterranean ports. In the bad old days, it held a slave market as important as Ghat or Ghanases, the enormous square filled with buyers and sellers, shackled slaves and preparations for their future transport. The whole town was built of adobe brick, I was privileged to see, as in biblical times.

We arrived at a marvelous and historic moment—it was raining. For the first time in more than seven years, torrents poured down on the city, turning the streets into a sea of mud through which what appeared to be the whole population was sloshing joyfully. Faces turned to the pouring sky were wet not only with rain but with tears of thankfulness as they opened their mouths to the water of life. I received a lot of muddy kisses from the exalted populace.

However, it was impossible to stay in "Tam" and the army post, which is responsible for travelers, directed us to a camp of sedentarized Touareg further north.

Volumes have been written about the fabled "Blue Men" of the Sahara, from Pierre Louys' *Atlantis* to the writing of Pere du Foucauld, venerated as a *marabout*, or muslim hermit, by the locals, and that of numerous ethnologists. The Berber origin of the Touareg is undisputed, their history obscure, their caste system and customs, including women's rights and responsibilities, well documented though still mysterious. For centuries, they were proud masters of the endless desert, preying on caravans of gold, salt and slaves, exacting tribute—mafia-style protection—from rival tribes. There are indications that they may have been

Christianized before converting to Islam. They seem to have cheerfully assumed the rites and ceremonies of other religions without renouncing their own customs and traditions.

Two African countries have taken opposing attitudes to the problem of what to do with this roaming tribe of warriors. Algeria has a program of sedentarization, settling the Touareg in towns or oases, while Niger has agreed to allow them autonomy over the administration of a large tract of desert and semi-desert in its northern territory. There the Touareg continue to live as nomads, displacing themselves and their chattel, which includes creamy white camels and goats, in a spartan life on the edge of hunger. They maintain their well-defined caste system of warriors, nobles and vassals in an economic time warp.

The Touareg do not really accept being immobilized, settled down or turned into gardeners. They despise farming and some have managed to find work in the oil fields, which is considered a more manly occupation, at Hassi Messaoud. In the past, raiding the slave caravans was a source of considerable wealth and supplied them with their own slaves. The last officially recognized slave caravan was in the early 1930s. Slavery was legally abolished in Algeria in 1962.

We visited a colony of sedentarized Touareg north of Tamanresset in the late sixties. The Touareg warriors (even if their occupation is gone) still have a lordly, aristocratic bearing. I appreciated the courtesy and condescension of the tall, handsome men, their eyes flashing above their veiled faces, elaborate turbans increasing their height.

At the Touareg camp, I accompanied the women to the well, which offered a social occasion for the exchange of gossip and news. Carrying bright green or yellow plastic buckets on their heads, they made a wonderful ballet of strong, upright, blue-clad figures as they walked back to the settlement, children scuffling around them.

Amina drew me gently into the shade, explaining that she had been taught to speak French by the "white sisters," missionaries, no doubt, whose presence apparently had been both intermittent and effective over the years.

"You could teach French," I suggested.

"I do teach," she said. She went into the hut and returned with a booklet issued by the Tourist Ministry, printed in a strange language of straight lines with no arabesques that bore no similarity to oriental

Arabic or Persian scripts, or any other that I knew.

"This is our language—Tifinagh," she said. "It has always been exclusively understood, written and taught by women. Men were excluded from written language. Now it is a tourist curiosity and eventually will disappear. Would you like to watch a lesson?"

A group of girls—preteens—gathered around Amina, and she scratched the strange linear figures in the sand, making the girls copy them and repeat their lesson. It was a serious occasion, the young women understanding that this was a precious heritage that they had to preserve.

Amina stood up, laughing. "Tonight I will fetch you to a group of women in a tent outside the camp. They want to ask you questions, learn about your life, tell you about theirs—become sisters."

This seemed a lot more interesting than reading the plentiful government statistics about Touareg agriculture—the hard work, I observed, being mainly performed by the dark-skinned descendants of slaves.

I wandered off from the camp in the direction of a couple of black goatskin tents to enjoy the glorious sight of a herd of camels, creamy white to dark beige, roaming freely in search of pasture. Camels are still essential to desert transport, although being replaced by Jeeps and Land Rovers. Caravans still set out from sub-Saharan Africa to fetch provisions and a biannual camel market is still held at Tindouf—a rowdy, exciting occasion combining festival and heavy bargaining with crowds of buyers and sellers from Morocco to the Sahel, hundreds of noisy camels, mounds of sugar and salt and loads of transistors. It is a wild, unforgettable scene.

Just before sunset, tall, regally beautiful Amina took me by the hand along a stony track to a big tent nearly a mile from the camp. Inside, a number of young women were lounging on cushions and folded carpets. Dressed in dark blue with black kerchiefs lightly placed on their heads, they wore traditional heavy silver necklaces, often ending in the Southern Cross with its loop at the top. Resembling the Egyptian ankh, the Southern Cross is also worn by French colonists as a Christian emblem. Heavy earrings, bracelets on graceful, polished arms, delicately worked sandals—what a garden of beauties. I was welcomed with loving smiles and pats.

"Now for the questions," said Amina. And thick and fast they came: How many children? Was I still married? Where did I live? How many sons? daughters? How did it happen that I, a grandmother, had undertaken this trip? They asked questions about health care for children and spacing births. Amina acted as interpreter. When the tide receded, one young girl started to play a haunting melody on a stringed instrument made from a turtle shell.

In the distance I could hear singing and laughter approaching the tent. A handsome young man stood at the entrance; a group of youths, all dressed in their best, stood behind him. Amina stepped forward and invited them to enter and in they swarmed, smiling, respectful. Two pretty girls appeared with a tray covered with tiny metal cups and another fetched a coffee pot. Music was played, and guests mingled with the hostesses.

Amina pointed out a tall, fierce-looking young man. "Perhaps we will marry," she said. "He works at Hassi Messaoud—there is housing and schools there—but it would mean such a changed life."

I saw that I was becoming *de trop* and said I was tired and would like to return. "I will take you," Amina said. So I made my farewells, touching everyone's hand, being embraced by the girls. Amina and Bachir, her betrothed, escorted me back. "Bachir will help preserve what we can of our customs, history and traditions. Wherever we are, we both will always belong to the desert." I watched them disappear, the moonlight glinting on Amina's silver jewelry.

The whole episode had surprised, delighted and almost shocked me. Islam usually conceals its women and immures its daughters, who often see their bridegrooms for the first time at the wedding. What I had seen reminded me of an English or American presentation of debutantes—in reverse. The girls had been looking over the eligible young men and making choices, decisions. Amina had shown her preference clearly.

We left very early the next morning, and I did not see her again, but gathered from Bou Salem that the party had gone on until the small hours. Bou Salem disapproved of the whole thing, considered such behavior immoral and "backward," primitive. I was fascinated to see the persistence of what some ethnologists have called a matriarchal social order; I was certainly happy to see mutual respect and pleasure between the sexes. It seemed less fraught than a debutante's presentation, but this was only my impression. That women have the right of choice in their society was clearly evident.

It was hard to leave with so many questions unanswered; there was so much to learn. I felt love and admiration for Amina and for all those beautiful, strong, young people. Gaiety and enjoyment are not usually found in Islamic society in a respectable gathering of both sexes. Nor are they easy to achieve when a centuries-old way of life is fast disappearing. The Touareg hope not to become a tourist attraction like the Pueblo Indians. Despite Amina and others anxious to preserve Touareg life and customs, it is possible that these legendary desert warriors, the lords of the Sahara, may be destined to linger on the edges of miserable desert settlements, scraping a living from tourists. I recall the men, in full panoply of blue robes, veils, towering turbans, spears, daggers and elegantly worked sandals, dancing at the First (and last) Pan-African Cultural Festival, the dance platform shuddering with their stamping feet, their élan carrying them more than an hour over their allotted time—perhaps one of their final appearances as a proud, triumphant tribal entity.

Akbar says: "Culture and Peace may at any time be overthrown by Barbarians." None of the remedies proposed—abolition of private property, letting untrammeled greed sort things out, dictatorship whether of tsars or the proletariat has been effective. Relying on the disciplined force of the Third Augustan Legion, Rome maintained comparative peace and prosperity in North Africa for nearly three hundred years. Remnants of their remarkable buildings survive, but peace and prosperity were swept away with the fall of the empire. These were my fleeting thoughts as I left Cleopatra's Tomb, a strange beehive-shaped monument thought possibly to be the tomb of Cleopatra Selene, Caesar's daughter.

I was en route to Dar el Deida to catch a military transport for the West Sahara, scene of a local territorial dispute that was struggling for international recognition. Unless something important such as control over supplies of oil, bauxite or other potentially useful raw material for the military is involved, such local wars have little chance of interesting Western media, but this one concerned two important North African countries with covert sponsorship from rival great powers.

The former Spanish Sahara, wedged between Morocco and Mauritania, is forbidding and empty enough. It is mostly beige sand thickly sprinkled with black rocks, as if from a giant pepper mill. Gloomy and mournful, I found it hard to believe that such abandoned emptiness could be desired by anyone. Unrelievedly black, why was it called El Hamra, "The Red"? Then, at sunset, the crystalline, ore-bearing rocks picked up the last rays, glowed a deep purple-red and turned the hostile desert into a magic, jeweled carpet.

Our news-gathering trip, sponsored by the Government Ministry of Information, was assembled at the airport at seven in the morning, in pouring rain. It was easy to spot my future companions: Jiri, a melancholy Czech with wispy blond hair and an expression of bewildered disgust who looked as lost as I felt myself; Dieter from East Germany, a rock-hewn, indestructible blond; two Spaniards; a Russian from Pravda; and two government people from the Ministry.

Getting there was fraught, uncomfortable—dangerous, actually, when gasoline cans leaked in the back of the Land Rover, forcing us to leap out hastily; I was the only nonsmoker. The whole trip took nearly two days, permanently shepherded by our Ministry guides who never left us alone.

We reached the refugee camp and started to film at once, as the light was going. Our local guide, Zachariah, proudly strapped on his cartridge belt and picked up his rifle—a Kalashnikov—to take on a tour, immediately revealing his vanity and ineptitude. However, we were directed to a bunch of boys and succeeded in filming a meeting of women sitting in a circle, some with small children, being harangued in Hassani—the local Arabic speech—by a Saharan Pasionaria.

We were settled in a ruined hut with blankets spread on the floor, lit by an old Army kerosene lamp hanging on a string which revealed the handsome, fierce faces of our hosts, their dirty feet and unwashed hands—as indeed so were our own; water was too precious to be used for washing. It was a crowded picturesque scene. I had warned Jiri *not* to refuse tea, as this would have been an awful insult, and he gloomily took his turn at the communal glass. The armed nomads retired with their weapons when food—a big dish of overcooked spaghetti with a few lumps of camel meat—was brought in. I managed to get a rather battered plastic spoon, but it was mostly finger food. Jiri shuddered and swallowed a vitamin pill.

We settled to sleep on the blankets in bitter cold. It was so crowded that the driver decided to sleep in the Land Rover. I envied him. Tomás the Catalán, nicknamed "The Philosopher," tried to discuss the comparative merits of Nietzsche and Marx. Dieter started to say in his slow, deep voice, "It's all nonsense," but Tomas interrupted him, saying "Let me speak," though he said nothing else.

Jiri and the Russian had to be returned to the north, unable to stand the discomfort or eat the food.

To me, it all seemed like a dream or an adventure story I was being told, the daily miseries and dangers to be endured for the sake of exotic wonders to come—a pilgrimage in a way. A series of strange adventures, crowded like the strands of a carpet so brilliant it's hard to distinguish the pattern, found me somewhere in the Dar in a desert hollow filled with dead or dying acacia trees. There must have been a well somewhere, as we had water and even tea to drink. In the eerie starlight, dim gray figures were scooping what looked like a series of shallow graves out of the dune above the hollow, the sand already icy cold.

"No scorpions," said Sayeed, who somehow had managed to be designated as our guide. Oh, charming, cheerful Sayeed with his incongruous knitted cap perched on luxuriant black curls, his perpetual smile, his inefficiency—we became attached to each other, meeting again unexpectedly in different places and circumstances, including Paris, sort of an aunt and naughty nephew!

Thankfully, I wrapped myself in my *djellaba* and stretched out in my "grave," only to be told I must reverse myself, as all heads must be pointed toward Mecca. Dimly visible in the silver starlight, soldiers laid aside their weapons for the last prayer of the day before retiring, leaving two sentries on duty. It was completely peaceful and silent. I was glad that only the cameraman and I were there to enjoy that strange night under the stars with our Reguibat friends sleeping beside us.

Despite being involved in that armed struggle for the empty, stony desert, after touring the dunes in a captured Moroccan Army jeep and entering El Aioun just after the Moroccans abandoned it with war planes circling above, I was enchanted by the wonderful peace and silence of the desert. I never felt so serene and calm as on that night spent with a detachment of guerrilla fighters in the trackless immensity of the desert.

The Reguibat are the dominant tribe in the West Sahara, which they consider their ancestral domain. They purchased part of it from hostile

tribes in the twelfth century, and their ruling status has not been challenged since, except during Spanish colonization. They claim kinship
with the Almoravid caliphs who reigned in Cordoba from 1036 to 1147,
an important part of the Moorish occupation that left Spain with architectural marvels as well as an agriculture that fed everyone, and a method
of water distribution to farmers still in use in Andalusia as well as in
some Saharan towns—this from my own observation.

The Reguibat, therefore, are not just unsophisticated nomads. They
consider Spanish rule over the Río de Oro and El Hamra as a brief
episode in their history, and refuse annexation by Morocco, claiming
an independent West Sahara. They wage a typical guerrilla war of swift
raids, which avoids a direct confrontation with the Moroccan Army to
whom they would inevitably lose. "Spain sold us like a package of tea,"
said an officer manning a machine-gun post just outside El Aioun.

I was in a Land Rover with seven Reguibat guerrillas—or rather, six
because Sayeed was jammed in with the rest of us. I was the only one
without a weapon and ammunition belt, crushed in the back with weapons, food supplies, spare gas, other passengers and a goat. In the front
seat were four older men, one in a blue turban who seemed to inspire
respect bordering upon awe. Even frivolous Sayeed touched his turban
reverently when Mansour spoke.

They all asked me questions, and when I mentioned that I had several grandchildren, Mansour turned to me and spoke in Arabic. "To
us," he said, "you are young and beautiful because you have made the
hard journey to come here and tell people about us."

It was a long trip but made easier because my companions sang,
shouted and laughed most of the way. "What we want," said Mansour,
"is a Sahara without frontiers where one can travel from the Atlantic to
the Gulf without papers."

We swung round in a ninety-degree curve and stopped, confronted
by a steep, impassable sand dune. My companions grabbed their weapons and jumped out. On the summit of the golden dune, a Toyota and
two armed soldiers looked down on us.

What now? Captured by the Moroccans? I thought. But it turned
out to be a hiding place for Moroccan prisoners, whom we interviewed.
I thought them mostly Mauritanians. Then we all had a picnic, captives
and capturers sharing the hapless goat in a *mechoui*.

The desert dwellers, whether Touareg or Reguibat, are very interesting and attractive, lean, hard and handsome, honed to a fine edge by desert wandering, which they love. Tribal warfare and raiding has always been an accepted feature of their lives. They are unfailingly courteous and controlled. Discipline is unswerving—a mistake or dereliction of duty may mean death in the desert. All is changing with terrible swiftness. The caravans of camels, men, women, children, goats become rarer as Land Rovers take over, and airplanes cut the weeks of a voyage to hours. The golden dunes, as changeable and unchanging as the sea remind me not to believe all I read in the newspaper. We encountered caravans and nomad camps in our rather circumscribed wanderings. Coming down a steep, apricot-colored dune, I once saw a man in Saharan dress walking rapidly, alone. He climbed over the next orange dune and the next and disappeared, a tiny, enigmatic figure in the immense emptiness, another desert mystery.

It was time to start our return northwards—file copy, ship film, struggle with telephones. The cameraman was fussing about shipping film and sound tapes. Finally, we got the promise of a Cessna plane to fly from Tindouf to the Mediterranean airport.

We started the long trip back in another Land Rover, ex-Spanish Army this time. A day's bumping over hard laterite rocks brought us to the border. We slept in a big army tent with a lot of other people including government workers and a million flies.

I insisted on saying good-bye to my Reguibat friends who had all been so loving and respectful throughout my travels. The young men were particularly affectionate, all thanking me for the effort of coming. We got hold of some coffee and sat drinking it.

"Why always three cups?" I asked.

They answered in Hassidi, which ubiquitous Sayeed translated: "The first is as bitter as life, the second as sweet as love, the third as insidious as death."

They all embraced my shoulder as I left for "civilization," taking with me forever those silent, starlit phantoms of the magic Saharan sun.

WHITE THIGHS

Trish Ingersoll-Adams

There was no wind, no cloud or hesitation as we crawled on and on, immutably, up this Alaskan mountain. The struggle was so consuming that what seemed to be only minutes passing had really been hours. We were hip-deep in snow, eight hundred feet up the initial two thousand-foot couloir of Mount Hunter's Southwest Ridge: outside time, outside familiar space, and outside self. Above us lay our immediate goal, Camp I at 9,500 feet. It was a vague spot on the map, all too remote to even imagine.

How to explain the desire to start such an adventure?

To journey beyond our ordinary lives had always held a spell for our little party of three: Len, Ramin and me. I had known Len, a radiation physicist, off and on since 1968 when he had emigrated from England to the United States, looking for work. During the "off" years he disappeared to climb in South America, Africa, Turkey, Iran and Europe. Then, through the grapevine, word would come that he was back in England teaching high-school math or working construction to finance another expedition. In 1977, these years culminated for him in the last climb of Nanda Devi sanctioned by the Indian government. Since then, he had woven smaller trips into his family and working life.

Ramin grew up in Iran before the revolution, spending summers scrambling in the foothills of the Alburz Mountains behind his grandmother's house in Nivaran. Later he attended school in England

and college in Scotland, where epic ice climbs honed his skills for the Arctic-ice conditions of New England and climbs he pursued after graduate school in engineering at MIT. We had climbed together for five years.

My climbing started in the early 1960s when I spent two high-school years in Switzerland. During the summers I lived with a family in their small mountain village near the Furka Pass. Their son and I pursued one goal: to climb the big ones. First we had to get fit. We trained by hiking to the region's huts at breakneck speed. I remember feeling incredible pride as I carried the nylon rope up to the hut of my first alpine climb. It must have been a very easy route because this rope, tied around our waists, was all we used to anchor ourselves to the blocky mountain; there was no other protection. We had improvised our way to the top. I was exhilarated and free. Some wild thing in my gut had been set loose. I returned home to the U.S., to redirect this passion, studying composition at the New England Conservatory and then ceramic sculpture at the Boston Museum School. I taught ceramics at various colleges and started a family.

Twenty-three years later a restless longing for the mountains came back to stalk me. I returned alone to Switzerland for a week, the summer of my fortieth year, leaving a slightly confused husband, two small children and a sitter (and back-up sitters). I hiked hut-to-hut in this region I had known so well. As I scrambled up rock faces laced with wire cables, I let loose a long dormant cry of joy. "A joy," as Goethe said, "without peace." I returned home with a vivid sense of what I needed to learn: rock and ice climbing. I took courses in New Hampshire till I knew enough to be on the "sharp," leading, end of the rope. Since then, my two friends and I have laughed and clawed our way up the wild winter ravines and rock faces of New Hampshire, the grand ice routes on Mount Katahdin in Maine, some classics in Europe and out West.

Mount Hunter, 216 miles from the Arctic Circle at a latitude of 63 N (compared to 27 N for Mount Everest), presented a very different arena. We studied this Southwest Ridge route, viewed slides and discussed its features with a New Hampshire guide who had been turned back, last year, by storms and avalanches at Camp II. We discovered that this route was not yet popular, low in altitude and technically interesting.

So a plan evolved, at least on paper. We would fly to Anchorage from Boston toward the end of April, the time of year when we might get the most fair-weather days. Early May would still be cold and windy (negative ten degrees to negative forty degrees Fahrenheit), though not quite as violent as winter; we anticipated the snow bridges over crevasses, the windswept cornices and hanging seracs, to be safely frozen. The twenty-one hours of light would allow us more flexibility to accommodate the changing weather, the time needed to prepare meals (melt snow) and break camp (three to four hours twice a day).

Getting to Anchorage was a twelve-hour ordeal of missed connections and computer-inspired reroutings. At one in the morning we landed and were met by a childhood friend of mine and her husband, with a huge van rented just for all our gear. From their apartment we could see the Denali massif held in the momentary glow of sunset. It then turned gray, unearthly, and finally black, an accurate vision of the hostile ground we were about to enter. I wondered not so much about this unknown world, but more about the unknown me. I wanted to stay and visit with my good friend, hear her tales of being the head of the Environmental Protection Agency here in the Northwest and her new life in Alaska, but I longed to be in the wild mountains, homeless, and committed. Here, in this limbo-land of before-a-climb, lurked fears, and the furies pulled at me to leave the familiar; I was ready to follow.

After a short sleep, we were up early to repack and drive the two-and-one-half hours to Talkeetna where we had to register with the park rangers and load up the Super Cub that would fly us to Mount Hunter. The small air field was shared by four air services and the paraphernalia of their many clients. We were glad to be already packed and could thus start loading the plane immediately. Our pilot, Cliff Hudson, guided this feat with such precision that when we crawled into our spots to buckle up (back seats removed), not a centimeter was unused. Consumed by our gear, the impending adventure and the ear-numbing roars that underscored the power needed to make lift off, we suddenly, without warning, were gone.

5 minutes: We follow winding, white glacial tributaries to the frontier mountains of Denali Park.
10 minutes: A narrow breach appears in the rock barrier and we

glide, straight and low, through Gun Shot Pass, wing tips seemingly only yards from the jagged rock walls.

15-20 minutes: We range above giant coursing glaciers, rising higher and higher with the maze of mountains, till we reach the head of Kahiltna Glacier, a massive flow from Denali.

25-35 minutes: Mount Hunter rises before us and we circle a couple of times, looking down on the snow and ice conditions along our route. No blue, hard ice or double cornices (big trouble).

40 minutes: One final pass over the Kahiltna to check that ice blocks are not on the glacier where we are to land (bigger trouble).

Here at 20,000 feet we looked down onto the Southeast Fork of the Kahiltna Glacier where we would land and set up Base Camp at 6,500 feet. The glacier was surrounded by an amphitheater of peaks 11,000 feet high. The choreography of our future climb lay before us. From Base Camp we would ski the mile up the glacier, deposit our skis, climb the two-thousand-foot couloir, exit onto the ridge and place Camp I at 9,500 feet. Camp II, at 10,500 feet, would be at the end of this cor-niced ridge in a saddle below the thousand-foot rock and ice wall. Above this wall we would find a site for Camp III at 11,600 feet. Then, the final push to the South Summit at 13,966 feet. The descent would retrace our steps. Allowing for bad weather, we were taking provisions for seven days, but these could be stretched to ten.

Reality proved something else altogether!

We were deftly deposited onto the glacier at midafternoon. The tiny plane quickly vanished, and we were alone with the results of our months of planning: two hundred or more pounds of gear (seventeen days of food and fuel, stoves, pots, ice screws, rock gear, ice axes, helmets, har-nesses, shovel and saw, tents, sleeping bags, one-piece insulated suits, insulated gaitors and gloves, general clothes, cameras, boots, crampons, packs, skis, ropes, pitons, pickets and slings. We figured the total cost of gear accumulated over the years equaled a small down payment on a house). The complete isolation of our position settled on me and the exquisite silence sank into every pore. It was a gargantuan, breathing silence coming up from the depths of the glacier, oozing up the ancient rock walls where it had been held for eons. I felt an urgent need to do something familiar, such as focus on the brute effort of moving all our stuff to the Base Camp site. This done, we set up our tent, at a cordial distance from the vacant tent we had seen from the air, and began sawing snow blocks to build a six-foot-tall protective wall around our compound.

Without warning, we were hit by a tremendous pressure blast. It was followed instantly by the shattering rapport of calving seracs and avalanches. They plunged down onto the glacier where we had just landed and came rushing toward us. We dove into our tent. It deflated with a suck, then inflated, choked with fine snow. No time to think. Was the wave of snow about to engulf us? Then all was quiet. I could only hear pounding: my own heart. Welcome to Alaska. This was a chilling explanation for the name of the mountain trembling above us to our south: Thunder Mountain.

By eleven o'clock at night in Arctic twilight, we had finished our compound, complete with a sculpted snow dragon perched on the block wall and overlooking the latrine (lined with plastic bags to be flown out). We were a dot on the glacier dominated by Mount Foraker towering over us at 14,000 feet, and still bathed in warm, golden luminescence. I felt strangely at home after a mere six hours; even frequent avalanches went unnoticed.

The pattern of the next three days was frustrating as clear mornings repeatedly gave way to midafternoon snow. Each day we would optimistically ski the mile up to the couloir, stash skis, rope up, cross the tiny snow bridge spanning the dark bottomless *bergschrund*, and, keeping safely away from the avalanche path, climb until snow enveloped us. Hastily, we would cache our loads here at 8,000 feet, and rush back down to our skis before avalanches began scouring the couloir. After three days, we had now ferried from Base Camp all the supplies we would need on the climb. Champing at the bit, we were feeling well acclimatized and fit.

Day four dawned cloudy. We reached the couloir in light snow and began climbing. Given our previous forays, we assumed we had plenty of time before snow could accumulate and avalanche. But two hundred feet into the climb, a cataclysmic explosion ripped apart these assumptions. Is this why mystics come to the mountains: to have the mind so completely separated from the body? In this case, transcendence by fear not by contemplation. The hanging glacier next to our couloir had broken off in sections, five stories high, setting off an avalanche that engulfed our morning ski tracks. We watched in awe, trying to adjust to the magnitude of this magnificent menace. Then, throughout our couloir, came a grinding roar, as still more avalanches broke free. One funneled down on us faster and faster. Helpless wonder immobilized us in a weird breathless silence. Giddy with fear and relief, we then saw how close we had come to this astounding force. It had missed us by three feet! When the tension subsided, I noticed a strange, familiar reaction to such events: an increased commitment to the climb.

Finally on the fifth day, we got a settled forecast for forty-eight hours: no new snow overnight. This was it: our chance! With light packs we quickly reached the couloir. Once more, we labored up to the cache. Only this time, here at the edge of the avalanche trough, the snow was chest-deep. The three-foot garden wands that marked our cache were completely buried, forcing us to spend precious hours searching and digging for our gear. I was anxious about this lost time. Nearby, the incongruous chirping of a lost finch brought a moment's distraction in this lifeless world. Then we shouldered our huge packs and I began to lead up the twelve hundred feet of steepening ice, desperately trying to overcome the constant feeling of instability. My body was charged with adrenaline; it tightened my muscles. I had to remember: three deep breaths in, then slowly exhale, relax. I tried to keep my senses separate from my mind. I knew that if they came together it would be anarchy, panic. We took turns leading, and halfway up passed the only other team on the route. They were descending from Camp II, where they had sat out the last five days in storms, then run out of fuel.

Near the top of the couloir, rock walls closed in to form a barrier of steep, icy gullies. Our map showed the route as a vague black line leading onto the ridge. The trick now was to pick the right exit gully. We had been climbing for twelve hours and I wondered about our judgment. Thus, on emerging from our chosen bottleneck, I had a tremendous feeling of being freed. We looked down over the other gully "choices" and saw nothing but vertical walls. It was two o'clock in the morning, dimming to dark. We settled into Camp I and could only laugh in disbelief. We were dramatically perched on the dividing ridge of Mount Hunter, "The Throne of the Gods." The following morning, our camp looked an unlikely sight: first a blue and then a green speck of tent shaking off a dusting of snow, amidst a circle of garden wands sprouting frozen socks, hats and gloves. It resembled some ancient burial ground, a thousand feet above converging glaciers with mountains surging off to the horizon. Len was moved to add to the architectural splendor by building an elegant snow cave (his preferred place of rest) with such fervor that I worried about this passion to burrow. We languished in the sun's warmth at zero degrees, raving about hot jello. Eventually we proceeded to scout out the next day's route till heavy mist rolled in and spooky snow conditions returned us to camp.

Early the next morning, we headed up to Camp II as the sun thinned the mist. We climbed easy-angled yet questionably stable snow, along sublimely sculpted cornices. We tiptoed across snow bridges spanning crevasses large enough to hold a freight train and placed garden wands to mark these dicey spots of the route for our descent. Unimaginable joy came as I watched the surrounding peaks sink farther and farther below. I felt an unabashed sense of omnipotence on the one hand, followed instantly by a vivid understanding of our minuscule presence in this game with an indifferent player; I hoped we knew the rules.

Throughout the day we followed the narrowing ridge till it merged up against the rock and ice wall. In bitter cold, we placed our second camp. Len dug his small cave deep into the bowels of this saddle which dropped three thousand uninterrupted feet to the glacier below. We set up our tent. This rock wall section would be the most technical and physically demanding of the climb. We decided to spend the next day protecting and fixing ropes in the hope of assuring a safe, fast ascent with our heavy packs. But the negative forty degrees Fahrenheit made for very slow progress, especially across a thoroughly unstable, airy traverse. Had I fallen here the frozen ropes would have held. But given my lack of dexterity, it seemed unlikely that I could have climbed back up the overhanging traverse. Cold and weary, we retreated in frustration to await the evening weather report. It was not good.

Dawn winds at three o'clock in the morning were strong and a dark sky was building all around us. We had just finished the necessary two hours needed to melt snow and dress when the gale hit. Securing everything, we went about placing food and fuel by the door, heightening camp walls, wanding a path to Len's cave and the latrine and basically trying to create some kind of comfort.

Here at 12,000 feet, life became a slow undulation of eating, sleeping and eliminating. This last business took extreme care to execute and was avoided as long as possible. White-out conditions made for epics to the "pot," so near and yet so far. But safety was only half our worry, as the whimsy of erratic winds merged with pee, and toilet paper was useless. All decorum was lost. Above all, though, we cursed the complicated act of just getting in and out of our three-pound expedition tent. No amount of diligence could keep out the snow.

The storm not only raged on, but rose to new heights, sounding suspiciously like howls of laughter or eerie, annoying, undecipherable cries. Days passed. Our actual appearance began to speak more for the changes than we let on. Somehow, the men took on that L.A. movie-star look with their nine days of unkempt beard and untameable looks. I, on the other hand, became more Druid-like: eyes all whites, endlessly searching the roof of the tent for frozen condensation just waiting to come tinkling down into my sleeping bag. Indifferent to pain? Yes, but not to the small miseries.

Periodically we would consider our pathetic perch, how alone we were. But that was actually hard for us to grasp, packed as we were so tightly against each other. In fact, we found our existence quite lovely for a while: no plans, no phones, no work, no worries. We lived to eat, talk about food and tell silly, perverse jokes. Imagined feasts from our various backgrounds (British, Persian and American) were described in minute detail. Our adaptability amazed us.

It was only temporary.

The demonic wind left never a moment of silence and conversation became increasingly difficult. Spirits dwindled into scatological mumbling about feral odors. Sometimes the closeness became unbearable, especially during cooking. If one had to move, to relieve some intolerable cramp or such, extensive warnings had to be given. The threat of instant immolation was all too real. I took relief in my journal; snuggled into my bag, I was warm and private. Tours of useless shoveling were a mild diversion, and the tent poles were undeniably starting to go, as was the tent. We obviously had to do something. Boredom and the great precedent set by Len's previous snow caves finally motivated us. We began enlarging his snow hole.

In the end, our large icy "retreat" offered room for any number of activities, but all we wanted to do was crawl into our sleeping bags and lie, as if buried alive, in this cold, blue silence. Outside, the storm fumed and bellowed. We fell into lethargic sleep, almost missing the weather report: "short clearing spell followed by another big storm."

Dully, we grasped the meaning of this news: we had to retrieve the ropes and gear, still in place on the wall above, and get off the mountain, quickly. Pathetically clumsy from days of cold and inertia, we dug ourselves out of the cave. All possibilities for the summit were gone; we felt heartbreak and yet relief. Would we ever be able to give it another try physically, mentally or even with a semblance of the same exhilaration and comradeship? Did we know too much? Or not enough? No, we had to believe we would be back someday. And this deception made it possible to head down.

The storm's five feet of new snow made descending the ridge breathtaking but alarmingly unfamiliar. Where were the wands marking the crevasses and our route? In the lee of each rolling cornice crest, we had to shovel away the chest-deep snow, just to move forward. Thus we took on the battle to get off this corniced ridge, never questioning our slow progress or what would happen if we had to descend the whole ridge like this. It would have taken fifteen hours. Fortunately, after six hours of maniacal wading, we reached firm, windswept snow and could move quickly.

Back at Camp I, new problems arose. Len's crampon broke, and his feet felt desperately cold. But to feel cold feet meant no frostbite, not yet. So, despite his wrathful curses and hatred at the melting snow pouring into his boots, we continued: down the bottleneck into thigh-deep snow, and into the veiled night-shade of the southwest couloir. We could not see down the two thousand feet of darkness to the sprawling glacier below, nor assess its dangers.

What can one feel other than confidence? We did not expect to fail. Yet I worried. Did the frightening conditions make us vigilant enough? Or were we being overly confident?

Tensions increased as we descended. Bound together, exhausted and out of sync, we tempted the Fates. Yells of "Slow Down!" were followed by homicidal tugs on the rope. We were beyond words. Now and again, spindrift avalanches swept over and around us. Mad paddling kept the snow from building up and taking us down, but left us spent. By the end of this two-thousand-foot shoot, I became increasingly suspicious of dangers lurking in the *bergschrund*, even though it was now nicely filled in with snow. Tears froze on my cheeks. I could barely force myself down over this final hazard. The dark, ugly labyrinth of my mind and this sinister crevasse were melding with the utter fatigue of my senses. I could not see out, only inward: chaos.

Safely back at our skis, all reasoning failed me: how to put on my skis while carrying my huge pack; or, how to put on my pack and then skis. In either case I would end up impaled, face down on the icy crust. I left the skis and walked the mile down to Base Camp, postholing through the thin crust, fiercely grumpy.

We had been on the mountain eight days. It was now three in the morning: we were "home." All that mattered was sleep, but the ordeal had left us tense and restless. I could now think of my family, and missed my children passionately. Len went about fixing food, changing clothes and rearranging things. Ramin and I watched dumbfoundedly, then thankfully dropped into a dreamless sleep. By six o'clock the tent was an inferno. The sun lulled in a cloudless sky. Mad unzipping sounds revealed our decrepit, dripping bodies crazed with hunger. It would be hard to conjure up the squalid, barbaric manner in which we attacked the bagels, spaghetti, butter and other delights. The loud gurgling noises were such that I barely heard the approaching plane. How unjust to interrupt our "feed!" I deeply regretted the "pick-up" call we had made yesterday to an overhead plane. This last day, I had imagined having plenty of time to linger and slowly pack, to mull the unsolvable mysteries of the world, but not this abrupt ending.

Then I remembered my skis.

Joyously, I escaped the confusion of dismantling the camp. I retraced our ski tracks, hiking back up into the silence, into the shadow of Hunter's Ridge, to stand awhile below the couloir I knew so well. These massive rock forms seemed to embody some simple truth, forming and re-forming, inexpressible. I now knew what Camus meant when he proposed, "Imagine Sisyphus happy."

Climbing Terms

anchor: a way of securing a climber to rock, snow or ice by means of protections

bergschrund: a crevasse caused by an abrupt change in incline, for instance, between a glacier and a rock face

bottleneck: a restriction in a gully

cornice: an overhanging, wind-carved formation of snow found on tops and ridges of mountains. Usually on the opposite side of the prevailing wind

couloir: a snow-filled gully

crevasse: a deep fissure in glacial ice

fixed rope: rope laid up a mountain to aid ascent

lead: to be the first on a climb

protection: equipment (rope, slings, gear) placed to safeguard the climbers

serac: an ice cliff

spindrift: very fine windblown snow

swing leads: to take turns leading

traverse: to move sideways

HAVE SADDLE, WILL TRAVEL

Maxine Kumin

This poetry business is a curious occupation. You cannot make even a modest living writing poems, but you can keep body and soul together nicely by reading them out loud to people. Over the last thirty years I've flown from Boston or from Manchester, New Hampshire, to every contiguous state in the Union except Oklahoma and Wyoming to give readings and conduct workshops. Lately, po-biz has begun to seem onerous, requiring a higher level of mobilization of my resources than I feel up to. My notion is to lighten these trips away from the farm by "horsing around" whenever I get the chance.

At five this morning, in almost total darkness, I separated the mare and foal into two stalls for their hay and grain, then tossed extra hay to the others in the upper pasture for my husband to bring in after he had made the airport run with me. We have an hour's drive to Manchester. Once it was a little rural airstrip with propeller flights to Boston; now it is served by three major carriers and crammed at 6:45 A.M. with people as intent on going places as I am.

In Pittsburgh the airport corridors look like central Manhattan at the noon hour. The volume of traffic moving through this airport is overwhelming. Commuter flights are relegated to a lower-level holding pen. Testy announcements admonish everyone to pay attention. If you are not ready when your flight is called—if you're in the bathroom or on the telephone—you have missed your flight. No second chances. I practice deep breathing in the midst of this controlled bedlam and try to stay alert for the sound of Lynchburg on the PA system.

At least half the expendable energy of po-biz is taken up with this kind of rackety travel. I am clutching a sheaf of tickets, my toilet articles, and my books, having trepidatiously checked all else. I used to travel light enough so that I could tote all my possessions on board (and shoulder them through airports on the long hike from Gate 1 to 99). But once I added a saddle to my necessary equipment I decided to entrust my suitcase to baggage handlers.

My lightweight synthetic saddle, foam over fiberglass, adapts to the narrow and broad-of-beam equine without difficulty. It is seemingly indestructible. Ads show a truck driving over one side of it. And an old friend, a poet from Salt Lake City, gave me her saddle carrying case into which I can fit not only the saddle and girth but also my schooling helmet and boots. These last in turn are stuffed with two pairs of socks, rolled-up breeches, and a T-shirt.

It's October. Lynchburg, Virginia, is golden with autumn haze. The Sweet Briar official greeter waves to me. The saddle has also arrived safely.

"What kind of musical instrument is that?" a gentleman asks as I reach down to grasp the strap.

"Tuba," I tell him. He nods, then walks off looking thoughtful.

Although visitors to the stables at Sweet Briar are not generally welcome except as observers, the rules have been gently abrogated in my favor. At 2 P.M. I am signed over to a trusted student, one of the college's top equestrians.

For a while we stand in the outdoor ring and watch an intermediate class learning how to execute turns on the forehand. The students are impressive, riding with relaxed agility and near-perfect form. Most of these horses were tax-deductible gifts to the riding program. Some came off the racetrack, others were hunt-club mounts. A few students have brought their own horses to Sweet Briar, but it's a heavy added expense.

Immense, well-lighted, immaculate, the indoor facility creates for horse lovers an ambience that could be compared to that of the Four Seasons or Lutèce for gourmets. The barn makes me think of the old

Bonwit Teller store, gracious and elegant purveyor of women's apparel, giving off a quiet aura of fame and propriety. The horses are stabled in large, airy stalls, bedded on crushed peanut shells, which the staff assures me are both absorbent and edible. Stall doors are customized mesh so as not to impede air flow. Saddle pads are laundered on a daily basis. Tack is cleaned almost immediately by its user in a washroom appointed with dozens of glycerine soap bars and sponges, towels and polish and neat's-foot oil. Outside, two wash areas for the horses have hot and cold water, hoses, buckets, sweat scrapers. In short, except for a lack of open space for horses to be at leisure in, paradise.

My guide and I set out for a lazy cross-country hack, over rolling terrain where Holstein cows from the college dairy graze. The fields are divided by counterweighted gates you can tug from horseback so as not to have to dismount to open and close them. The succession of pastures is also accessible via chicken-coop jumps, but students are not allowed to leap over these except under supervision. I am somewhat relieved. My jumping skills are rusty and those of the rotund Appaloosa under me unknown. His trot is longer-strided than I expected from my ground-level view of him, and this is pleasing. His canter is rollicking and rideable. His attitude—school horses all too seldom get out of the ring—is that of an enthralled tourist. Except for his breadth (he weighs 1400 pounds) I am enjoying the trip.

By nightfall my hip joints ache. It is the familiar ache of encroaching arthritis, clamorous enough to merit two rounds of ibuprofen. Usually I try to avoid such sprung-ribbed horses, but when you are a guest you take what you get. It is humbling to be mounted on something so broad and massive and to strive, for the sake of my reputation, to maintain a balanced seat thereupon. But it is good for poets to undertake prose from time to time, and it is good for the rider to adapt to a different way of going.

Transient humans at Sweet Briar are housed in capacious, attractive motel rooms on campus. The sliding glass door of mine leads onto a patio. Beyond are mixed oak and tupelo woods, sunlight streaming through the now-depleted branches and lending a glimpse, this late afternoon, of two deer. They are smaller than the New England deer in my home woods, but they provide the accidental-tourist touch that enhances my sense of comfort.

In this calm twilight before the dinner before the reading, I am able to stretch out and catch forty winks. In the background, persistent cicadas strum. They are certain to go down tonight in the predicted hard frost.

The ability to nap before a reading has only come to me in the last five years or so. My anxiety quotient seems to have receded gradually. I still welcome a serious drink or two, or at least a carafe of wine at dinner—for it is the rare reading that is not preceded by dinner with several faculty members, and/or students—but the Old Devil Panic has been superseded by nothing more than nervous tension.

Sometimes I wonder if that old terror of podium and microphone hasn't been subsumed by the total jitters I feel at the start of every competitive trail ride. Trying to stay in possession of myself and an overeager horse while waiting for my number to be called is harrowing. The first five miles of the ride are just like the first poem.

Every poetry audience is different. Some are formal and ominously silent. Others laugh easily, carry your books, and read them. There is no way to predict how it will be. You take a deep breath and begin . . . in a matter of minutes, you know. In the first five miles your horse comes to terms with the fact that he is surrounded by other horses; he settles down. Or doesn't.

This evening's reading goes well. Everyone connected with the program seems pleased by the size of the audience and the enthusiasm of students who linger for the reception. Many of them have studied some of my poems in class, which always defuses the tension associated with having to sit still for the distant poet, isolated on stage. There are books for sale and lots of people want theirs signed.

Next morning, after breakfast, the quick run to the airport. I hate to leave this landscape of rolling hills and pale autumn foliage. I fly, wrong way, it seems, south to Charlotte, then north to Newark, once again entrusting my luggage to the airlines.

A young woman from the College of St. Elizabeth meets me, recognizing me easily, she claims, from the publicity photo. It is always a relief to be plucked out of anonymity by the unknown person delegated to meet your plane. We proceed to the baggage-claim area, where my saddle, still snug in its vinyl case, rides up the conveyor belt almost immediately.

A long and anxious wait for my other bag ensues. The conveyor belt finishes its task and is shut down. Just as I am about to seek someone official, an attendant rushes up to me.

"This yours?"

The look on my face is his answer.

"It didn't get off-loaded with the rest. Got stuck behind the cargo door; I just found it."

I thank him profusely. I've lost bags in Gainesville, Austin, and Miami that I can remember. Selective amnesia is shielding me from other occasions; I'm grateful this is not to be a rerun.

There are no horses associated with this small women's college in New Jersey. For exercise, though, I get an hour's walk on a gravel strip designated as a bike path along the New Jersey rail line. A mockingbird greets and follows me for a bit. Several trains clatter past, both express and locals. I feel dizzy; I am nowhere. In *A Bend in the River*, V. S. Naipaul says, "The airplane is a wonderful thing. You are still in one place when you arrive at the other. The airplane is faster than the heart."

A glass of wine and a sandwich before the reading, which takes place at 7 P.M. to accommodate commuting students and the many continuing-ed students, older women, who attend college on a variety of schedules, nights and weekends.

The room is jammed with enthusiasts, filled to overflowing. The nuns seem a little startled by the turnout. My companion, who made the arrangements, was responsible for the publicity and she is of course delighted too. Alas, she has failed to arrange for books to be sold, always a downer for the traveling poet. But the evening ends early and I have a quiet night, broken every hour or so by the invasion of trains crossing the foot of my bed. Next morning my friend is punctual and drives me back to Newark Airport in good time for my early flight west.

A long day's travel to El Paso, with a change in Dallas. I have again checked saddle and suitcase through to my destination. The connection is smooth and my El Paso host meets me at the gate. We drive to her charming little house on the larger ranch of a cardiologist/gentleman farmer. I am to spend tonight here in the desert to facilitate an early-morning ride tomorrow. This afternoon there is time for a brief nap before supper and the reading. I don't sleep but am soothed by the sound of the wind in the cottonwoods imitating rain, and by the presence of a big house cat, Gamine, who seeks me out at once and lies purring beside me.

In spite of overlapping the World Series (postponed by the earthquake to this date), the reading draws a good audience. Books are for sale there, and at a private party at a student's house after the reading, the dining table groans with homemade delicacies. But by 10 P.M. jet lag has overtaken me. And three readings three nights in a row, no matter how you vary the poems, take their toll. Moreover, tonight there was no microphone. The acoustics in the auditorium were splendid, but I feel extra fatigue from having had to project my voice beyond its usual range.

Driving back from town into the desert I am not too tired to note a beautiful, healthy-looking coyote with a great bush to his tail. He stands transfixed in the head lights as we turn up the driveway; rarely, says my chauffeur, do they look so well fed and bold.

Finally, to bed! Sleep carries me off almost instantly. I come awake a few hours later to the several voices of coyotes, at first barking in concert like dogs, then building up the scale to a series of yelps that precede the full-fledged howl. This cacophony entertains me; I am not unhappy to be wide awake in the desert. When the orchestra finally fades, I am able to sleep again.

My host and her neighbor have planned for the three of us to ride up the mesa, make a broad circle, and descend the other face. I am to ride a borrowed polo pony, a 15 1/2-hand Appendix Quarterhorse-Arab cross. This eight-year-old gelding is rigged like a battleship, with breastplate and draw reins attached to a Pelham. This is slightly off-putting to me, as our endurance horses go in snaffles with a figure-eight noseband to keep their mouths closed on the bit. Sometimes in early spring when they are rambunctious, we switch to a Kimberwicke and curb chain. But I often question whether the additional control outweighs the added fussiness. I haven't ridden with double reins since I was a child in suburban Philadelphia, and was taught to ride saddle seat, hands high and legs parked straight out in front of me.

It is a splendid morning, warming, but with a good breeze. We all walk for about a mile, loosening up. My mount starts out a little behind the formidable bit but soon rounds over, gratefully dropping his nose to my light contact. He is a comfortable fit and instantly responsive to my legs. Going up through dense scrub growth of mesquite and creosote, we sight at least a dozen jackrabbits. They leapfrog in front of us, close enough so that I can see the veins coursing inside their fluted ears, which stand straight up at a considerable height. New England rabbits are smaller and furrier; they carry their ears at an angle and slick them back as they run.

Soon we pick up a steady trot. Everyone breaks a sweat; we all feel good. My horse has a high, competent stride. I concentrate on changing diagonals round every swerve and keep my hands light to encourage him to take more of the bit. We canter a long stretch. This is clearly his most secure gait and it is very comfortable. I really love this guy!

In about an hour we come out on top of the mesa, from which we have a 360-degree view. The Franklin Mountains are on one side, the Organ Mountains on the other. We can see El Paso spread out beyond us in the valley. Except for the city, miniaturized from here, the area feels timeless. The mesa and its arroyos have been here since the Ice Age, unchanged and unchanging.

A drivable dirt road winds its way up here. I am startled to see a pickup truck emerge out of a dust cloud and bear down on us. A little farther on we come to a dump—the polite term is landfill. My host says she found a dead calf up here one day. She circled it, repelled, thinking it would decay and stink. But each day as she rode back to inspect the corpse she found it further diminished, odorless, soon reduced to its essential bones. Dry air, hot sun, possibly turkey vultures?

Her allegiance to the desert is touching. Like so many other transplants I meet out here, she has bonded to the landscape. She loves the subtle changes from daybreak to dusk, season to season. My eye is not practiced enough to see gradations of brown and gray. The desert saddens me, at least on this limited acquaintance. The view looks static, like clay contoured by a careless hand. It feels depleted, if not dead. There are no birds, little wildlife. We see no road runners, no wild pigs, no rattlers. It is too late in the year for snakes. People wander out here casually to shoot their guns. Someone is always conducting target practice. The *thunk!* of rifles accompanies us as we cross the mesa and start down the other side.

Back on the valley floor, we ride around a big Quarterhorse ranch, with some very well-made horses following us curiously along the pipe rails. Yearlings cavort in one corral. Weanlings are in separate pens, wearing halters with long ropes attached. My companions explain that this is the western way of breaking them to the lead rope. They are invited to step on it and come to an abrupt halt. Back East we would decry this as dangerous. Horses seem more expendable here, to my biased easterner's perception.

As we travel single file along this sand track, I realize how much my eye depends on the sight of companionable horses, grazing, moving from hummock to knoll, to pine grove and back. These great dry paddocks with wire fencing depress me.

Much as I love to roam the woodlands of New England on horseback, pastures are even dearer. I see the landscape with the instincts of a farmer. Now that we're back down in the valley, cantering on the berms of great irrigation ditches, I feel lighter-headed, more at home. There is iceberg lettuce in the field still. Most of the cotton has been harvested, but here and there a section waits to be picked by huge mechanical pickers.

Out here, alfalfa is a major irrigated crop, grown as a perennial. Cut and laid in windrows, it is baled soon thereafter. The climate is so dry that spoilage is seldom a problem. Alfalfa will cure in the bale, they assure me. I see it stacked two stories high under a covered pavilion on farm after farm.

On the way home we detour slightly so that I can see someone's pet llamas in their enclosure. Four or five of them stand looking bored in their sandy pen. In the far corner one llama seems to have his head down under the door to the storage bin.

"Is that guy stuck?" one of my buddies asks, immediately concluding that he is. She does a flying dismount, throws me her mare's reins, and shinnies up the chain-link fence, under the electric wire—I never find out if it's turned on—and drops into their pen. Because she is horsewise, instead of tackling him frontally she circles around the critter, slips into the storage area through an adjoining stall, and opens the door from the other side. The poor prisoner recovers his neck with the head still attached, blinks, and stands perfectly still, giving us the once-over. No sign that he had ever been pinioned in that awful cramped position.

"Lucky we made the detour. The owners don't visit every day," my host says.

I ride back silently cursing absentee animal ownership, these casual possessors of creatures they have so little feeling for. If only you needed a license to own a horse or llama, like a driver's license. . . . If only the world were kinder and people more educable. Horses die out here from sand colic, which is another name for dying of boredom and neglect. With nothing to forage for in their bare paddocks, unable to crib on wooden fences or tree trunks—vices we do not condone but under-stand—some horses ingest sand particles as they nose about their en-closures. Impaction colic can result.

That evening we cross the border into Mexico to meet some stu-dents for dinner in Juarez. We spend an hour or so cruising through the local museum and then the state-sponsored crafts shops. Faced with handsome examples of Mexican art, my sales resistance wavers, then holds fast. Enough baggage!

My colleague escorts me to a downtown hotel from which, she as-sures me, there will be limo service early the next morning for my 6:30 flight out. I leave a wake-up call for 5 A.M. and secure everything for a dawn departure. I am still a bit anxious about the supposed limo. I've experienced their late or non-arrivals elsewhere and spent a day fuming, trying to find other connections out.

The next morning I discover I had nothing to worry about. The pilot of my flight to Dallas, as well as several other pilots and flight attendants, slept here, too. We all get a cup of coffee in the lobby, then board the same limousine. They are very chatty, want to know what brings me to El Paso, what is my line of work.

What a strange life! Horses appear in it wherever I go. It turns out that the pilot has a Morgan mare. He's thinking of breeding her to an Ara-bian stallion and asks my opinion. His daughter rides English and wants to learn how to jump. As tactfully as I can, I counsel him to look for a different stallion, a Thoroughbred if possible, to provide the kind of bone a jumper will require.

I almost never have to admit I am a poet in public. When asked "What do you do?", "I raise horses" meets with interest, even approval. "What do you do?" "I'm a poet" invariably invites, "That so? Ever published anything?" If you say you are a doctor or a lawyer your credentials go unchallenged, but to be a poet is immediately to be set apart as somehow incomprehensible.

When I deplane in Dallas to reconnect to Newark and finally to Manchester, the pilot/horse owner is waiting for me at the door of the plane. To my astonishment he is holding a copy of my book, *Nurture*, with my photograph on the back. "I knew I'd seen you somewhere. My daughter went to your reading night before last." He creases the book open to a particular poem, "Sleeping with Animals." And then I remember the adolescent girl who asked me to sign her copy on that page.

I've been found out.

"Have a good trip back," he says. "It's clear weather, all the way."

DRINKING THE RAIN

Alix Kates Shulman

I was nearing the cabin with a bucket of clams in one hand and a giant strand of kelp in another when I tripped and fell on a rock. Somehow, by letting the seaweed go, I managed to break my fall with one hand and prevent my head from cracking, but my torso smacked into the rock, scraping along the sharp barnacles, and the clams flew from the bucket and scattered. I got to my feet and retrieved the clams; and as I cleaned off my bloody body I thought how lucky I was to have escaped with nothing but a skin wound.

That was yesterday; today I'm in pain. As soon as I try to get out of bed, knives start at my side and rip up toward my teeth. I crawl to the aspirin. No help. When I try to lie down again, it's excruciating.

Shall I be afraid? Over the years I've noted how visitors' fears of the solitary life have generally divided by sex. Men fear injury—the broken limb with no one around to care for them—while women, traditionally the caregivers, instead fear the stranger, the hacker. Men fear "nature"; women fear men. Now, with no stranger on the horizon, I follow form, despite the pain.

I soon conclude I've broken a rib. My aged father, who has several times cracked his brittle ribs, once told me there's nothing a doctor can do about them except send you home to heal. Since I'm over fifty myself, I figure mine will probably take some time. Hoping to tame my pain, I study it. Upright I find it's tolerable, but raising or lowering my torso is agony—so I devise a way of sleeping with my back propped against a mound of pillows. I'm okay if I avoid sudden motions and certain specific rotations. Soon my pain is as much a part of me as the calluses on my feet, as familiar as my hands with their blue veins. Whoever I was before, this is who I am now—and managing. Since walking slowly is not unbearable and neither is squatting, I'm able with care to continue gathering my food. Each successful meal reconciles me to the person I've become; instead of damaged I feel accomplished—the opposite of obsolete.

But several weeks later my confidence is tested as, feeling the floor suddenly begin to shake, I look out to see a stranger climbing the stairs. Forgetting myself I leap up, sending a sharp reminder shooting up my side, and rush onto the deck to meet a man dressed, astonishingly, in jacket and tie.

"Morning," he says, thrusting at me a card identifying him as Ethan Groate, Tax Appraiser. I examine it, then reluctantly invite him in.

Perspiring from his long walk across the sunny beach, though it's already mid-September, Ethan Groate stands dazed for a moment in the center of the room, holding his attache case. His spare middle-aged frame is topped by a large head with sallow cheeks, thin lips, and receding chin. Blinking behind his glasses, he pulls from his breast pocket a plaid handkerchief, shakes it open, and mops his skinny neck. Then he slowly looks me over before turning his appraising glance to the cabin, which he begins to circle. I watch him take in the open shelves, the cast-iron stoves, the chunky pink piano, the old seaside scenes from St. Joseph the Provider that I've tacked up here and there.

"When was this cottage built—turn of the century?"

I'm amazed that someone in his line of work could be off by more than half a century. "Nineteen sixty-five," I say, pointing to the framed Certificate of Occupancy, and wonder how old he considers me.

He looks from the document to me and around the room, shaking his head. "Nothing much here but the bare studs and rafters," he says to excuse his error, waving at the uninsulated walls and ceiling. He looks at the mess in the kitchen where I've just been peeling a pot of the small sour apples suitable only for cooking that I gathered from under my tree. He pokes his head into the storeroom: tools and towels hang on nails, miscellaneous supplies in empty coffee cans and boxes are piled neatly on deep shelves, and a salvaged bathroom sink stands beneath the window looking past the outhouse far out to Dedgers. Here's where I take my semiweekly sponge baths by the old-fashioned pitcher-and-basin method, using a pot for pitcher and the sink for basin, and when I'm done I let the water run out the drain that empties through a hose out a hole in the wall. On hot days I sometimes dip in the icy ocean or else shower with water heated in the sun in a giant black plastic douche bag called a "sun shower" that I suspend from a hook over the sink. On cold days I may soak my feet in a tub of luxuriously steaming water, my make-do version of a hot tub.

Ethan Groate tries the faucets, but nothing comes. "No plumbing," he accuses. I shake my head and indicate the outhouse. He opens his attaché case and jabs down a few notations, then closes it and heads out the back door.

From the deck I watch him negotiate the path to the outhouse, his mouth turned down distastefully. He takes a cursory look inside, then hurries back to the cabin. Fixing me with a suspicious stare, he asks, "No septic tank?" I shake my head. "No electricity? No telephone?" I keep on shaking no. "Pretty spartan here, wouldn't you say?"

Spartan? I don't know what to say. This cabin is furnished with everything I could want for my luxurious life and seems anything but spartan. The luxuries I live with are circa 1910—hand pump, gaslights, woodstove—but they're luxuries no less. Still, I'm glad the Tax Appraiser thinks it's spartan, and like a wily merchant consummating a shady deal I readily agree.

He makes some final notes and looking past or through me mutters, "You'll be hearing from us," as his footsteps boom down the stairs.

While I finish the applesauce and clean up the kitchen I try to imagine how this cabin must appear to Ethan Groate. The porcelain surface of the secondhand kitchen sink reveals a network of fine surface cracks distinguishable from dirt only by one who scrubs it. Wiping the long counter, I notice it crumbling near the pump; soon I'll have to replace it. Both cast-iron woodstoves are relics: to use the Franklin stove safely I must frequently mend it with stove cement, and the elegant Queen Atlantic that now serves merely as a countertop has long since rusted out of use. Only one of the burners on the gas stove that replaced it can be turned down to simmer without going out and the door to the oven won't open all the way. The ancient gas refrigerator sports a screwdriver for a door handle. In the eight storm doors on the long sides of the cabin, two panes have been cracked forever, but I've never thought to replace them since they keep the rain out well enough. The screen inserts have all been patched. The doors themselves need painting. The pink piano, which once boomed out rousing accompaniments for our weekend songfests, has four dysfunctional keys and no more pedal or cutoff. In fact, except for the faded canvas director's chairs and the walnut medicine cabinet I once salvaged from the dump, then stripped, oiled, and reglazed, not a single piece of furniture in the motley collection would be presentable anywhere else. The remnant rugs are unraveling, the wood chests have holes, the desk chair has a loose castor that falls off if you move a certain way, the side tables, consisting of driftwood boards set upon boxes, are tippy, the cots sag. The doors stick when it rains, and water stains—remnants of violent storms that drove the rain in under the doors and around the windows—rise up the raw wood walls and spread out on the floor. Windows don't match, deck boards are loose, and battens are gradually coming unnailed.

A ruin!—as perhaps I too appear to Ethan Groate. Yet, like the unexpected reflection I sometimes catch in a window, which looks more like my aging mother than myself, I've come to cherish it no less. Waking in the early light, I study the long rafters and studs like ribs and bones, the grains of the varied woods like networks of nerves, knots like eyes, arteries of copper tubing that rise from the propane tanks beneath the deck and snake along the rafters and down the walls to each lamp. Listening to the pulse of waves against the shore, I feel the house come alive as each day awakens in song.

Sometimes I'm startled awake by the thump of heavy gulls landing on the roof, once by a woodpecker hammering on my ear through the bedroom wall, occasionally by barn swallows chattering on the porch railing outside my window. Without insulation, the roof reverberates like a sounding board, a drumskin, a set of strings stretched across the rafters to catch the staccato-clear splatter and plink of each individual drop when it starts to rain, until, as the rain falls harder, the roof gives back a trill, a tremolo, a chord, a roll. And beneath the chorus like a ground bass beats the complicated rhythm of the sea, thundering at high tide or murmuring at low, gentle as brushes or furious as cymbals, as it laps protected Singing Sand Beach to the north, crashes on the rocks of Dedgers to the east, and pounds against South Beach, stretched out along the back of the nubble.

I gather up the apple peels and step out on the deck to toss them, in the direction of the apple tree, down into the dense acre of brush and shrubbery that surrounds the cabin. What would Ethan Groate have to say about this? "No garbage can? No compost heap?" The whole nubble is my compost heap as I fling what little garbage I produce in as wide an arc as I can to join the apples, bay leaves, and rose hips already rotting on the ground.

Beyond Dedgers there's a boat anchored, with two people in wet suits going over the side. Heeding a call of nature, I head for the privy, where I can watch them dive. Back in the days when the cabin was crowded with visitors, this outhouse was my refuge—like the bathroom of my childhood, the one lockable room in the house, the only place where privacy was guaranteed. Architecturally a puppy of the main cabin, identical in its board-and-batten exterior and the low pitch of its roof, the outhouse has two small rooms: one the woodshed, the other the throne room. Except on the rare, still summer day, the single hole, freshened by ocean breezes, collects few foul smells, no flies.

Whereas in the city, despite the most lavish bourgeois bathrooms, using the toilet is considered at best indecorous, using this privy is one of the day's most satisfying interludes. (So it must have been in the grand Roman imperial privy, mosaic-adorned, that I once saw in an excavation in Rome and again in a bathhouse in Pompeii, with holes for perhaps a dozen people to sit and shit together in council; so was it for the Queen in the excavated toilet chamber at the palace of Knossos on the isle of Crete.) From this perfect bird blind of a privy, built on a platform with a protective roof and open front facing the sea, I can watch the swallows feeding their young in the rafters, or follow a marsh hawk glide in slow easy loops around the nubble as it hunts field mice. From this pew I have marked the progress of the seasons in the flower-crammed brush: fiddleheads and berry blossoms in early spring, wild roses, nightshade, and touch-me-nots in summer, goldenrod and pale purple asters now in fall. Knowing I can see them but they can't see me on my shaded seat, I watch the yellow-slickered lobstermen standing in their boats to haul in their traps, rebait them, and toss them back into the ocean. Sometimes I watch sailboats race across the horizon from Falmouth to Monhegan Island and back again and, at night, the clouds racing past the moon.

Recently a contest was held at the island store to see who could identify the greatest number of the island's outhouses pictured in a long row of snapshots tacked up on a wall. I was told that people generally agreed the view from the nubble outhouse is one of the best on the island—an opinion seconded in the grateful graffiti left by occasional winter visitors—*pace* Ethan Groate.

His contrary response reminds me of an incident that occurred on a visit I made years ago to the great eighth-century Buddhist temple of Borobudur on the island of Java. In ninety degrees of muggy heat, sweat streaming from my pores, I climbed the steep shadeless hill up to the temple, then on around the temple's lavishly carved walls, examining the thousands of narrative and decorative stone bas-reliefs as I spiraled slowly up toward the summit. Growing progressively abstract and spiritual as they approached the top, the sculptures were so transporting that even the most obdurate materialist must feel the holiness of such a place. Back at the bottom, where a protective park with refreshment stands, parking lots, and rest rooms surrounded the temple, I stopped at a kiosk to gulp down a tall glass of hot lemon, and another, and yet another, then walked to the toilets before leaving. Squatting inside a booth, I overheard an American woman, one of a new busload of tourists, tell her companion that she'd rather hold it in for another hour than use these awful toilets. I was surprised: the tourist facilities in the park were modern and impeccable, the toilets scrupulously cared for, like everything at that holy site where UNESCO had carried out a careful restoration, hoping to preserve the temple and its grounds for another thousand years. "None of the toilets flush, they don't even have seats," wailed the tourist to her companion. Now, it was true that the toilets had no mechanical levers to release a rush of water—often far in excess of what might be needed—like those the tourists were used to. But there was plenty of clean water: in each booth, beside the toilet, stood a deep tiled cistern with a faucet that could be turned on as needed and a long-handled ladle for transporting the water to the toilet in the exact quantity needed for flushing. And a pair of slightly raised footrests were positioned for comfortably squatting over the low toilet bowl. An efficient sanitary system—like my privy, unfairly scorned by Ethan Groate.

As I sit high in my outhouse on the smooth seat, watching the frog-suited couple dive from their boat for sea urchins destined for the lucrative Japanese market, I'm both sitting and squatting. Since my midwife friend Margaret convinced me of the natural virtues of squatting to expel an object from the lower body, I've placed a four-by-four on the floor as a footrest, so my knees are raised to the level of my waist, I can rest my elbows on them, chin in my hands, and push. In our first summer here, we always threw a ladleful of lye down to the ground below before leaving the outhouse, as someone had advised; but with so few odors or insects, I no longer bother. Why fill up the space any sooner than neccssary? When I decide to plant a garden, it will be behind the outhouse, where the rich night soil trickles down and enormous black-berries are just now beginning to ripen. I pick two, press them against the roof of my mouth with my tongue to release the juices, and savor them slowly as I walk back up the path to the cabin.

When the kettle is boiling I place a dishpan in one half of the double sink, fill it with warm soapy water, and pile in the dirty dishes. In the other half I set another dishpan under the pump for rinsing. The capacious cistern that serves as rain barrel holds more water than I'm ever likely to need; I've never once run out. All the same, I try to use the minimum. The pleasure is as much aesthetic as practical. Sinking my hands in the warm suds and reliving the meal as I whoosh away the remains, I think of the years in New York when I washed dishes with the taps wide open and the water running down the drain, oblivious of the energy required to purify an urban water supply, and then of other years when I routinely piled dishes into an electric dishwasher, though the time required to scrape and rinse them, then load, start, run and empty the machine, compounded by the excess water and energy, the detergent pollution, noise, wear on the dishes, the cost of purchase, operation, and repair, and the eventual problem of solid waste disposal washed away the advantage unless I had been feeding a mob.

Yet, if it hadn't cost half a fortune to get a rig up on the nubble for digging a well or to bury electrical and phone lines under the beach, Jerry would probably have installed all the standard equipment for an up-to-date life under late-twentieth-century capitalism, and I would never have discovered how gracefully one can live without them.

I empty the dishwater down the drain and wipe the sink, focusing not on the hairline cracks but on the islands of porcelain gleaming between them. Let the Tax Appraiser file his report. This cabin, however scarred or outmoded, miraculously renews itself. Like my rib, which will soon be healed.

It's October 18—later than I've ever been on the island. Dense foggy mornings, frosty nights, a lucent crown of brilliant red and golden leaves on the distant ridge. A stately great blue heron arrives at dusk to fish the cove; hundreds of ducks mass offshore in a huge black armada; two cedar waxwings with their masked faces and jaunty crests swing on the ripened goldenrod burning across the nubble in the cool October light; honking geese V southward overhead—all preparing for winter. Soon, alas, I too, succumbing to the cold, will have to pack and leave.

A storm rages that night, bringing heavy winds and choppy seas. When it clears, the normally white beach is littered with masses of dark seaweed thrown up from the deep and other interesting debris that cause bathers to think post-storm beaches "dirty." (One summer, in fact, the city of Portland hired teams of teenagers to rake up and burn all the seaweed, driftwood, and refuse that had accumulated on South Beach during the previous winter, only to see much of it replaced during the next big storm. The one lasting result I could see of all that fruitless effort was the pitiful waste of the driftwood fuel I'd come to count on.) According to a booklet on seaweeds Jerry has kindly mailed up to me, many species of seaweed are exposed only after a storm; so at the next low tide I go down to the beach in my poncho to investigate.

The shore is strewn with great balls of Irish moss, immense blades of smooth long-stemmed kelp, similar to the Japanese kombu, and several long whips of the rare sea plant I'd longed to find, alaria. This brown seaweed, sometimes called honey kelp, winged kelp, or, in Japanese, wakame, looks very like ordinary long-stemmed kelp but for the delicious hollow rib which is actually a continuation of the stem, or stipe, running from the holdfast all along the blade to the very tip and which, when sliced into a salad or stew, adds a sweet tasty crunch, something like water chestnuts.

When I've gathered all the alaria I can find, I crisscross the beach several times more looking for tangle and dulse, but without success, and pass up two more left-handed fisherman's gloves at their historic spot. Heading up the beach toward the nubble, I notice what looks like a giant quahog, the largest I've ever seen, lying alone like a rock in the midst of a great expanse of white sand at the top of the beach, far from the water.

I stoop to examine it. Its shell is open about half an inch, revealing the firm plump flesh of a living clam. I pick it up. Measuring eight or nine inches across, it lies in my hand like a stone weighing several pounds—equivalent in size to perhaps a dozen of my ordinary, laboriously procured clams. As soon as I poke the flesh the quahog snaps closed its shells, clamming up tight. I drop it into the bucket.

For years I've seen only ashtrays in those largest of all empty clam shells strewn along the shore, have passed them in ignorance, like most beachcombers, oblivious of their species or how they got there. I suppose I assumed they'd been snatched from the ocean gulls and dropped from the sky—even though their smooth shells offer no purchase for a beak and seem far too heavy for a gull to lift. Now, remembering that storms can toss entire armadas onto shore, I wonder if perhaps the ocean itself hasn't somehow hurled it here.

Can it be safe to eat? With plants the trick is to avoid harmful species; but with shellfish it's the tainted individual one must guard against by making sure each specimen is alive and healthy when caught. This is not always as easy as it appears; it takes some practice to discover each species' telltale vital motions. Most creatures naturally retreat or flee when they sense danger: clams clam up, periwinkles slam shut their operculas, crabs scram; but (as humans have sometimes observed closer to home) some live creatures act dead and some dead ones look alive. Crustaceans that have just shed their shell go limp and simulate corpses, while lifeless empty bivalve shells are sometimes misleadingly glued shut by a cement of water and sand. To guard against these traps, I've learned to cook my bivalves separately; then, if an individual fails to open, or if a sand-filled one finds its way into the pot, I can removed the duds, let the sand sink, and skim off the good broth. Ordinarily I wouldn't consider eating a creature lacking any means of surface locomotion found so far from its underwater habitat; but this particular clam is so clearly alive and so loaded with meat—big enough for an entire meal—that I decide to risk it.

That evening I turn my catch into the sweetest chowder I've ever had. In the pot, it gives up a rich aromatic broth and yields over a cupful of nutty meat. I thicken the strained broth with gelatinous Irish moss (the same agent used commercially to thicken ice cream), add the chopped meat, flavor it with sea rocket, garlic, and angelica, and garnish it with six inches of crisp stipe of fresh alaria that I sliver with a paring knife. To the accompaniment of foghorns and buoy bells, beside a crackling fire, I slowly eat my dinner.

The next day I'm down at the shore hunting again. I find three more specimens of the giant clam, and the following day, two. I scrub them, steam them open, and anatomize them, examining each intricate organ before I eat them. I'm so absorbed that not till the third day do I turn to my books to see what I can find out about this newest and easiest catch. Gibbons, in an entire brief chapter devoted to its praises, tells me I have found not a quahog but a surf clam, the largest clam species on the Atlantic seaboard. Like so many wild foods, the surf clam is widely scorned by all but a few initiates—including Gibbons, and now myself. I'm pleased to find I've been chopping into my chowders parts of the clam that even Gibbons disdains as tough. From him I learn to sauté and savor unadorned the large tender cylindrical abductor muscles, the very part of the scallop we consume and prized by Gibbons in the surf clam as sweeter than the sweetest scallop's.

Tomorrow, according to the forecast, begins another week of cold with intermittent rain. Having already felt the first premonitory chill of winter, I'm resigned to boarding up and leaving for the city in at most a week. In the few remaining days I concentrate exclusively on surf clams, snatching them from cresting waves before the undertow can push them out again. As I toss the empty shells out to sea, I wonder if and where they'll wash ashore to be collected for ashtrays by day-trippers ignorant of what they've found—like me until just this week. It troubles me that though I read Gibbons's book straight through, I never before noticed a surf clam. What other edible species may be lying unrecognized at my feet?

On Friday the sea turns calm, and there are no more clams.

. . .

Bundled up on the deck in parka, muffler, and gloves to capture the few precious hours of remaining light, I seem to have entered a new mode. I glance up from my book to notice the apple tree heavy with ripe fruit. But instead of being small and green, the apples are yellow, some tinted with delicate pale-pink stripes, some as large as market fruit. My surprise registers more as a feeling than as a thought. I reproach myself for having made no more than half a dozen apple pies this year, as many batches of applesauce, two apple cakes, only three jars of apple chutney, a few experimental savory dishes—and all mainly from windfalls, since I couldn't bear to pluck a fruit before its prime. And now the most perfect apples will go uneaten. (If I had a family to feed we could store our apples for the winter in bins, or dried, or preserved in chutneys, jams, and sauces. But alone I'm able to eat just so many apples.)

Seeing this vast casual waste, I feel a pang of regret—fleeting and dismissible, since I've had all the fruit I want. I let it go and return to my book. But glancing up to reflect on a passage, I see again the groaning tree and the pang returns, this time closer to a thought. Each time I look up it nags at me, expanding bit by bit into the space between my other thoughts, until finally I put down my book and try to grasp it. I focus on the feeling as I fill in one small gap after another, connecting what have hitherto been disparate, even contrary, takes, until finally it's there before me, full-blown as the apple tree itself: a long thought that lengthens and spreads like the sun's rays at day's end till it tints the entire sky—surely the kind of thought Ouspensky means by "long":

This island, which has been my refuge from the waste that is the other side of glut, produces excess of its own. There are all those apples, finally ripened to perfection, and they will not be eaten. Everywhere I look I see a world of astonishing abundance, wild extravagance, glorious waste. Hundreds of thousands of dock seeds, my muffin enricher, fringe the bluff. Touch-me-nots (or jewelweed) fling their edible seeds into the air at the merest touch of a bird or breeze. Brilliant red rose hips, my staple tea, my daily hit of Vitamin C, now entirely surround the cabin. They're already perfectly preserved, and though birds will feed on them all winter there'll still be plenty for me when I return in spring. Countless seaweeds, naturally dried and salted, line the shore; blackberry leaves, goldenrod, bay all beckon me to harvest and dry them for winter infusions. Everywhere I turn I see abundance and overflow—

as excessive as the glut I deplore in the city, but with the crucial difference that here it's all biodegradable. Whatever I leave behind far from
being wasted will nourish the soil and grow again.

From a few isolated tentative flashes, my thought has lengthened
into an awareness of abundance that replaces the pang of regret with a
purr of joy. And still, as long as I concentrate, it has plenty of room to
grow—and will continue to grow and stretch until, after many more
meals and years, it will eventually encompass a great cornucopia of edibles
in perfect ecological balance spiraling in circles downward to the sea
within a ten-minute radius of my hearth. Before I'm done I will have
found and eaten: elderberries, raspberries, blackberries, huckleberries,
currants, shadberries, rose hips, jewelweed, fiddleheads, goldenrod, sheep
sorrel, charlock, bay leaves, all from the brush surrounding the cabin;
then just down the stairs above the beach: angelica (for parsley), Scotch
lovage, dandelion, chicory, beach peas, red clover, orach, lamb's-quar-
ters, strawberry goosefoot, goosetongue, sea rocket, strand wheat, yellow dock, apples; in the tidal flats and among the rocks: steamer clams,
quahogs, surf clams, green crabs, blue mussels, horse mussels, periwinkles, dog whelks, moon shells, sea urchins, lobsters, eels; in the tidal
pools that form my seaweed garden: sea lettuce, tiger moss, Irish moss,
tangle, bullwhip kelp, long-stemmed kelp; and strewn across the beach
after a storm: alaria, purple dulse, laver or nori, and colonies of arame;
then venturing across the beach up the path, onto the dirt road: a dozen
other varieties of apples, as well as pears, cattails, pineapple weed, juniper berries, serviceberries, cranberries, chokecherries, strawberries, stag-
horn sumac, Jerusalem artichokes, acorns, chestnuts; and in the woods:
wild ginger, blueberries, mint, ground nut, wood sorrel, and various
edible fungi. All are part of the living cohort I first glimpsed on the
subway in its human manifestation and now see daily in myriad forms
everywhere I look.

Not only on the nubble but everywhere, once I've learned how to
see. In the cracks of city sidewalks, on the Colorado Rocky
mountainsides, in the lawns of Cleveland Heights and the yards of Santa
Fe, in the gutters of Honolulu, on the trails of Oahu, sprinkling the
desert and lining the riverbanks, I see endless offerings of discarded or
unharvested food: pigweed, nasturtiums, laurel, mint, watercress, prickly
pears, plums, apricots, avocados, guavas, cherries, crab apples, oranges,

lemons, pomegranates—a garden of delectables unrecognized, snubbed, forgotten by a world that goes to the store.

I decide to fill a garbage bag with a selection of dried seaweeds and a few small bags with dock seeds, rose hips, and bay leaves to take back to the city as a reminder of the difference between abundance and glut, between a long thought and a short one.

Now the wild spinach has all gone to seed and the nights have turned so cold that I fear the water will freeze and crack the cistern. I drain it, pack my bags, close off the propane, and before dusk falls reluctantly board up the cabin.

As I look back at the nubble from the end of the road where I wait for Lucy Chaplain to pick me up in the island taxi to take me and my gear to the ferry, I see the great blue heron light again at the base of the Shmoos. I unpack the binoculars to watch him fish. How majestically he stands on one foot in the roiling surf as the tide flows in. He wades through the water so slowly that his movement is almost imperceptible, though once I see him swat at something in the air with his great wing, then snatch it with his beak. Mostly he just waits and watches, patient and still, until the moment comes to plunge his head into the water to grab his prey and then, throwing back his head, consume it in a few snaps of his long beak. I watch his darkening silhouette with its stilt legs and slender throat until there's barely light to see by.

I want my thoughts to be as patient and slow as the heron standing at the water's edge fishing the incoming tide for as long as it takes to catch the treasures swimming by. Or, I want them, like the barnacles opening up to feed when the tide comes in, to filter the plankton newly streaming around me, so rich and abundant that what I can't find here hardly seems worth wanting.

POLAR BEAR PASS

Helen Thayer

In 1988 Helen Thayer set off to do what no other woman had ever done: ski to the North Pole. Planning to make the journey alone, at the last minute she was persuaded to take along a black husky she named Charlie.

Day 3

At 6:00 A.M. I was awake but not rested. It had been a tense night listening for bears. Charlie had made no sound and I hadn't heard the dreaded sound of a bear. As I lay in my sleeping bag trying to persuade my reluctant body to move out of the tent into the cold to begin a new day, I thought of yesterday. But my mind rebelled and I resolved not to dwell on the past. No more thinking of the yesterdays, they were gone. Instead I would save my emotional energy to think and plan ahead. I needed to travel as many miles a day as possible to move quickly through this heavily populated polar bear area. Having set a firm course of action in my mind I crawled out of my warm sleeping bag into the bleak cold of the early Arctic morning.

My first job was to take stock of my hands. The bloodblisters were larger and redder than yesterday and both hands were more swollen. My usually large hands were now very large and certainly weren't candidates for a beauty contest. There was no sign of infection. Surely no self-respecting bacteria would live in this cold place, I thought, as I gritted my teeth and squeezed my swollen hands into blue liner gloves that now seemed two sizes too small.

I unzipped the tent door, grabbed my warm parka, and stepped outside. I looked quickly around for bears while I walked across the ice in my camp booties, sliding into my jacket as I went. Charlie had just got up and was stretching and yawning. I hugged him good morning. "Did you sleep OK, Charlie?" A lick across my face with his big soft tongue told me "yes."

The first long golden rays of the new day's sun were already washing over the tent, turning the tiny ice crystals covering the blue nylon into dancing, sparkling diamonds. I fumbled around trying to make my hands cooperate so I could light the stove. The pain in the tips of my fingers made that out of the question. I had to devise a method of using the palms of my hands and my wrists to connect the fuel bottle to the stove. With some patience it worked. The stove roared to life as loudly as a blowtorch and I moved to where I could see Charlie in case he warned me of a bear. It was impossible for me to hear anything over the roar of the stove. I quickly put a pan of ice on the stove to melt while I fed Charlie. I was in a hurry to leave this place and find smooth ice again with better visibility. It was spooky in this icy forest.

The water was barely warm when I poured it over my granola. I ate fast, then gulped down one cup of hot chocolate and began packing my sled as more ice melted to fill my thermoses. In another forty-five minutes all was packed and Charlie and I were ready to leave.

The rough ice stretched ahead as far as I could see but it was possible to ski around the mounds now. Charlie and I zigzagged back and forth, finding narrow gaps between the pillars of ice, which allowed our sleds to slide through without jamming. Suddenly Charlie let out a blood-curdling yelp. I almost had a heart attack. I thought a bear had got me. Then I realized I had stepped on his front paw with my ski. He stood holding his foot up and I stopped and rubbed it to make sure it wasn't cut. "I'm sorry, Charlie," I said. Then miraculously it was instantly well. Amazing what a little attention can achieve.

Another hour went by and I could see about half a mile ahead to where the maze of pillars appeared to end at a long east-to-west ridge of ice. It was a ten-mile pressure ridge, stretching snakelike all the way from Bathurst Island to Kalivik Island, about ten feet high with some peaks reaching fifteen feet. Pressure ridges form when the leading edges of two ice floes or bodies of ice meet, coming together under tremendous pressure, crumpling and grinding upward to form rough, jumbled, jagged ridges. Sometimes the pressure is forced downward, creating a pressure ridge beneath the water. I hadn't expected to find a ridge of this size in this area, but the ice pack is unpredictable and changes every year. I was halfway between the two islands. Here, the ridge appeared to be at its highest. Away off in the distance it was lower closer to Bathurst and Kalivik. But it was a long way to ski to the lower ends. Perhaps I could find a gap close by.

The tracks of a large polar bear and the tiny tracks of an Arctic fox crossed our path. They looked only a few hours old. I couldn't see any sign of the owners so I nervously kept going. Charlie exuberantly pressed his black nose hard down on the ice over the bear paw prints and tried to follow them. I yanked his chain as hard as I could with my right hand to stop him from pulling me off after the bear. It developed into a tug-of-war. I gained ground after shouting, "No, Charlie," and, "Come here, Charlie," several times. He conceded victory, but he gave me a long sideways look that told me I hadn't won any points for imagination. My unsportsmanlike conduct in not joining in the bear chase was clearly not appreciated. "Charlie, we're supposed to avoid bears," I said, "not look for them."

At a hundred feet away I still couldn't see any real gaps but there were snowdrifts built like ramps on the side of the ridge. Over to the left I spotted a small cave that had been lived in, but was now smashed inward. Bear and fox tracks ran everywhere. I saw a large splotch of blood and a mostly devoured seal three feet in front of the cave. Charlie was gleefully trying to pull me over there, so I gave in and joined the investigation. It had been a ringed seal breathing hole, which had drifted over with blowing snow to form a cave, with the unfortunate occupant having met a violent end.

Seals are the polar bear's main food source. The ringed seal, so called because of the pale rings on a dark skin, is the most common seal in the area. They live in the sea under the ice and come up for air through breathing holes in the ice pack, usually in cracks or in the thinner ice. During the winter when the ice becomes hard and thick, they have to keep their breathing holes open by constant scratching with the strong, curved claws of their fore flippers. Blowing snow drifts over the hole, camouflaging it. The snow becomes deep and hard-packed enough for the female seal to excavate a small snow cave or birth lair, in which she has her pup in the spring.

The snow cave is supposed to protect the seal and her pup from the prying eyes of a hungry polar bear. But polar bears have a remarkable sense of smell, and they can detect ringed seal breathing holes beneath a layer of snow as much as two or three feet deep. When a bear senses a seal breathing hole or birth lair, it smashes it with massive front paws and in a flash grabs the unfortunate seal or pup. The thick layer of fat beneath the seal's skin is the polar bear's favorite meal. Arctic foxes commonly follow polar bears to scavenge the leftovers of the hunt. By the looks of this scene a bear and a fox had eaten well.

Charlie was having a picnic scratching and chewing the bloodstained ice and eating a few scraps of leftover seal. When he tried to roll in the blood I decided enough was enough. A dog that smells like a seal might become an attraction instead of a deterrent to polar bears. There were probably more seal breathing holes around the pressure ridge, undoubtedly good hunting for polar bears, in which case this was definitely a place I wanted to leave as soon as possible.

To our right was a promising-looking ramp of hardpacked snow reaching halfway up the pressure ridge. On each side of the ramp the tortured, fractured ice was piled in an uneven mass of jumbled blocks, some six feet or more across. Leaving my skis beside my sled and using my ice axe for balance, I climbed the ramp looking for a way over the top. At the top four feet of unstable broken ice still had to be crossed. The only thing to do was chop a path over the top, pull my sled up, then lower it carefully down the other side.

After twenty minutes of chopping I formed a usable path. Climbing back down I tied a fifty-foot piece of seven-millimeter rope onto the front handle of my sled; then, grabbing the sturdy handle, I pulled it up the ramp. Now for the tricky part. Holding on to the sled with one hand and balancing myself so that I didn't end up at the bottom of the ramp again, I tied the rope around a three-foot block of ice. Then, carefully stepping around the sled, I got behind it ready to push it over the top. Suddenly, my feet shot out from under me and I somersaulted down the slope to land right under the nose of an astonished Charlie, who jumped back in alarm. Unhurt, I scrambled to my feet thinking dire thoughts about pressure ridges and sleds. Climbing up again, more carefully this time, I pushed the sled over the top, then slowly lowered it with the rope down the other side. Now for Charlie's smaller, lighter sled. It was quite easy to pull up and over, using the same system.

The pillars of ice were behind us now; ahead lay a smooth stretch of terrain. But as I was standing on top of the ridge, I noticed strange-looking bumps in the ice about half a mile out. It was 11:30 A.M. when I started off in that direction. The sky was still clear and the wind speed read twelve miles per hour. The temperature had lowered to 33 below zero, sending the wind chill to 60 degrees below zero. My face mask was covered with an inch-thick layer of ice that molded the mask to the shape of my face. My eyelashes were frozen. I was growing tired of looking at the world through a row of miniature icicles that hung down in front of my eyes. At first I tried to rub them off but each time an icicle came off, it brought with it an eyelash. The thought of returning to civilization with no eyelashes made me stop rubbing. Even out here by myself in the middle of this icy desert, vanity was still a factor.

I was anxious to reach the icy, dark bumps I had seen ahead of us. My curiosity was soon satisfied. I stood looking in disbelief across a sea of ice that looked as if it had boiled into giant bubbles, each bubble a solid mound of ice six feet across, two feet high, frozen in place. The snow had been swept away, leaving a smooth, shiny, dark blue-green surface with thin strips and circles of hard-packed snow around the mounds. It was old, multiyear ice, perhaps twenty feet thick, rock hard, worn smooth by the wind and sun, with the salt and air squeezed out.

The synthetic skins that I had started out with were still on my skis. They performed well, giving my skis the extra grip I needed to pull my sled. But these shiny smooth mounds would be a real test. Charlie had had no problem with traction so far, but I wondered how his feet would grip the hard, bare ice ahead of us.

We had already passed Kalivik Island. I could see nothing but mounds of ice to the east so I decided to angle west, closer to Bathurst, in search of a way around the strange mounds. At first I kept to the packed snow bordering the edges of each mound, trying to find extra grip for my skis. After spending hours weaving through the rough ice we had just left behind, I longed to ski straight ahead and make good time. I decided to tackle the mounds.

By standing solidly on the middle of my skis to gain all the grip I could, I managed to walk my skis up one side of a mound, then slide down the other with my sled teetering on the top before it came flying crazily down the slope, catching the tails of my skis. Meanwhile, Charlie was following at my side at the end of his chain. I was concentrating so completely on staying upright and dodging my flying sled that at first I didn't notice the sideways tug on Charlie's chain. Finally, he got my attention by jerking at his chain, stepping out to the right onto a patch of snow, and stopping. I was thankful he couldn't put into words what was on his mind. His eyes were gloomy and his ears drooped. His expression told me that he was not going to put up with these straight-ahead tactics any longer. He was having trouble gripping the smooth ice of the mounds, and the only way he was going to continue was to follow the snowy edges.

I had already begun to realize that my tactics weren't working. The flying sleds were dangerous. This was no place for either Charlie or me to break a leg. I felt terribly guilty at being so impatient and putting speed ahead of safety. It was time to stop and put matters right with Charlie. The best way to ask for forgiveness was with food. Releasing my skis and sled harness, I pulled the day's food bag out of my sled. Sitting on his sled with my arm around him, I fed him crackers and a few peanut butter cups. I told him, "I'm sorry," and patted his head as he ate. His gloomy look was immediately replaced with his begging look. Everything was all right between us again. I managed to eat a few peanut butter cups before he finished the entire day's supply.

On we went, pulling our sleds, following the snowy edges around the mounds as we gradually angled over toward Bathurst Island. I had already marked Kalivik Island to the east off my map, and now I could see Goodsir Inlet on Bathurst. The coast was still very low, and according to my map the inlet appeared to be almost at sea level for about a mile inland. The map also showed a river mouth there, but it was frozen and impossible to see in the afternoon's white glare. I was a mile offshore and still angling in.

The glare was a problem. As the afternoon wore on, I squinted more and more, trying to see through the bright reflected light for landmarks and bears. My double lens goggles were a nuisance. They kept fogging up and the fog quickly turned to ice. When I used the mountaineering trick of wiping saliva on the inside of the lens, it too instantly froze and had to be scraped off. The goggles were not the wrap-around kind and seriously inhibited my peripheral vision. They made me feel as if my world was closing in around me, and the thought that there might be a bear just around the corner where I couldn't see it drove me to distraction. But every time I tried to do without the goggles I could feel my eyes burning in the bright light and I was forced to put them back on. This was only day three and once again the polar bears were making me ride the fine line of survival. I reminded myself that only emotional discipline was going to get me to the pole.

About four hours after we first entered the ice mounds, they began to decrease, replaced with longer areas of packed snow. I was less than a half mile off the Bathurst shoreline, in the transition zone between the rough fractured shore ice and the older, thicker sea ice. Before I turned directly north up the coast, I checked the measuring wheel that was attached to the back of my sled. Each revolution of the metal wheel moved a counter that gave me the number of miles I had traveled. It was already four-thirty and today's mileage, so far, totaled only five. All that work for so little gain.

To make matters worse I could see more rough ice ahead. This area was supposed to be smooth—at least those were the reports from last year. I was the only expedition to travel to the magnetic North Pole this season so I hadn't been able to get any current ice conditions except for a report from the meteorological office and two of Bradley's pilots who had told me, "The ice seems to be more broken and pressured this year along Bathurst." So far they were right. Bezal at base camp had also warned me that the ice might be rougher this year. He was just as concerned about wind. He called the route to the magnetic North Pole a wind tunnel. As yet wind had not been of any significance. Perhaps I would be lucky for the entire journey. I decided to travel two more miles, then camp. My mask was cold and beginning to freeze to my face. Even so it still protected my skin from the cold wind.

I reached another pressure ridge, this one only three or four feet high with long easy gaps between the blocks of ice. "This is more our size, Charlie," I said with pleasure. But on the other side all I could see was a field of broken, jumbled ice stretching north, east, and west. The sun, low in the sky over Bathurst, was spreading a golden glow over the western sides of tall pinnacles of ice that cast long, dark, ghostlike shadows to the east. A fog of ice crystals, turned golden by the setting sun, was also spreading softly over the low coast of Bathurst. The scene before me was unreal, unearthly. A photograph could never capture the cold, naked beauty of a land and icescape untouched and uncomplicated by man.

Standing there beside Charlie, I was afraid to go through those silent, dark shadows that lay across our path. I wouldn't see a polar bear in there until he was too close. A feeling of vulnerability swept over me and thoughts of Bill sprang into my mind. He knew about the three bears yesterday and he would be worried about us. To add to my fears, Charlie had been sniffing the air to the east for the last half hour. I could see nothing, but did he know something was out there? As I stood leaning on my ski poles looking ahead to the shadows we must pass through, I spoke to Charlie, talking away my fears. "This is spooky, Charlie, but to get to the pole we have to cross through here. A few bears and a few shadows shouldn't stop us."

The sound of my voice bolstered my courage. I put my arms around Charlie and hugged him tight. Those shadows ahead didn't seem nearly as ominous now. It was time to go and we entered the first long shadows. It was still spooky, but I was in control again.

I kept going until we had passed through the shadowed area. Meanwhile, Charlie was still looking due east. He had me worried. What was he looking for? If there was a bear out there, it must be keeping abreast of us. Perhaps it was a fox. I decided that until proven otherwise it would be a fox. That was easier for my mind to handle.

There were a few smooth ice pans, some two or three hundred feet wide, between the leaning towers and blocks of ice. An iceberg, thirty feet high, lay ahead. It came from a distant glacier and stood trapped in the crushing grasp of the ice pack, a prisoner until the summer thaw. There was a wide apron of smooth ice around it, a good camping spot with good visibility.

The sun had slipped away and the temperature was dropping, although still only in the minus thirties. The extreme dryness of the air made it seem colder. I eased my face mask off without tearing my skin underneath. It was a cold, frozen lump. Tonight I would have to thaw my mask and fix my jacket. Ice crystals had built up between the jacket lining and the outside fabric. My arms could hardly bend because of the ice. It had become a straitjacket.

I went to work feeding Charlie, making camp, and cooking and eating dinner. But he was still uneasy. He ate a little dog food but left the rest in his bowl as he stood looking into the distance to the east. Something was bothering him. Even after the long day he wouldn't sit or lie down. I arranged my skis, axe, and spare ski poles in a circle fifty feet out from the tent. My theory was that a bear might be curious enough to stop to examine these strange objects before investigating the contents of the tent. The idea was just a little silly, because if a bear got that close, Charlie would have a fit and would warn me. However, it was a psychological help.

In my tent I kept an eye on Charlie while I thawed my mask over the stove, which sat in the doorway. The jacket was next. It had a hood and was made of a red-and-black windproof fabric with a zipper all the way down the front. There was a thick layer of ice along the zipper that thawed out in a cloud of steam that froze almost instantly into ice crystals and formed a frozen fog inside the tent. During the day the zipper kept freezing up and jamming. Now as I pried it open I had to be careful the zipper teeth didn't break. I found the jacket could almost stand up by itself because of the thick layer of ice between the lining and the shell. The lining was sewn shut so I slit the sleeve endings to allow the ice to fall out as soon as it formed. It looked a little ragged but would now be much more functional. It was a good traveling jacket. But when I stopped, I always put my big down jacket over the top of my clothing in an effort to keep the cold from creeping in. The down jacket was too bulky and warm to ski in.

At eight o'clock I called base camp to give Terry my position and sent a message to Bill. Terry told me Bill had telephoned and sent his love. These daily messages relayed by radio and telephone were a comfort that I looked forward to. When I signed off I noticed that Charlie was still standing guard. Sleep was out of the question for me until I found out what was out there. Wearing my big down parka, I sat on my sled, facing Charlie, with the rifle and flare gun close at hand, and wrote in my journal. The pen had frozen, so I took out one of the many pencils I had brought with me. My hands made writing difficult. As I held the pencil between the inside edges of my index and middle fingers, my usually bad writing was made worse, but it was important to write details of the events and my thoughts for the day. "After experiencing such awful mind-consuming fear continuously for three days," I wrote, "I wonder if the real definition of courage is the ability to deal successfully with one's fears. At the end of this expedition I hope to be not only alive, but also able to say that I have courage."

Suddenly Charlie growled softly. Dropping the journal, I grabbed the rifle and flare pistol and moved quickly to his side. I squinted through the gray light but could see nothing. Charlie growled louder. Then I saw a movement to the side of a small car-sized block of ice. It was an adult bear standing about two hundred yards away, looking straight at us. Charlie was motionless and quiet. I stood still and waited. When the bear began to walk toward us, Charlie sprang to life with a fierce snarling growl. The bear immediately backed up and, seemingly satisfied, Charlie stopped growling. The bear, still two hundred yards away, moved to the south of us, then stopped, as if to come forward again. Charlie was ready with another ear-tingling snarl. The bear appeared to think better of the whole situation and left, moving at a fast lope, going south. I guessed it had been following us some distance off to the east for several hours. Charlie apparently knew it was there but sensed that the bear was just curious and only growled when it took the liberty of moving toward us.

I was relieved beyond words and again thankful for Charlie. He was relaxed now and went about eating his dinner. He seemed satisfied that another bear episode was over. I gave him a good night hug just before he curled up to sleep. How I wished I could figure out these bears the way he did. He obviously could sense the difference between an aggressive, dangerous bear and one that was only curious. It was eleven o'clock. The pale light of a full moon sparkled across the ice. I felt confident that we had seen the last of the curious bear, so I climbed into my sleeping bag for my best night's sleep on the ice so far.

CONTRIBUTORS

Barbara Beckwith (born 1937) has written about her outdoor adventures for the *New York Times*, the *Washington Post, U.S. Air, Backpacker Footnotes* and *Adirondack Life*, and about women's issues for *Ms., Essence, Sojourner* and *Women and Health*. An outdoorsperson all her life, she has backpacked in almost every mountain range in the continental U.S. and has spent time rock climbing, white-water canoeing, winter camping and bicycle-camping in France.

Marcia Bonta (born 1940) has lived on her mountaintop for twenty-four years. She is the author of six books: *Escape to the Mountain, Appalachian Spring, Appalachian Autumn, Women in the Field, Outbound Journeys in Pennsylvania* and *More Outbound Journeys in Pennsylvania* and the editor of *American Women Afield*. She has published more than two hundred nature-related magazine articles in state and national publications, has a nature column in *Pennsylvania Game News* and is the editor of the University of Pittsburgh Press's Pitt Series on Nature and Natural History.

Marguerite Guzman Bouvard (born 1937) was born in Trieste, Italy. She is the author of three books of poetry and several books in the fields of women's studies, political science and psychology. Her latest book, *Women Reshaping Human Rights: Extraordinary Women Tell Their Stories of How They are Changing the World*, was published by Scholarly Resources, Inc. in April 1996. She was for many years a professor of political science and poetry, and was also a writer-in-residence at the University of Maryland. She is currently a resident scholar with the Women's Studies Program at Brandeis University.

Sally Carrighar (1905–1986) was born and brought up in Ohio. Her nature-writing career began while she was convalescing from an illness and she communicated with birds that perched on her windowsill to feed and a mouse that lived in her radio. She wrote books about the Sierras, the Tetons, the Arctic and Alaska.

Alexandra David-Neel (1868–1969), a Frenchwoman, had an early career as an opera singer. In 1923, having studied Tibetan Buddhism for many years, she became the first European woman to enter Tibet's forbidden city of Lhasa. She was fifty-five. Disguising herself as a pilgrim and accompanied only by a young Sikkimese lama, she struggled on foot through a harsh and dangerous terrain to reach her goal. When she returned from Tibet, she was awarded the Gold Medal of the Geographical Society of France and made a Chevalier of the Legion of Honor. In the remaining forty-five years of her life, she was widely regarded as a scholar and lecturer; at her death, she left four projects unfinished.

Elizabeth Evans (born 1941) is a professor of physical education at Springfield College, Springfield, Massachusetts. Since her Peace Corps tour of duty in Africa, she has traveled extensively in Europe, South America, China and Japan. In 1995, she was the director of the gymnastics competition in the Special Olympics World Games. Combining her background in physical education and physical therapy, she teaches primarily in the field of adapted physical education.

Wendy W. Fairey (born 1942), Professor of English at Brooklyn College, where she teaches English literature, creative writing and women's studies, is the author of *One of the Family* (W. W. Norton, 1992). She has published articles on George Eliot, Edith Wharton, Willa Cather and women's autobiography, among other subjects, as well as a number of creative nonfiction pieces. She is currently at work on a group of interrelated short stories about women turning fifty entitled *Menopause and Poker.*

Eirene Furness (born 1911) was educated at the Bedales School and the University of Edinburgh. Although the first article she submitted, while still at university, was accepted for publication in the local paper, she spent her early adult years employed in various other fields. In 1980 she left Algeria for Spain, eventually moving to France in 1982. Working as a writer and translator in Paris until 1991, she retired to Nice where she is now writing—slowly—the memories of a long life. She has three children.

Betsy Aldrich Garland (born 1939) completed the high-ropes course at United Methodist Camp Aldersgate in Rhode Island while serving as a "senior" counselor to high school age students. The Executive Director of the Volunteer Center for Rhode Island from 1975-1995, she consults and trains widely in the nonprofit sector on volunteer and board management. A 1990 master of divinity graduate from Harvard University, she also works with communities of faith and professional volunteer administrators on the empowerment of laity. But to preschoolers Marina, Celia and Alden, she is simply Grandma Betsy.

Trish Ingersoll-Adams (born 1944) graduated from the New England Conservatory of Music in Composition, married, joined VISTA and became a volunteer in El Paso, Texas. On returning to Boston, she was awarded a scholarship to the Boston Museum School in ceramics and worked as a production potter for eight years before joining the faculties at Radcliffe College and the Boston Museum School. In 1992, she was invited to work in a ceramic factory in Uzbeckistan; in the summer of 1996, she taught in South Korea. She now teaches in her studio, climbs whenever she can: a few weeks each summer in Europe, up north summers and winters and occasionally out West. She hopes for Alaska again.

Ruth Harriet Jacobs, Ph.D., (born 1924) is a sociologist and gerontologist at the Wellesley Center for Research on Women. She teaches at Regis and Springfield Colleges. Her eight books include: *Be an Outrageous Older Woman*, revised edition, 1993, and *Women Who Touched My Life*, 1996, both published by K.I.T. Publishers, Manchester, Connecticut. Her leaders' manual, *Older Women Surviving and Thriving*, published by Families International, Milwaukee, Wisconsin, is used to run groups in the United States and abroad.

Florence R. Krall (born 1926), author of *Ecotone, Wayfaring on the Margins*, is a teacher, naturalist and author who writes personal narratives of place. She and her husband, Paul Shepard, divide their time between a cabin in her native Wyoming and their home in Utah, where she is a professor emeritus at the University of Utah.

Maxine Kumin (born 1925) has published ten volumes of poetry, as well as novels, short stories and essays on country living. She was awarded the Pulitzer Prize for Poetry in 1973, has been a poetry consultant for the Library of Congress and Poet Laureate of New Hampshire. In 1993, she was awarded the Poets Prize. Kumin lives on a farm in central New Hampshire, the locale that informs the core of her writing.

Harriet Laine (1941–1995) was a freelance writer and an ex-academic. She had a Ph.D. in biology and, for several years, worked as a medical writer within the pharmaceutical industry. Her nontechnical work appeared in *The Advocate.* She lived and rode in Garrison, New York.

Judith Niemi (born 1941) retired from teaching literature almost twenty years ago and became a wilderness guide. She is the founder/director of Women in the Wilderness; her favorite destination and spiritual home country is the Arctic. She lives in Saint Paul, Minnesota, with too many phones and computers, about eighteen canoes and her understanding life partner. Their circle of outdoor friends, the Sturdy Girls, celebrate their fiftieth birthdays in a big way and are saving up some special trips (e.g., canoe routes without three-mile portages) for when they get old.

Ginny NiCarthy (born 1927) has written several books about the abuse of women, including *Getting Free, The Ones Who Got Away* and *You Don't Have to Take It* (for women emotionally abused at work, coauthored). She now lives in Mexico halftime, is writing a novel, as well as a non-fiction book: *Mostly True Travel Stories.* She travels whenever she finds a spare nickel. Writers' groups in Seattle—Judy Hume, Ellie Mathews, Patrick Preston and Eric Torskey—and in San Miguel de Allende—Reesha Browning, Francoise Dubois, Patricia Gonzales, Nora NiMahon and Mary Nolan—made useful comments on this story, as did K. C. Pilon and Louise Wisechild.

Deborah O'Keefe (born 1939) is an editor, writer and former college English teacher with a Ph.D. from Columbia. She is working on a book about girls' fiction written before 1950. Her writing has appeared in the *New York Times, National Lampoon, American Heritage* and *McCall's.* Based in Chappaqua, New York, and Ripton, Vermont, she likes to walk and travel.

Heather Trexler Remoff (born 1938) lives, writes and runs in Eagles Mere, Pennsylvania, with her husband, Gene, and her flat-coated retriever, Chuckles. Although her Ph.D. is in anthropology and her joy is in her children and grandchildren, she has always considered herself a writer at heart. Most of her published work appears in periodicals and argues that female choice in sexual selection is a powerful determinant of the speed with which humans evolve. Her book, *Sexual Choice* (Dutton, 1985), is a popularized account of how women select their sexual partners. More recently, her writing interests have focused on the outdoors and the neglected role of land in theories of economics and biology.

Alix Kates Shulman (born 1932) is the author of ten books. Her memoir, *Drinking the Rain*, was nominated for a 1995 *Los Angeles Times* Book Prize and received a Body Mind Spirit Award of Excellence. Besides four novels, beginning with the bestselling *Memoirs of an Ex-Prom Queen*, she has written two books on the anarchist Emma Goldman, several books for children and numerous stories and essays. She has been Visiting Writer at the American Academy in Rome and has received grants from the NEA and the Lila Wallace/Reader's Digest Foundation. Her work has been translated into ten languages. She has taught at New York University, Yale, the University of Hawaii and other universities.

Alice Kent Stephens (born 1938) was born in California into a large family. She is a Christian missionary and teacher who loves to travel and be with young people. She taught English as a Second Language in California, Thailand and Mexico. She is now retired and writes books from oral histories done with older people.

Elinore Pruitt Stewart (1876–1933) was born in White Bead Hill in the Chickasaw Nation, Indian Territory, the eldest of nine children. Her first published work appeared in the *Kansas City Star* in the form of short articles and letters to the editor in about 1906. She homesteaded her land in Wyoming in 1909. A prolific letter writer, her work was taken by one of her correspondents to the *Atlantic Monthly*, where it was accepted, and Stewart became prominent as a frontier spokeswoman and storyteller.

Helen Thayer (born 1938) is a professional mountain guide and former discus thrower, sled racer and U.S. National Luge Champion (1975). In May 1992, she and her sixty-five-year-old husband, Bill, became the first—and oldest—married couple to reach the magnetic North Pole on foot, unresupplied. When they're not fending off polar bears, fighting frostbite or climbing mountains, Helen, Bill and dog Charlie make their home in Snohomish, Washington.

Jean Hand Triol (born 1938) spent her early years exploring the fields and waterways of west-central New Jersey and, later, sailing Barnegat Bay. Her adult career has been devoted to cytotechnology, scientific writing and to husband Cal, their four children and five grandchildren. She now resides with Cal in Somers, Montana, on Flathead Lake, where she races a San Juan 21.

Wuanda Walls (born 1943) is an African-American writer who focuses on travel, art, culture, history and the culinary arts. Her work has been published in *Baltimore Sun Magazine, Pennsylvania Magazine,* the *Denver Post,* the *Rocky Mountain News, Essence, Modern Maturity, Emerge,* the *Arizona Republic,* the *Swarthmorean, Black Enterprise,* the *Boston Globe* and others. Trilingual, she has traveled to Europe, Africa, Central and South America, Asia, the Caribbean and the Middle East.

Nan Watkins (born 1938) was born in Bucks County, Pennsylvania, of Welsh-American descent, studied music and German literature at the University of Munich and the Academy of Music in Vienna and has degrees in those subjects from Oberlin College and Johns Hopkins University. As a translator over the past twenty-five years, she has published various works in *Dimension, Asheville Poetry Review, Nexus* and *Oxygen.* As a musician and composer, she is an active electronic-keyboard performer and organist, and has appeared on four recordings, the most recent of which is her first solo album of original compositions, *The Laugharne Poems,* released by Fern Hill Records in 1995. She has lived in the Great Smoky Mountains of North Carolina for the past twenty years, currently residing in Cullowhee, North Carolina, where she works as a reference librarian at Western Carolina University.

Betty Wetzel (born 1915) grew up working on her father's weekly newspaper in Roundup, Montana, and graduated from the University of Montana School of Journalism. While rearing four children—three (liberated) daughters and a (liberated) son, she worked as a newspaper correspondent and freelance writer, which she continues today. While living in the East, she was the first publicity director of Oxfam-America in Boston. When her husband (of fifty-five years) was assigned to an education project in Bangladesh (then East Pakistan), she worked at the Southeast Asia Cholera Research Laboratory. Since returning to Montana, she has been a regular writer for *Montana Magazine* and is the author of *After You, Mark Twain* (Fulcrum Press, 1990). "Near Eighty—and Tall in the Saddle" was originally featured in the travel section of the *New York Times*.

Evelyn Wolfson (born 1937) has taught environmental education in private and public schools throughout Massachusetts. While raising two children, she also skied the Rockies and the Alps; rafted the Colorado, Middle Fork of the Salmon, Green and Snake rivers; flew small aircraft over New England; canoed its rivers, lakes and streams; and hiked trails of the Appalachian Mountains. She is the author of nine books, eight for children, and has written for a wide variety of newspapers and magazines. She makes her home in Wayland, Massachusetts.

Tomasz Adach

Jean Gould (born 1939) is the author of a novel, *Divorcing Your Grand-mother* (Morrow, 1985), as well as a number of short stories, reviews and personal essays. "Aamaa Didi," her piece about climbing in Nepal, was anthologized in *Another Wilderness* (Seal Press, 1994). She has been the recipient of a grant from the National Endowment for the Arts in screenwriting, a fellow in the novel at Wesleyan University and writer-in-residence at Hollins College. A book review editor at *Sojourner: The Women's Forum,* she lives in Natick, Massachusetts.

Season of Adventure is part of Seal's popular line of books that celebrates the achievements and experiences of women adventurers, athletes, travelers and naturalists. Bringing women's sensibility to writing about activities once considered the domain of men—such as hunting, fishing, rock climbing, and solo travel—has produced refreshing prose and new ideas, adding dimension to the existing canon.

Adventura books feature women determined to go off the beaten track—whether to scale a mountain in the Andes, cast a line in a nearby brook, or explore Tibet without a guide.

Please peruse the list of books below—and discover the spirit of adventure through the female gaze.

SOLO: *On Her Own Adventure*, edited by Susan Fox Rogers. $12.95, 1-878067-74-5.

ALL THE POWERFUL INVISIBLE THINGS: *A Sportswoman's Notebook*, by Gretchen Legler. $12.95, 1-878067-69-9.

A DIFFERENT ANGLE: *Fly Fishing Stories by Women*, edited by Holly Morris. $22.95, cloth, 1-878067-63-X.

UNCOMMON WATERS: *Women Write About Fishing*, edited by Holly Morris. $14.95, 1-878067-10-9.

ANOTHER WILDERNESS: *New Outdoor Writing by Women*, edited by Susan Fox Rogers. $14.95, 1-878067-54-0.

LEADING OUT: *Women Climbers Reaching for the Top*, edited by Rachel da Silva. $16.95, 1-878067-20-6.

WHEN WOMEN PLAYED HARDBALL by Susan E. Johnson. $14.95, 1-878067-43-5.

THE CURVE OF TIME by M. Wylie Blanchet. $12.95, 1-878067-27-3.

DOWN THE WILD RIVER NORTH by Constance Helmericks. $12.95, 1-878067-28-1.

RIVERS RUNNING FREE: *A Century of Women's Canoeing Adventures*, edited by Judith Niemi and Barbara Wieser. $14.95, 1-878067-90-7.

WATER'S EDGE: *Women Who Push the Limits in Rowing, Kayaking and Canoeing*, by Linda Lewis. $14.95, 1-878067-18-4.

Seal Press publishes books by women writers, ranging in topic from popular culture and lesbian studies to parenting, health and domestic violence, and outdoor adventure. To receive a free catalog or to order directly, write to us at 3131 Western Avenue, Suite 410, Seattle, Washington 98121; email us at sealprss@scn.org; or call us toll free at 1-800-754-0271 (orders only). Please add 16.5% of the book total for shipping and handling.